X-MEN 2

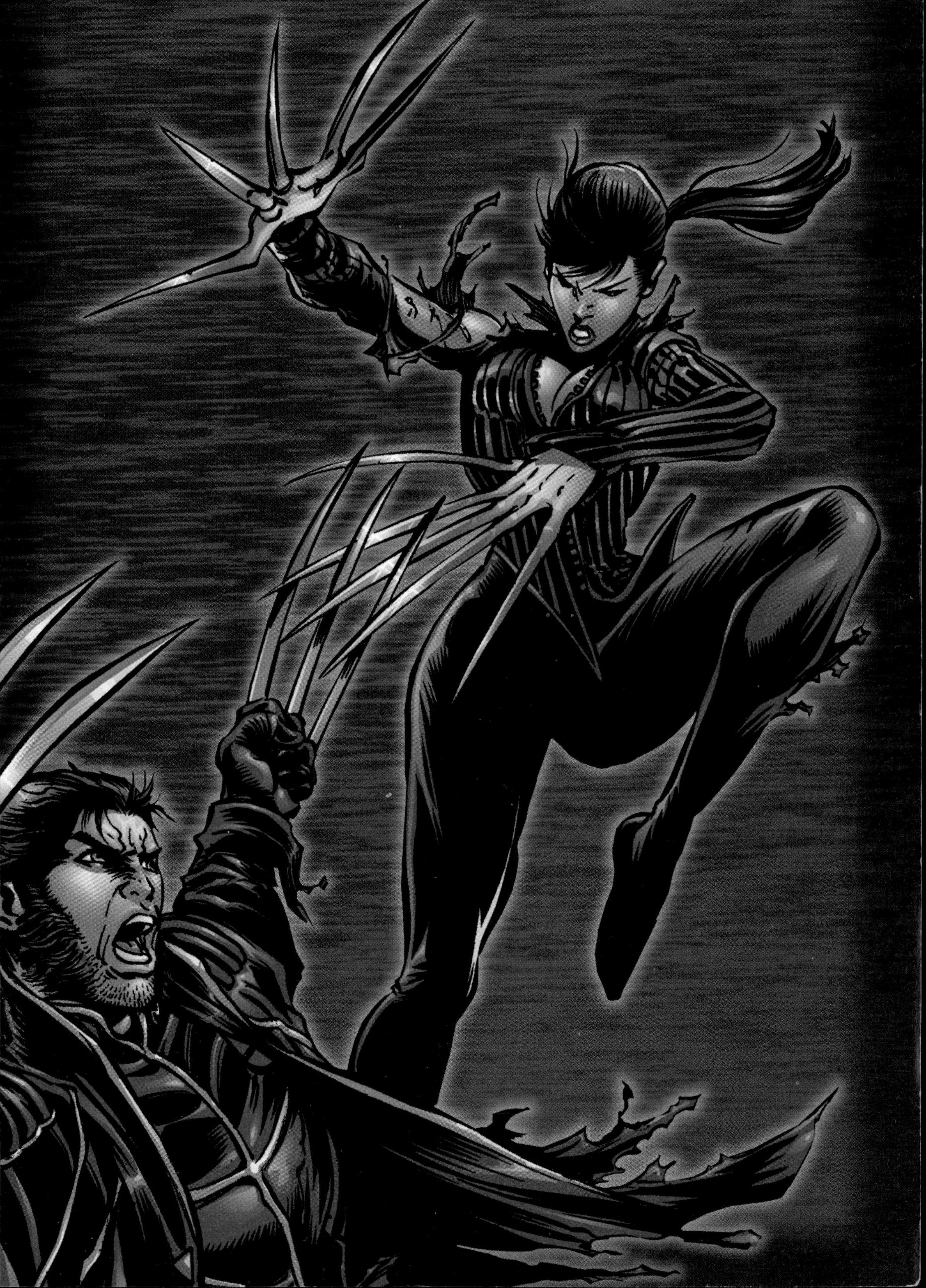

X-MEN 2

X2: THE MOVIE
writer: CHUCK AUSTEN
based on the screenplay by:
20th CENTURY FOX
pencils: PATRICK ZIRCHER
inks: LARY STUCKER
colors: AVALON STUDIOS' IAN HANNIN

X2 PREQUEL: WOLVERINE
writer: CHUCK AUSTEN
artist: KARL KERSCHL
colors: JUNG CHOI'S
TRANSPARENCY DIGITAL

X2 PREQUEL: NIGHTCRAWLER
writer: BRIAN K. VAUGHAN
artist: TOM MANDRAKE
colors: DAN BROWN

letters: PAUL TUTRONE

assistant editors:
MIKE RAICHT
NOVA REN SUMA

editor:
MIKE MARTS

editor in chief:
JOE QUESADA

president:
BILL JEMAS

X2: THE MOVIE. Contains material originally published in magazine form as X2: MOVIE ADAPTATION, X2 MOVIE PREQUEL: NIGHTCRAWLER and X2 MOVIE PREQUEL: WOLVERINE. First printing 2003. ISBN# 0-7851-1162-X. Published by MARVEL COMICS, a division of MARVEL ENTERTAINMENT GROUP, INC. OFFICE OF PUBLICATION: 10 East 40th Street, New York, NY 10016. Copyright © 2003 Marvel Characters, Inc. All rights reserved. X2: THE MOVIE: Copyright © 2003 Twentieth Century Fox Film Corporation. All rights reserved. $12.99 per copy in the U.S. and $21.00 in Canada (GST #R127032852); Canadian Agreement #40668537. All characters featured in this issue and the distinctive names and likenesses thereof, and all related indicia are trademarks of Marvel Characters, Inc. No similarity between any of the names, characters, persons, and/or institutions in this magazine with those of any living or dead person or institution is intended, and any such similarity which may exist is purely coincidental. Printed in Canada. STAN LEE, Chairman Emeritus. For information regarding advertising in Marvel Comics or on Marvel.com, please contact Russell Brown, Executive Vice President, Consumer Products, Promotions and Media Sales at 212-576-8561 or rbrown@marvel.com

10 9 8 7 6 5 4 3 2 1

PREVIOUSLY IN X-MEN: THE MOVIE

The X-Men are a group of heroes gifted with strange and fantastic abilities simply by virtue of their genetic makeup. They are Homo superior, born with the X-gene that makes them mutants. Yet in a world where mutants are feared and often hated by humankind, they must fight against discrimination and work to promote tolerance between humans and mutantkind.

The X-Men have been called together by their mentor, PROFESSOR CHARLES XAVIER, to the Xavier Institute in upstate New York. There, Professor X -- a mutant telepath of the highest order -- has opened a school to teach young mutants how to use their powers responsibly. But as mutant hysteria grows, Professor X's team of X-Men -- CYCLOPS, JEAN GREY, WOLVERINE, STORM and ROGUE -- are often called upon to protect the world.

Yet not all mutants promote tolerance. Professor X's most powerful enemy, MAGNETO, leader of the Brotherhood of Mutants, does not want to share the world with humanity. In a plan to exterminate the human race, Magneto and his Brotherhood -- including SABRETOOTH, TOAD and MYSTIQUE -- seek a brave new world comprised only of mutants. When Magneto captures the young newcomer to the Xavier Institute, Rogue, and uses her ability to absorb other mutants' powers to gain control over New York City, the X-Men are called to the rescue. In a heated battle at the Statue of Liberty, the X-Men succeed in stopping Magneto before his power grows strong enough to permanently harm the local human populace.

With Magneto now safely imprisoned by the U.S. government, Professor X and his X-Men are granted a brief moment of respite. But even though one battle has been won, there are new threats to the mutant race appearing every day...

WOLVERINE STORM PROF. X JEAN GREY CYCLOPS

ROGUE NIGHTCRAWLER MAGNETO MYSTIQUE STRYKER

CHUCK AUSTEN
writer

PATRICK ZIRCHER
penciler

LARY STUCKER
letterer

AVALON STUDIOS' IAN HANNIN
colorist

PAUL TUTRONE
letterer

MIKE RAICHT & NOVA REN SUMA
assistant editors

MIKE MARTS
editor

JOE QUESADA
editor in chief

BILL JEMAS
president

X2 Comic Adaptation based on a screenplay by 20th Century Fox

Mutation.

The result of a natural change in the genetic material-- the DNA-- of the human cell.

Mutation was beyond Darwin's knowledge when he formulated his theories of evolution.

But it is a common occurrence-- an everyday phenomenon--

--one that is generally unnoticed and largely harmless.

Or rather, it **was**. While mutation has always led to problems such as juvenile diabetes and multiple sclerosis--

--not long ago, mutations of a more **unique** power and variety--

--began to appear in certain individuals.

These individuals were branded with the catch-all label of "Mutants."

Since the discovery of their existence, they have been regarded with fear-- --suspicion--

--and often **hatred**.

Across the planet, the debate rages: Are mutants the next link in the evolutionary chain--

--or simply a **new species** of humanity fighting for their share of the world?

Either way, one fact has been historically proven, time and time again--

--sharing the world has never been a shining attribute of **humankind**.

To make certain that mutants are allowed their rightful chance at survival--

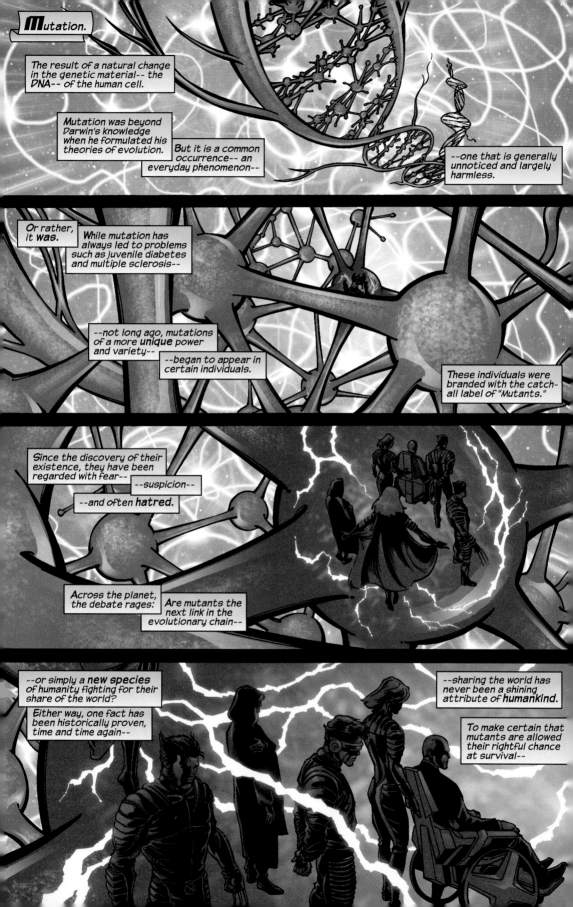

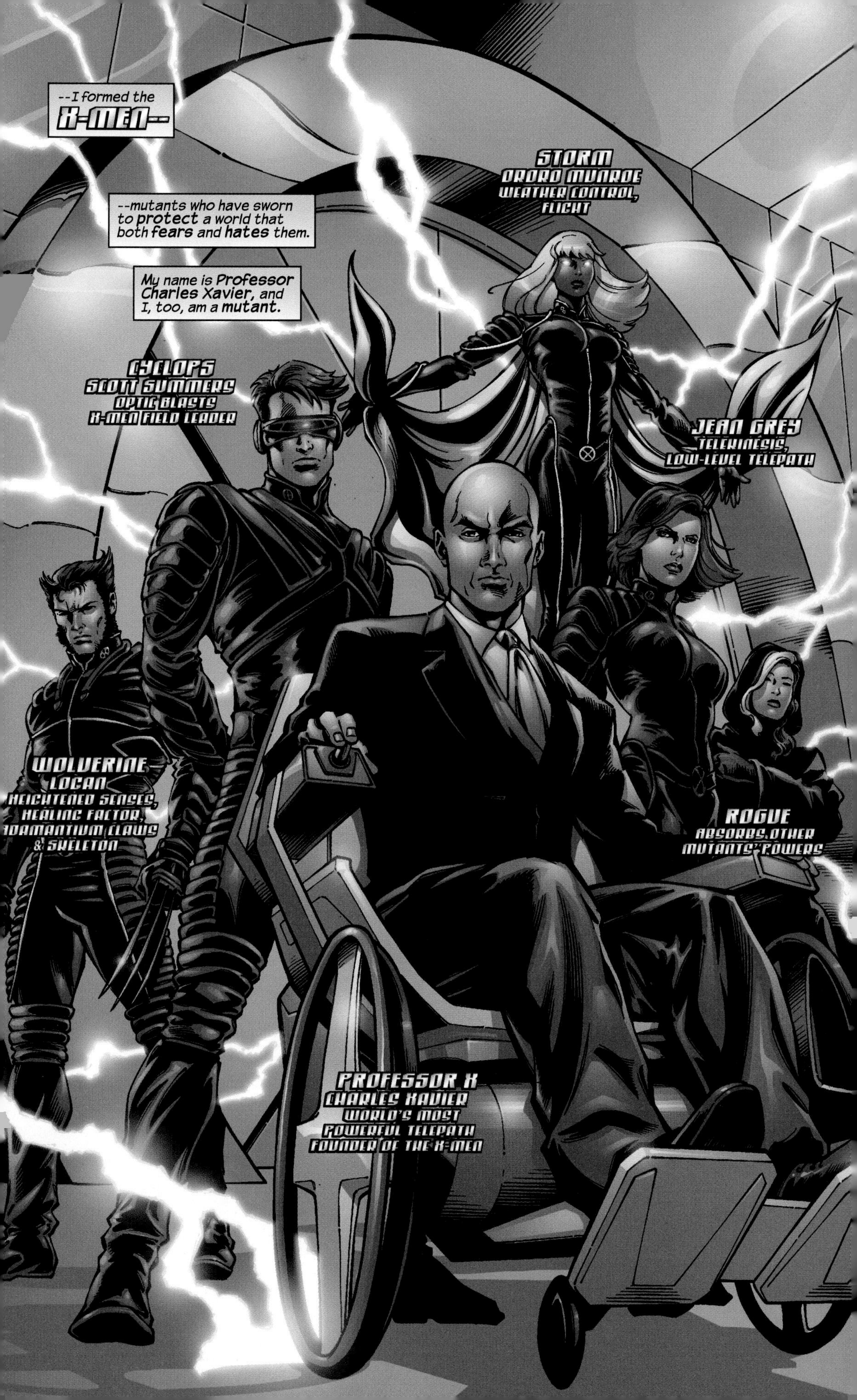
--I formed the X-MEN--
--mutants who have sworn to protect a world that both fears and hates them.
My name is Professor Charles Xavier, and I, too, am a mutant.
STORM
ORORO MUNROE
WEATHER CONTROL, FLIGHT
CYCLOPS
SCOTT SUMMERS
OPTIC BLASTS
X-MEN FIELD LEADER
JEAN GREY
TELEKINESIS, LOW-LEVEL TELEPATH
WOLVERINE
LOGAN
HEIGHTENED SENSES, HEALING FACTOR, ADAMANTIUM CLAWS & SKELETON
ROGUE
ABSORBS OTHER MUTANTS' POWERS
PROFESSOR X
CHARLES XAVIER
WORLD'S MOST POWERFUL TELEPATH
FOUNDER OF THE X-MEN

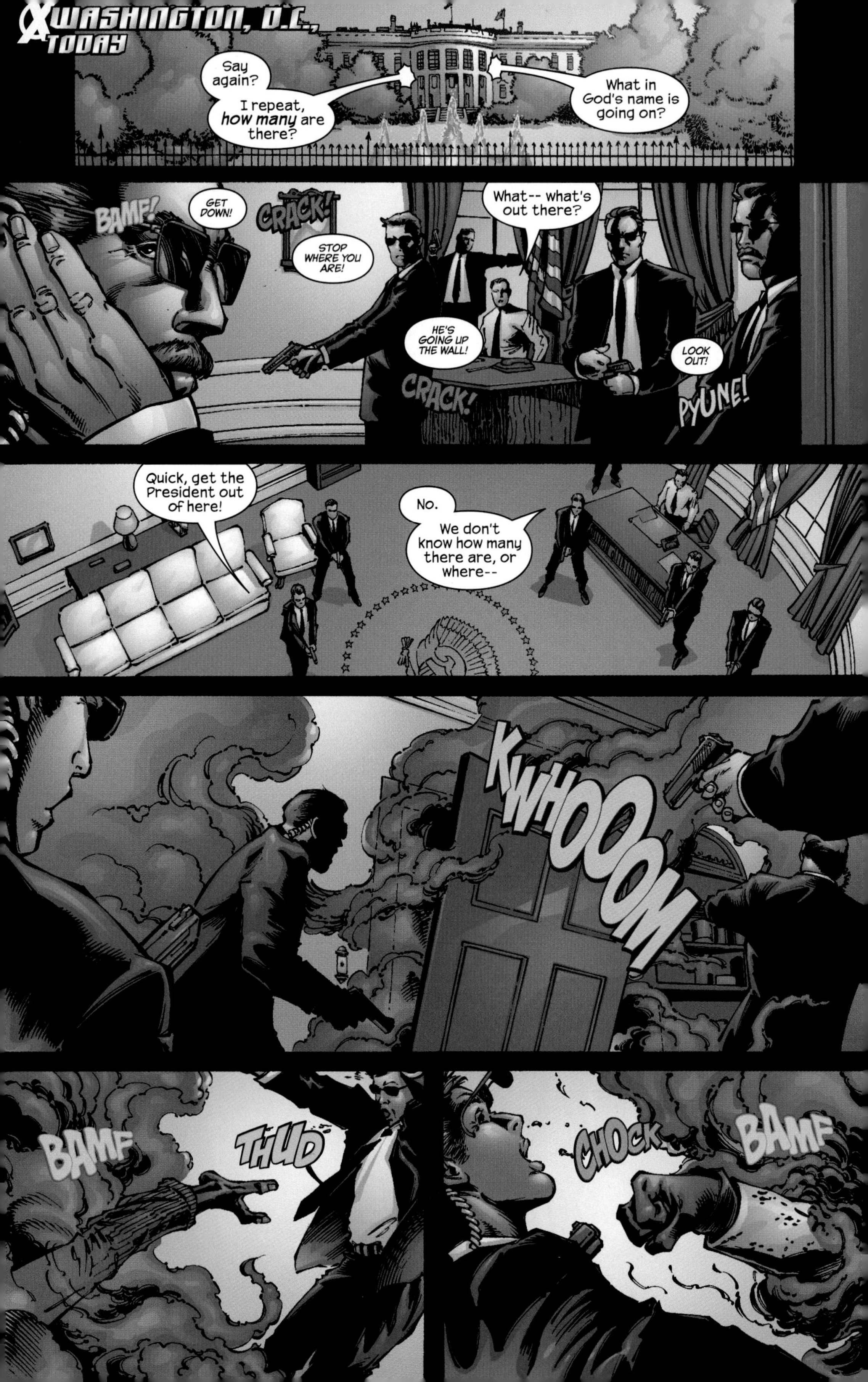
WASHINGTON, D.C., TODAY
Say again?
I repeat, *how many* are there?
What in God's name is going on?
BAMF!
GET DOWN!
CRACK!
STOP WHERE YOU ARE!
What-- what's out there?
HE'S GOING UP THE WALL!
CRACK!
LOOK OUT!
PYUNE!
Quick, get the President out of here!
No.
We don't know how many there are, or where--
KWHOOOOM
BAMF
THUD
CHOCK
BAMF

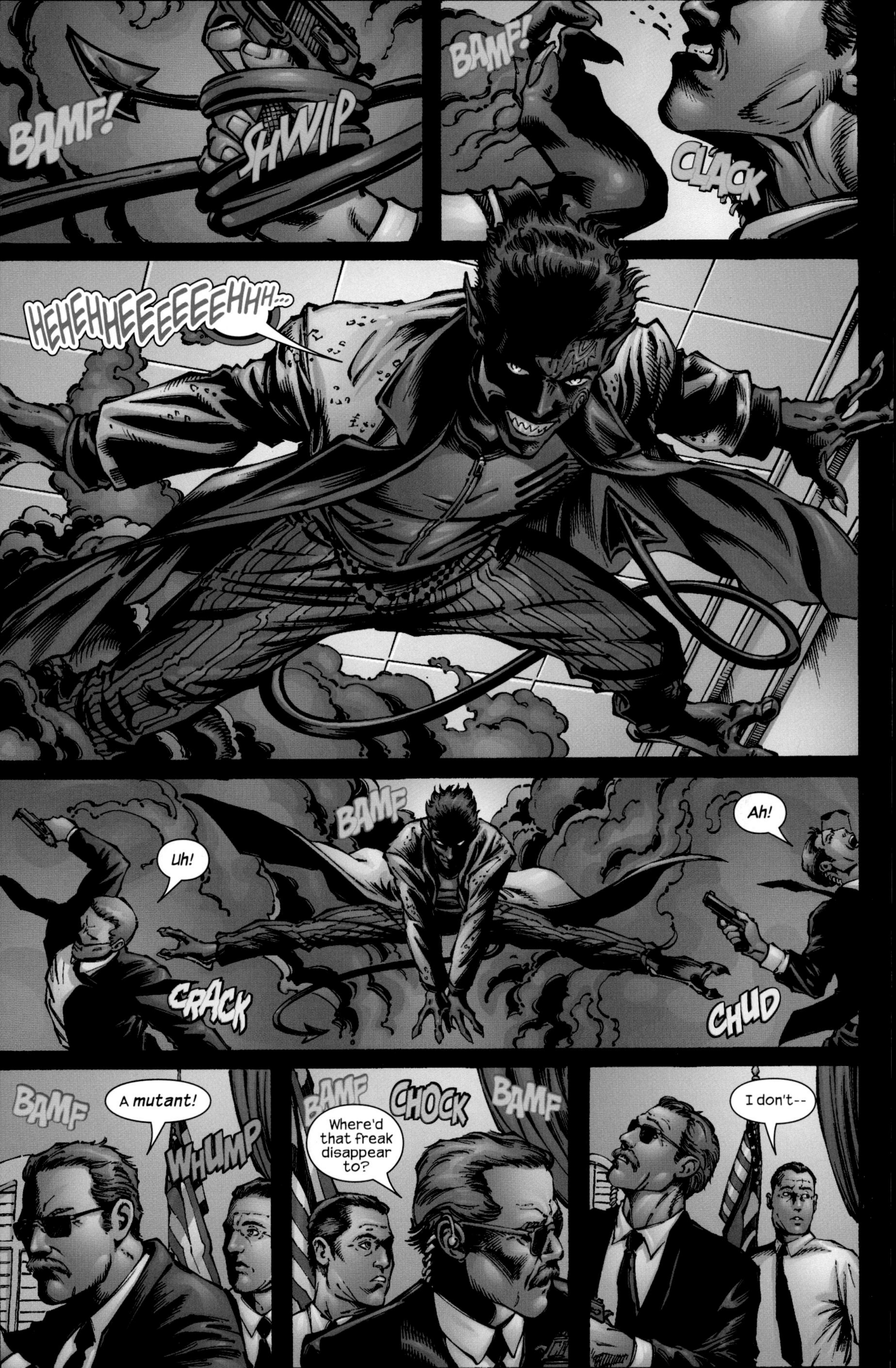
BAMF!
SHWIP
BAMF!
CLACK
HEHEHHEEEEEEHHH...
BAMF
Uh!
Ah!
CRACK
CHUD
BAMF
A mutant!
WHUMP
BAMF
CHOCK
BAMF
Where'd that freak disappear to?
I don't--

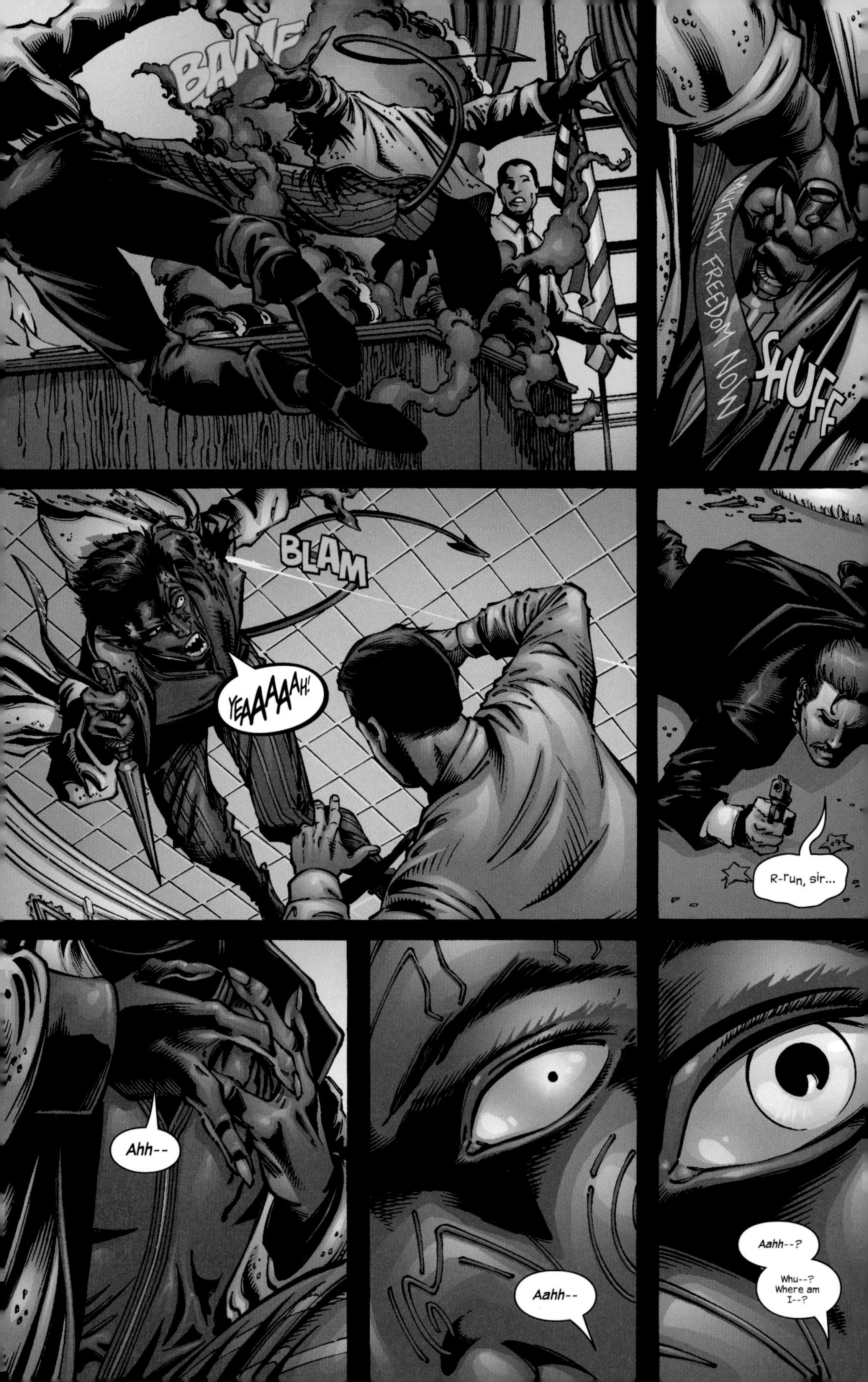
BAMF
MUTANT FREEDOM NOW
SHUFF
BLAM
YEAAAAAH!
R-run, sir...
Ahh--
Aahh--
Aahh--?
Whu--? Where am I--?

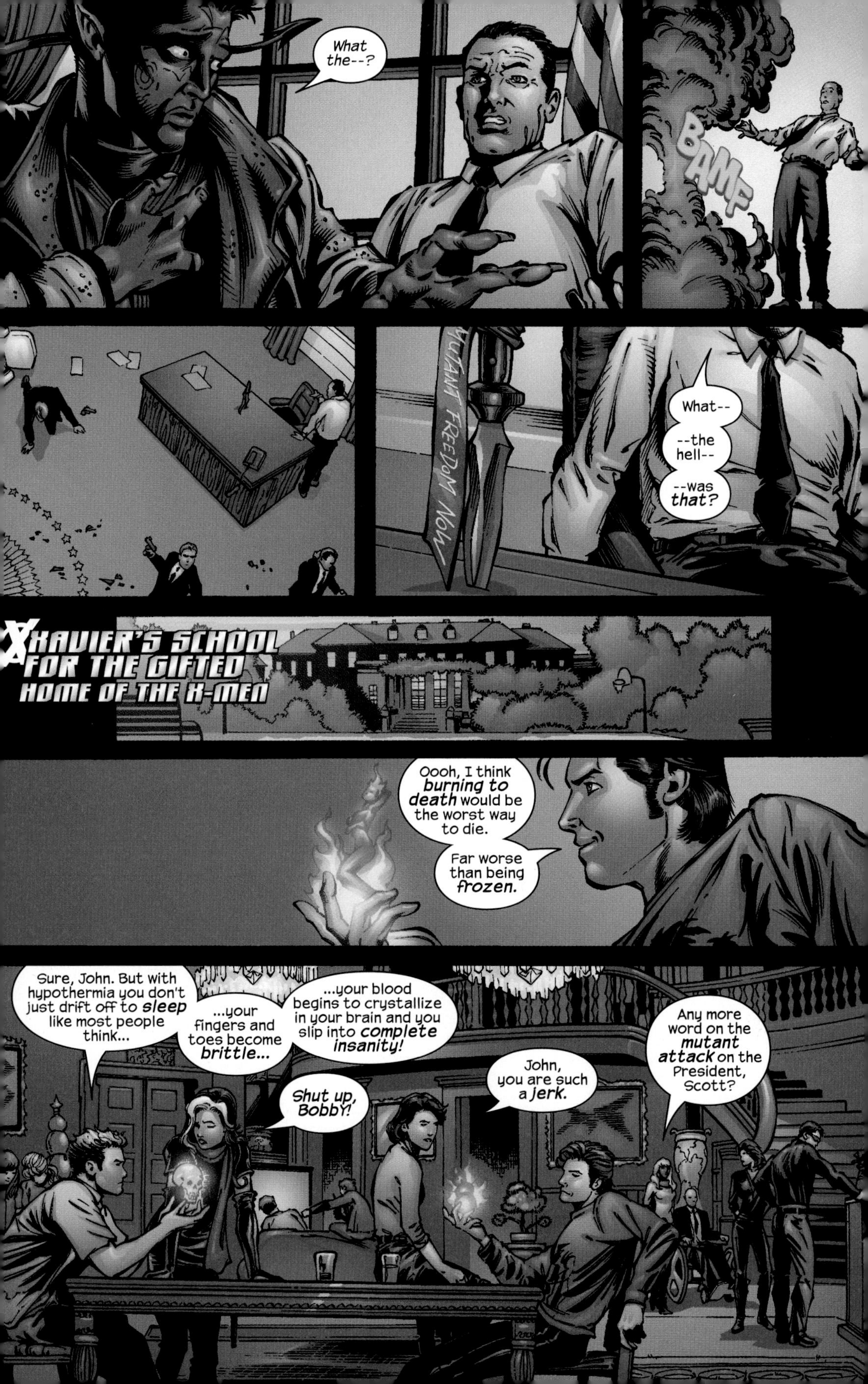
What the--?
BAMF
MUTANT FREEDOM NOW
What--
--the hell--
--was that?
XAVIER'S SCHOOL FOR THE GIFTED
HOME OF THE X-MEN
Oooh, I think burning to death would be the worst way to die.
Far worse than being frozen.
Sure, John. But with hypothermia you don't just drift off to sleep like most people think...
...your fingers and toes become brittle...
...your blood begins to crystallize in your brain and you slip into complete insanity!
Shut up, Bobby!
John, you are such a jerk.
Any more word on the mutant attack on the President, Scott?

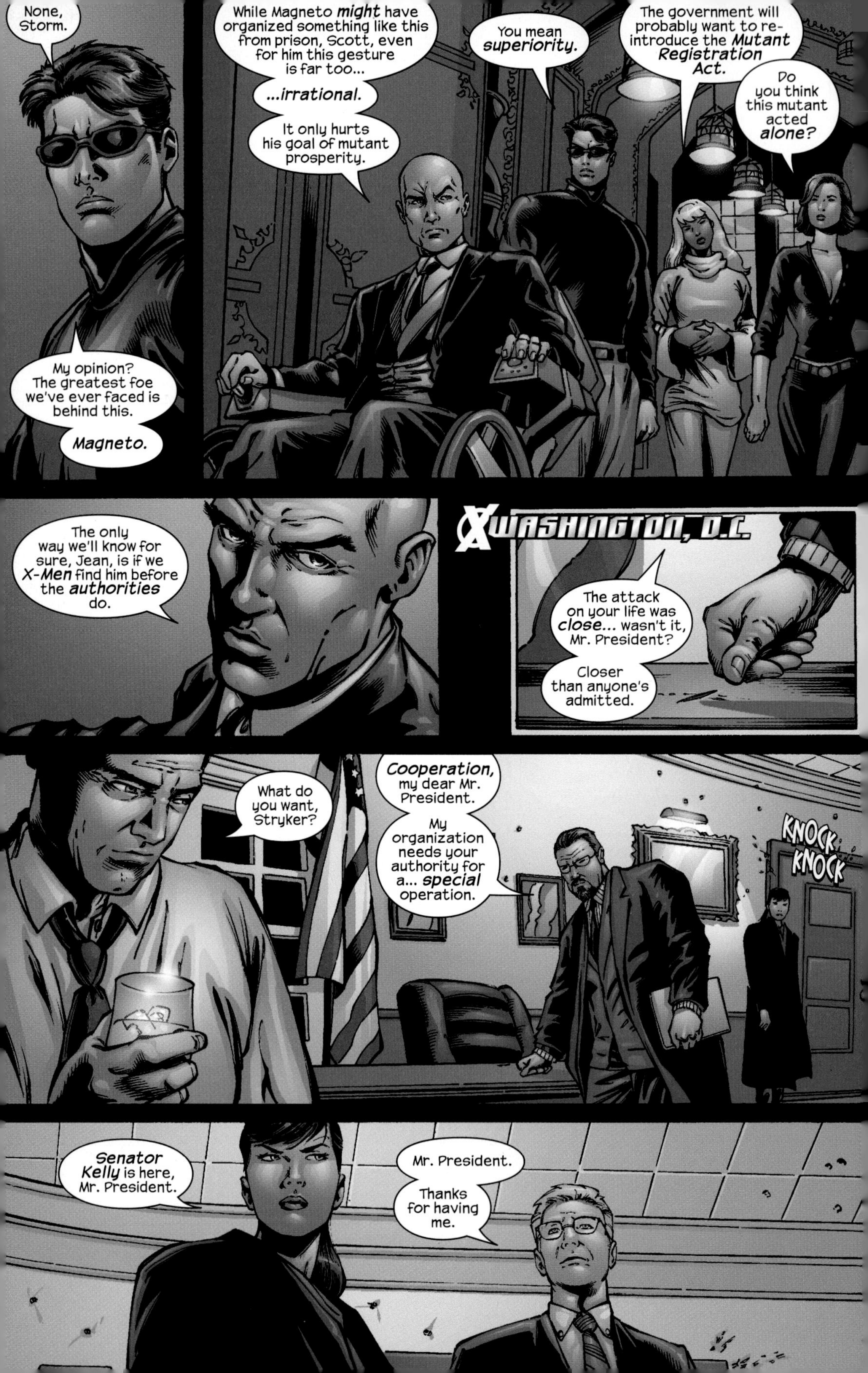

None, Storm.
My opinion? The greatest foe we've ever faced is behind this.
Magneto.
While Magneto *might* have organized something like this from prison, Scott, even for him this gesture is far too...
...*irrational*.
It only hurts his goal of mutant prosperity.
You mean *superiority*.
The government will probably want to re-introduce the *Mutant Registration Act*.
Do you think this mutant acted *alone*?
The only way we'll know for sure, Jean, is if we *X-Men* find him before the *authorities* do.
WASHINGTON, D.C.
The attack on your life was *close*... wasn't it, Mr. President?
Closer than anyone's admitted.
What do you want, Stryker?
Cooperation, my dear Mr. President.
My organization needs your authority for a... *special* operation.
KNOCK KNOCK
Senator Kelly is here, Mr. President.
Mr. President.
Thanks for having me.

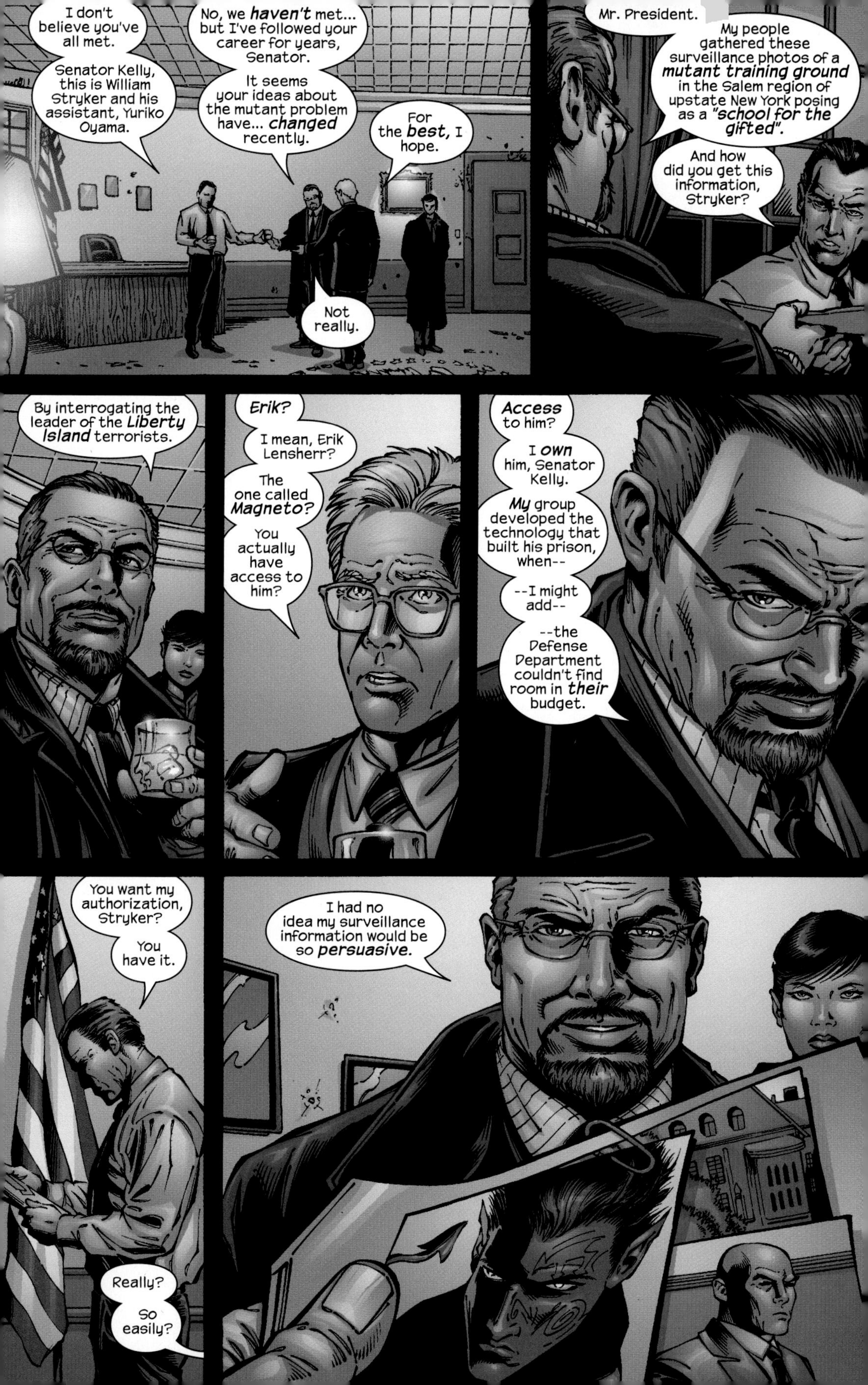
I don't believe you've all met.
Senator Kelly, this is William Stryker and his assistant, Yuriko Oyama.
No, we haven't met... but I've followed your career for years, Senator.
It seems your ideas about the mutant problem have... changed recently.
For the best, I hope.
Not really.
Mr. President.
My people gathered these surveillance photos of a mutant training ground in the Salem region of upstate New York posing as a "school for the gifted".
And how did you get this information, Stryker?
By interrogating the leader of the Liberty Island terrorists.
Erik?
I mean, Erik Lensherr?
The one called Magneto?
You actually have access to him?
Access to him?
I own him, Senator Kelly.
My group developed the technology that built his prison, when--
--I might add--
--the Defense Department couldn't find room in their budget.
You want my authorization, Stryker?
You have it.
Really?
So easily?
I had no idea my surveillance information would be so persuasive.

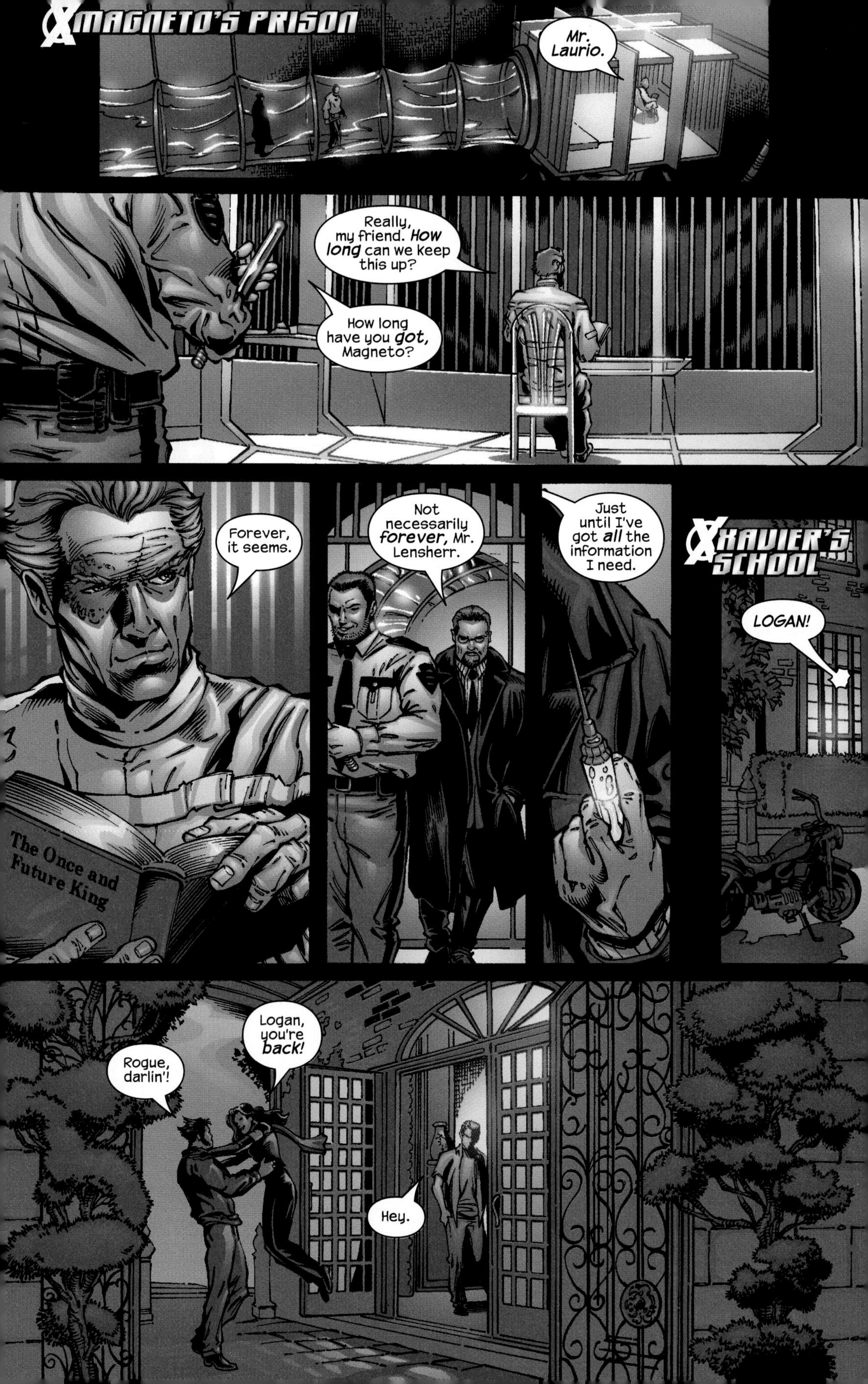
MAGNETO'S PRISON
Mr. Laurio.
Really, my friend. How long can we keep this up?
How long have you got, Magneto?
Forever, it seems.
The Once and Future King
Not necessarily forever, Mr. Lensherr.
Just until I've got all the information I need.
XAVIER'S SCHOOL
LOGAN!
Logan, you're back!
Rogue, darlin'!
Hey.

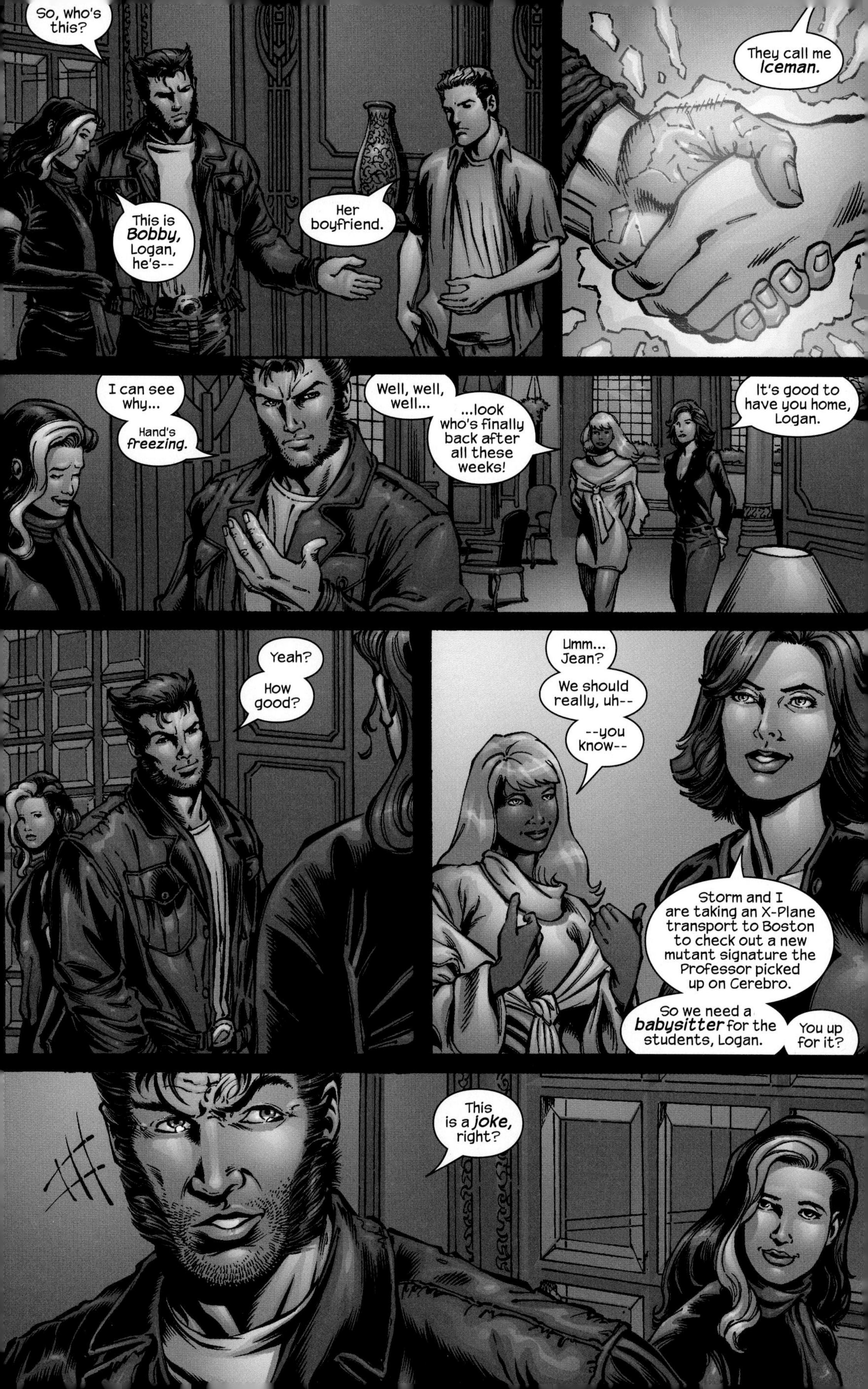
So, who's this?
This is *Bobby,* Logan, he's--
Her boyfriend.
They call me *Iceman.*
I can see why...
Hand's *freezing.*
Well, well, well...
...look who's finally back after all these weeks!
It's good to have you home, Logan.
Yeah?
How good?
Umm... Jean?
We should really, uh--
--you know--
Storm and I are taking an X-Plane transport to Boston to check out a new mutant signature the Professor picked up on Cerebro.
So we need a *babysitter* for the students, Logan.
You up for it?
This is a *joke,* right?

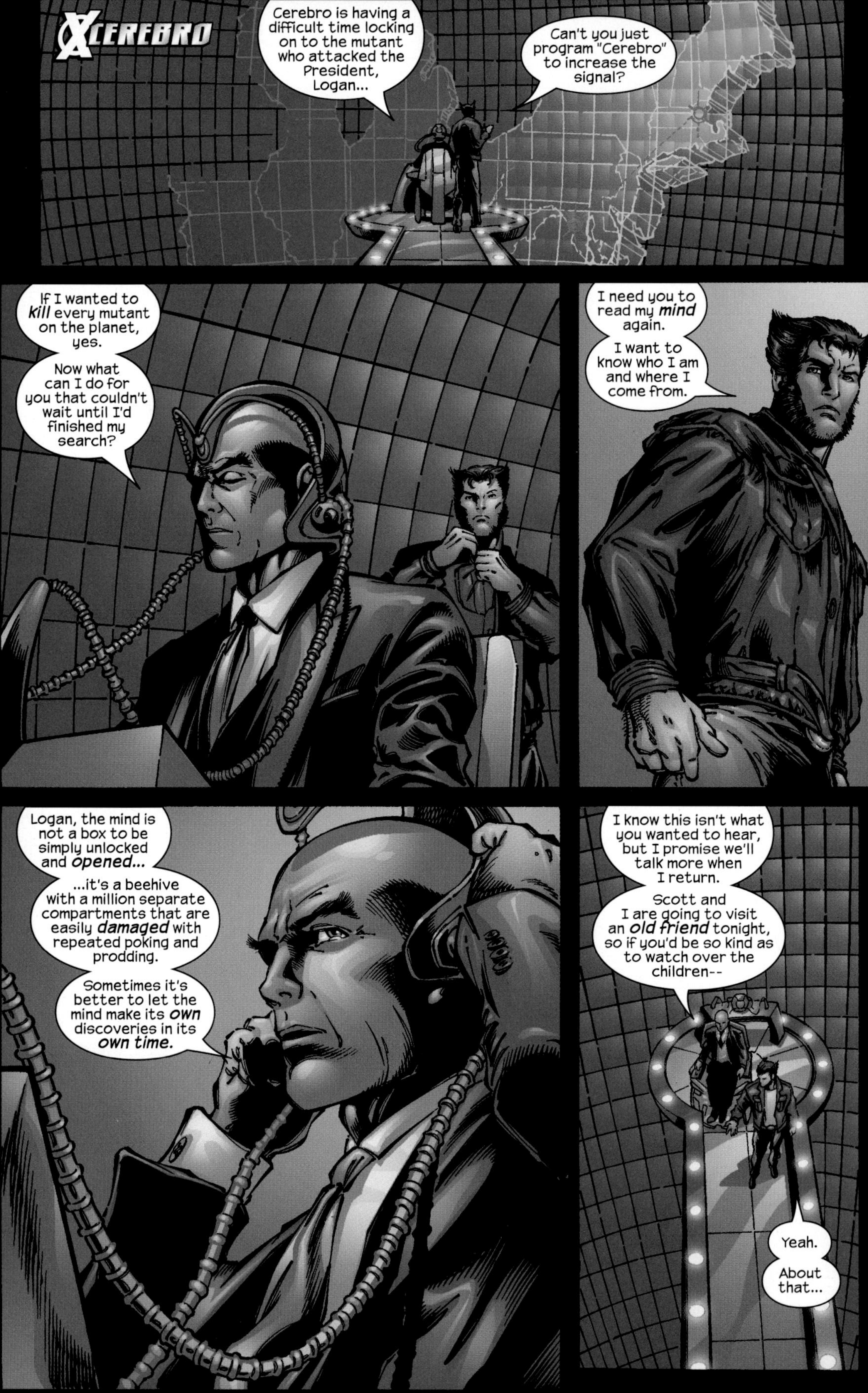

CEREBRO
Cerebro is having a difficult time locking on to the mutant who attacked the President, Logan...
Can't you just program "Cerebro" to increase the signal?
If I wanted to kill every mutant on the planet, yes.
Now what can I do for you that couldn't wait until I'd finished my search?
I need you to read my mind again.
I want to know who I am and where I come from.
Logan, the mind is not a box to be simply unlocked and opened...
...it's a beehive with a million separate compartments that are easily damaged with repeated poking and prodding.
Sometimes it's better to let the mind make its own discoveries in its own time.
I know this isn't what you wanted to hear, but I promise we'll talk more when I return.
Scott and I are going to visit an old friend tonight, so if you'd be so kind as to watch over the children--
Yeah.
About that...

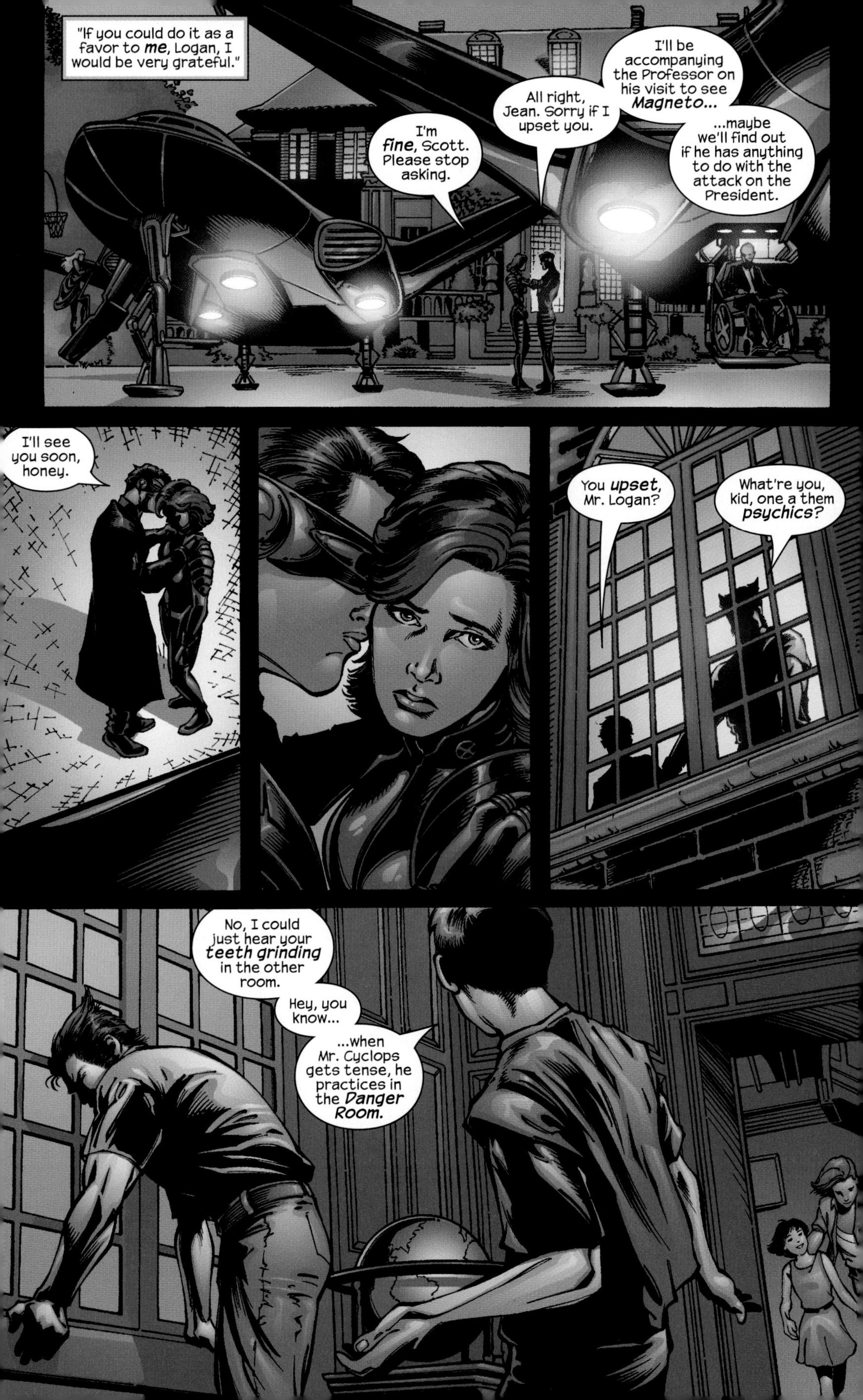

"If you could do it as a favor to *me*, Logan, I would be very grateful."
I'm *fine*, Scott. Please stop asking.
All right, Jean. Sorry if I upset you.
I'll be accompanying the Professor on his visit to see *Magneto*...
...maybe we'll find out if he has anything to do with the attack on the President.
I'll see you soon, honey.
You *upset*, Mr. Logan?
What're you, kid, one a them *psychics?*
No, I could just hear your *teeth grinding* in the other room.
Hey, you know...
...when Mr. Cyclops gets tense, he practices in the *Danger Room.*

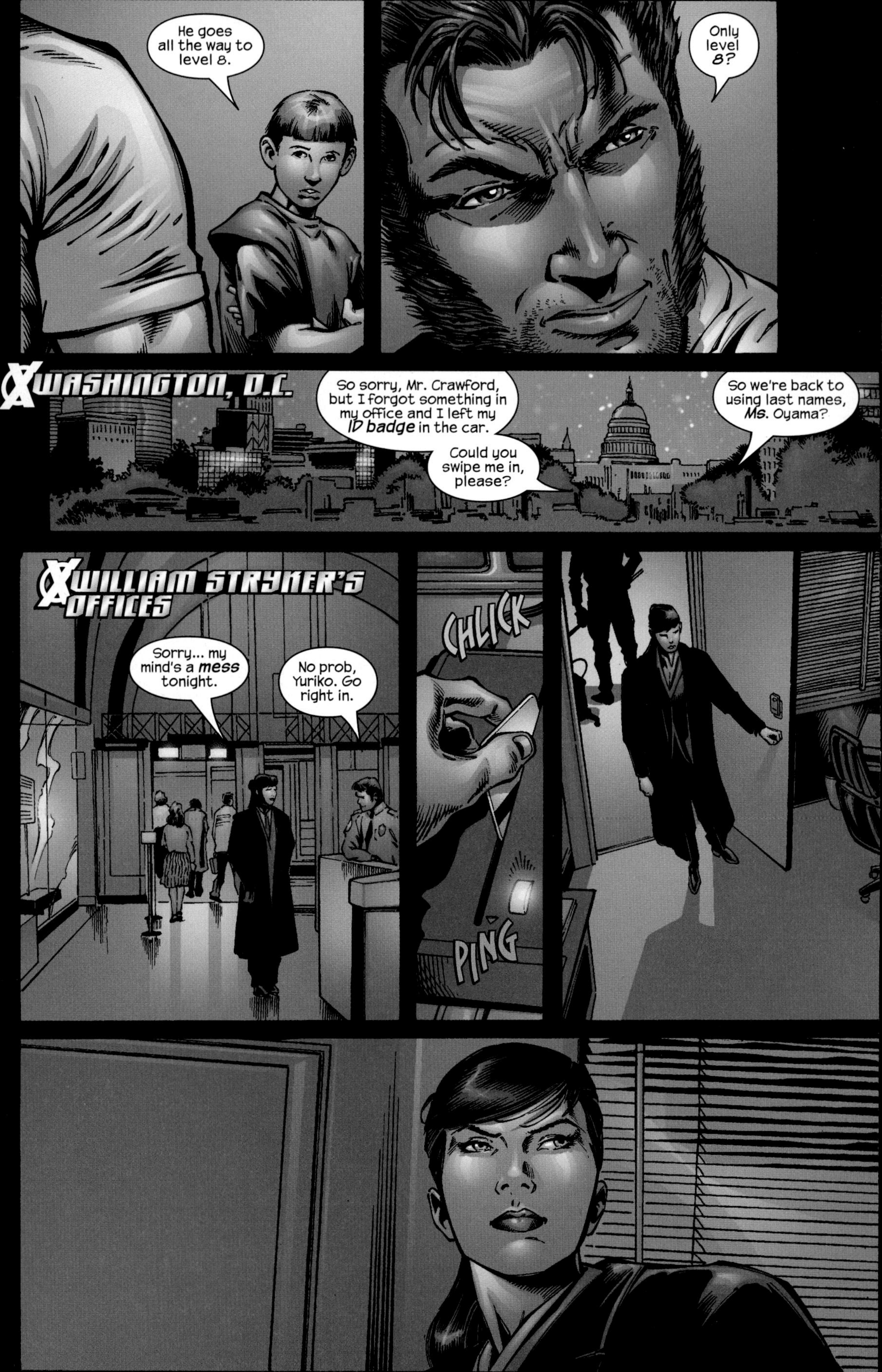
He goes all the way to level 8.
Only level 8?
WASHINGTON, D.C.
So sorry, Mr. Crawford, but I forgot something in my office and I left my ID badge in the car.
Could you swipe me in, please?
So we're back to using last names, Ms. Oyama?
WILLIAM STRYKER'S OFFICES
Sorry... my mind's a mess tonight.
No prob, Yuriko. Go right in.
CHLICK
PING

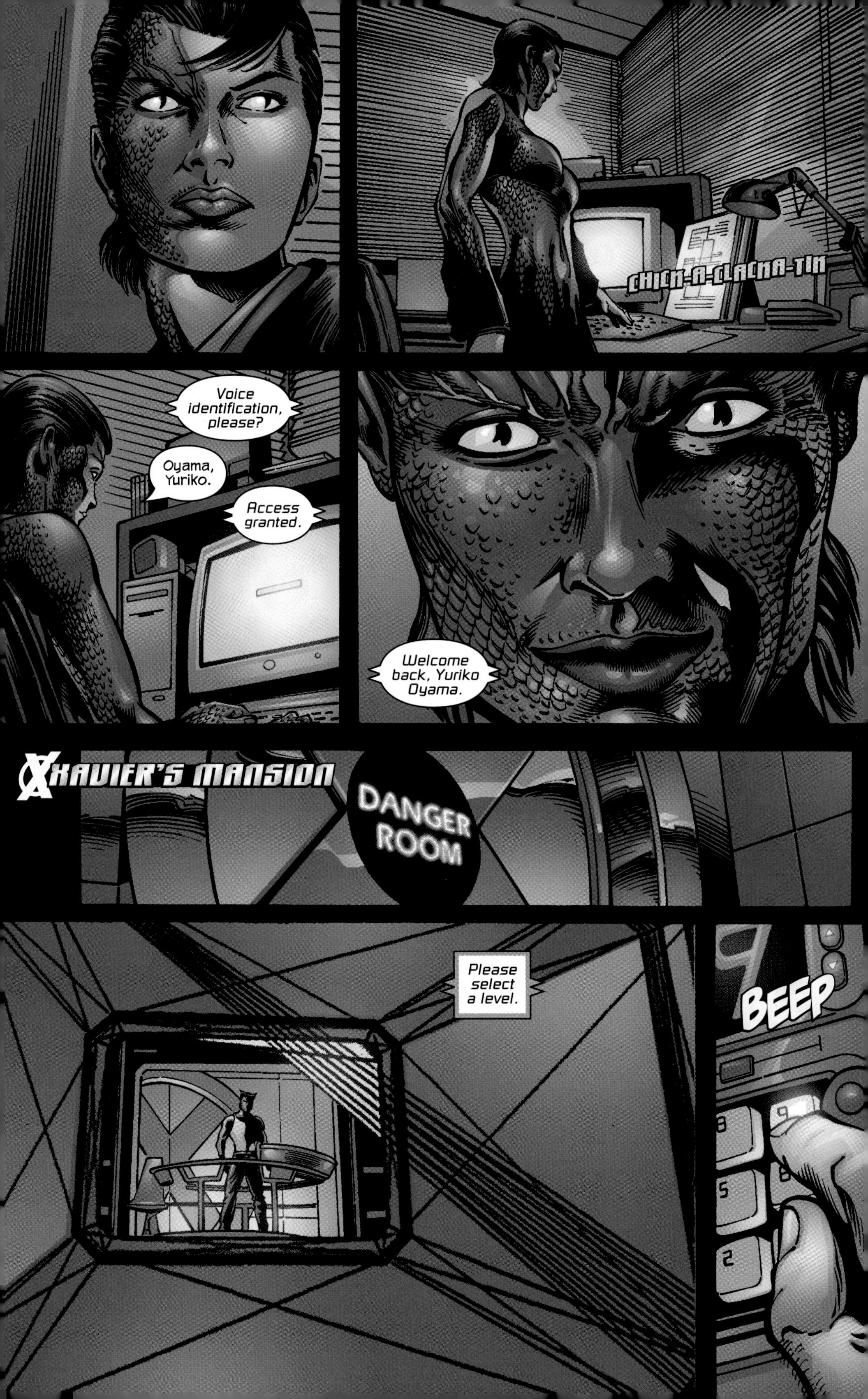
CHICK-A-CLACKA-TIK
Voice identification, please?
Oyama, Yuriko.
Access granted.
Welcome back, Yuriko Oyama.
XAVIER'S MANSION
DANGER ROOM
Please select a level.
BEEP

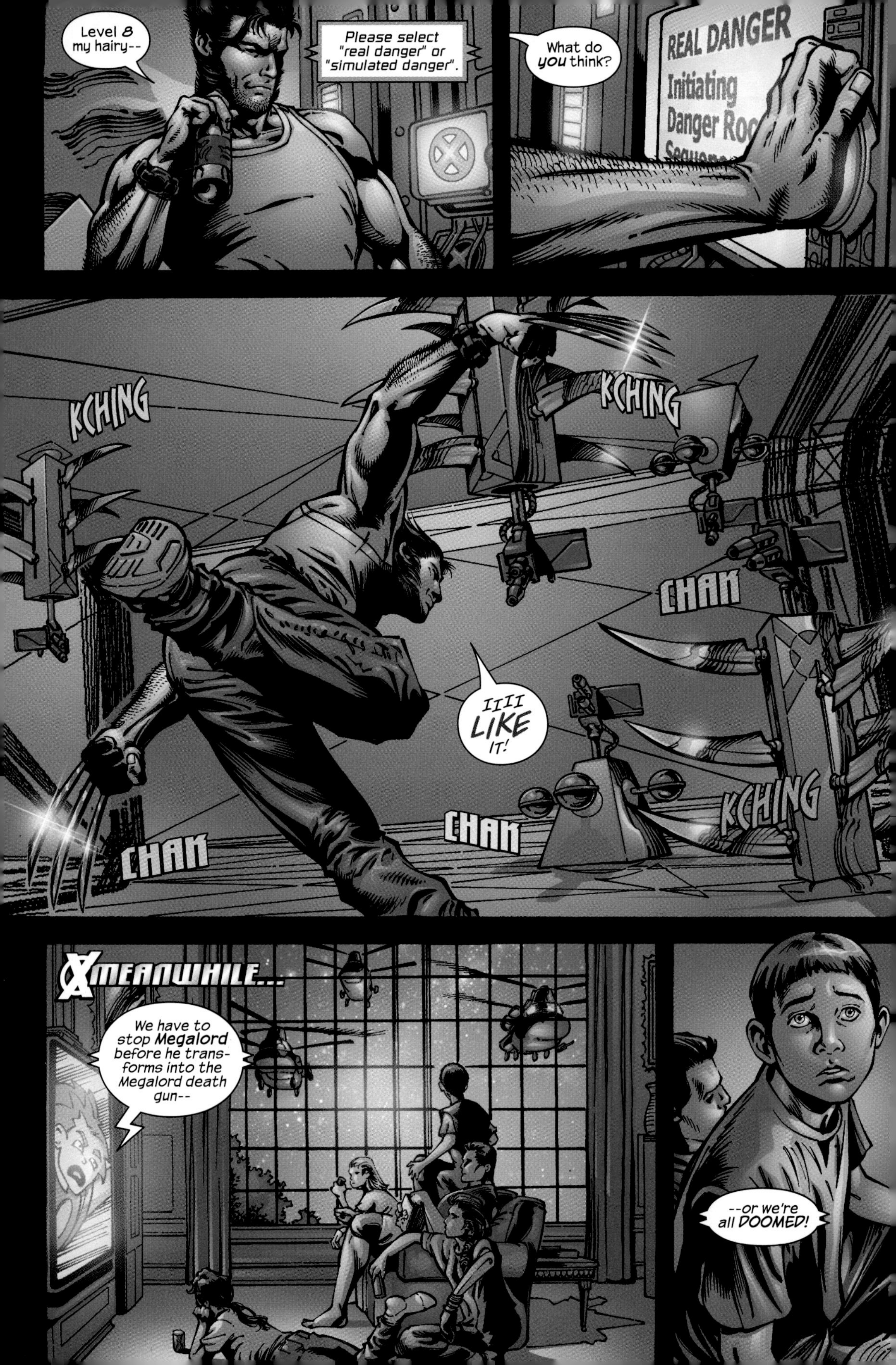
Level 8 my hairy--
Please select "real danger" or "simulated danger".
What do you think?
REAL DANGER
Initiating
KCHING
KCHING
CHAK
IIII LIKE IT!
KCHING
CHAK
CHAK
MEANWHILE...
We have to stop Megalord before he transforms into the Megalord death gun--
--or we're all DOOMED!

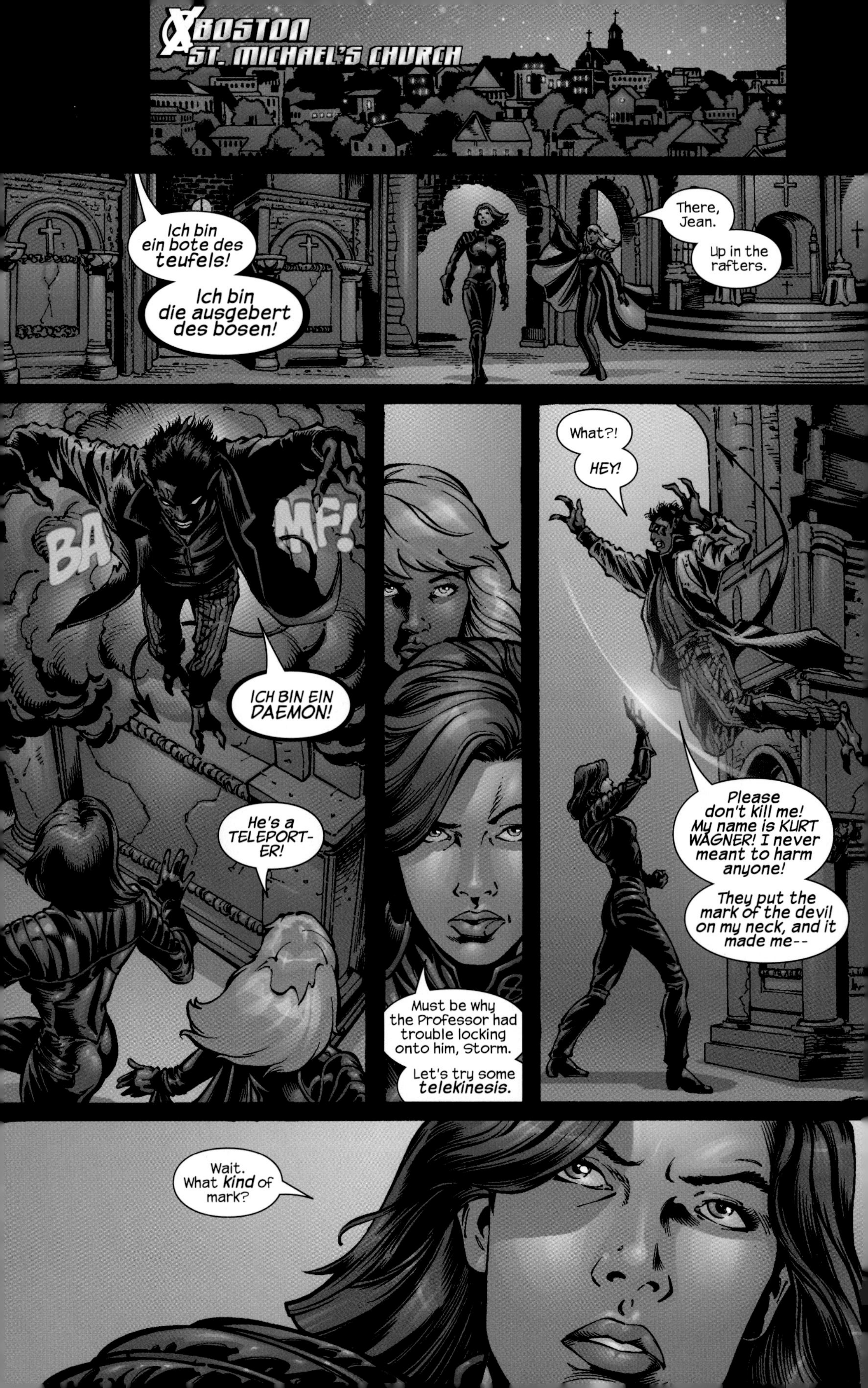
BOSTON
ST. MICHAEL'S CHURCH
Ich bin ein bote des teufels!
Ich bin die ausgebert des bosen!
There, Jean.
Up in the rafters.
BAMF!
ICH BIN EIN DAEMON!
He's a TELEPORT-ER!
Must be why the Professor had trouble locking onto him, Storm.
Let's try some telekinesis.
What?!
HEY!
Please don't kill me! My name is KURT WAGNER! I never meant to harm anyone!
They put the mark of the devil on my neck, and it made me--
Wait. What kind of mark?

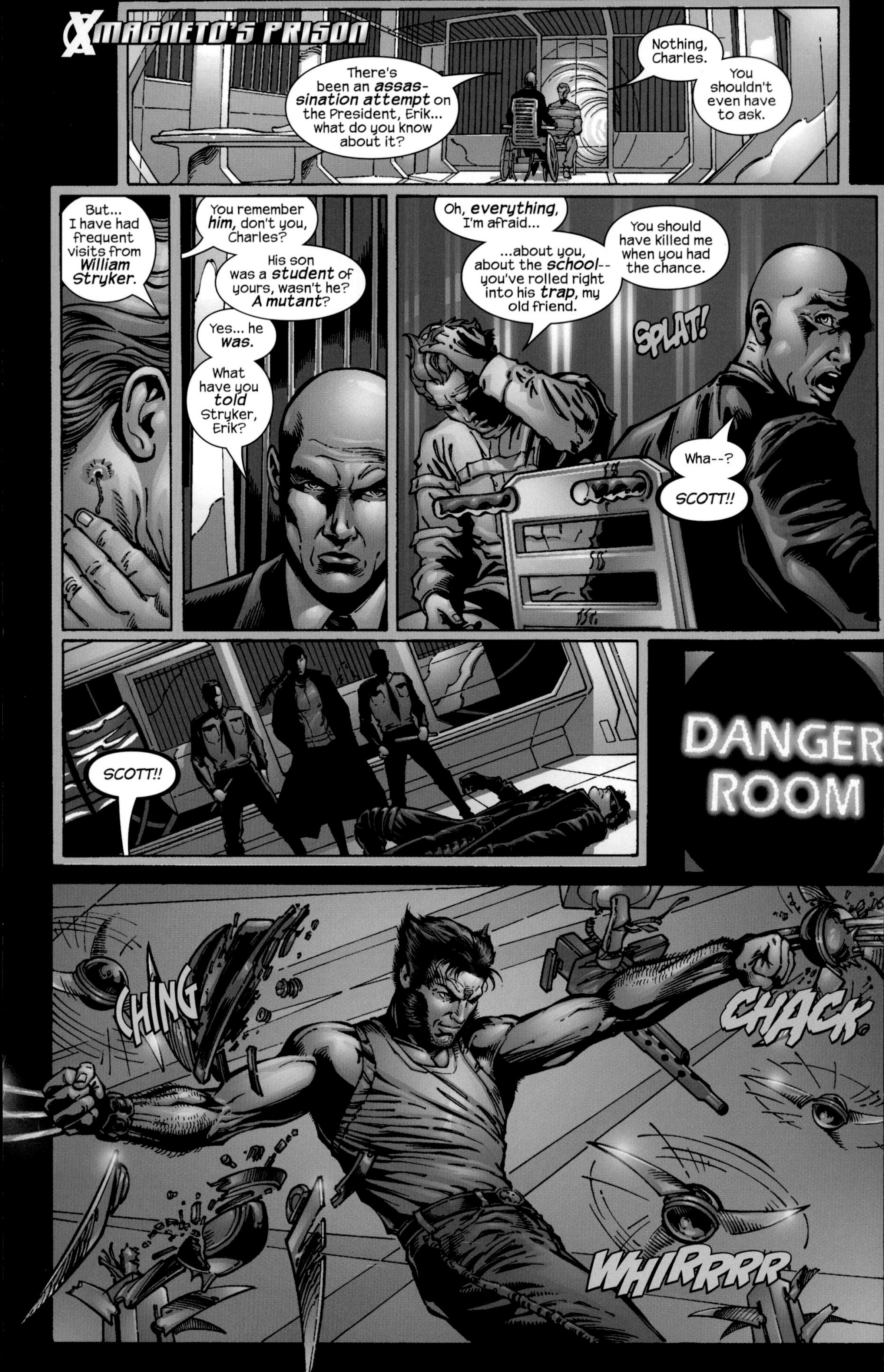

MAGNETO'S PRISON
There's been an assassination attempt on the President, Erik... what do you know about it?
Nothing, Charles.
You shouldn't even have to ask.
But... I have had frequent visits from William Stryker.
You remember him, don't you, Charles?
His son was a student of yours, wasn't he? A mutant?
Yes... he was.
What have you told Stryker, Erik?
Oh, everything, I'm afraid...
...about you, about the school--you've rolled right into his trap, my old friend.
You should have killed me when you had the chance.
SPLAT!
Wha--?
SCOTT!!
SCOTT!!
DANGER ROOM
CHING
CHACK
WHIRRRR

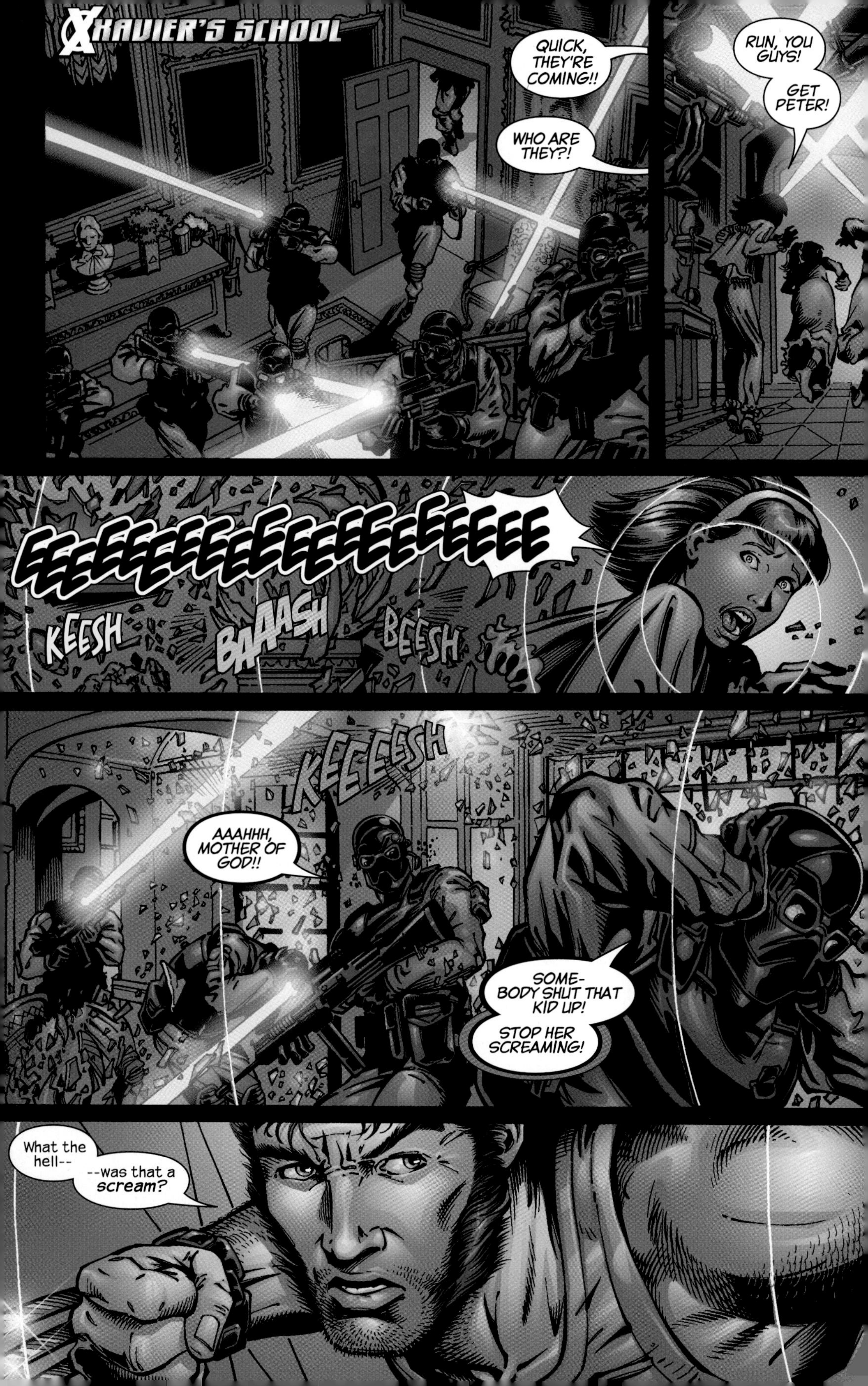

XAVIER'S SCHOOL
QUICK, THEY'RE COMING!!
WHO ARE THEY?!
RUN, YOU GUYS!
GET PETER!
EEEEEEEEEEEEEEEEEEEEEE
KEESH
BAAASH
BEESH
KEEEESH
AAAHHH, MOTHER OF GOD!!
SOME-BODY SHUT THAT KID UP!
STOP HER SCREAMING!
What the hell--
--was that a *scream*?

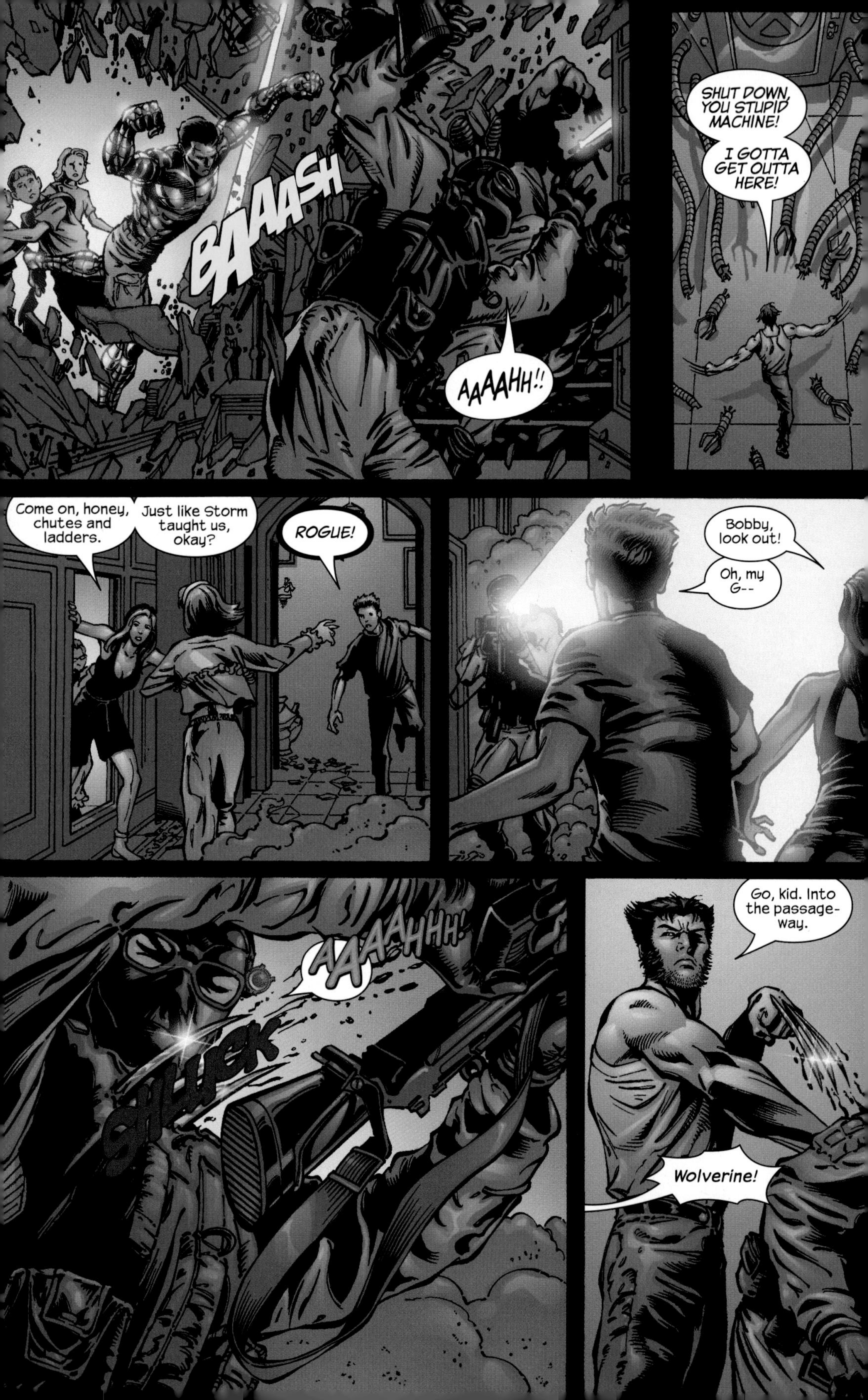
BAAASH
AAAAHH!!
SHUT DOWN, YOU STUPID MACHINE!
I GOTTA GET OUTTA HERE!
Come on, honey, chutes and ladders.
Just like Storm taught us, okay?
ROGUE!
Bobby, look out!
Oh, my G--
SHUCK
AAAAHHH!
Go, kid. Into the passage-way.
Wolverine!

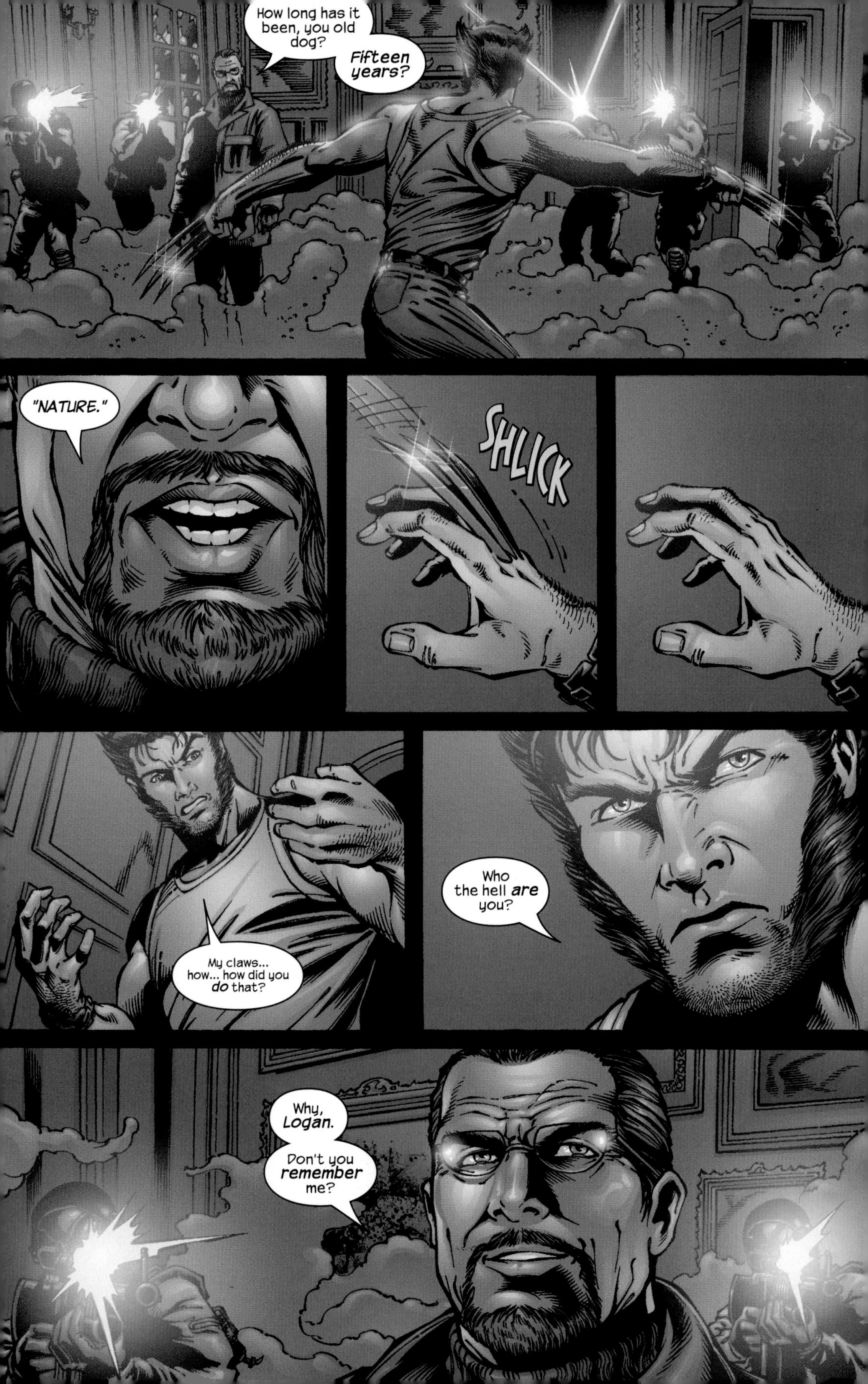

How long has it been, you old dog?
Fifteen years?
"NATURE."
SHLICK
My claws... how... how did you do that?
Who the hell are you?
Why, Logan.
Don't you remember me?

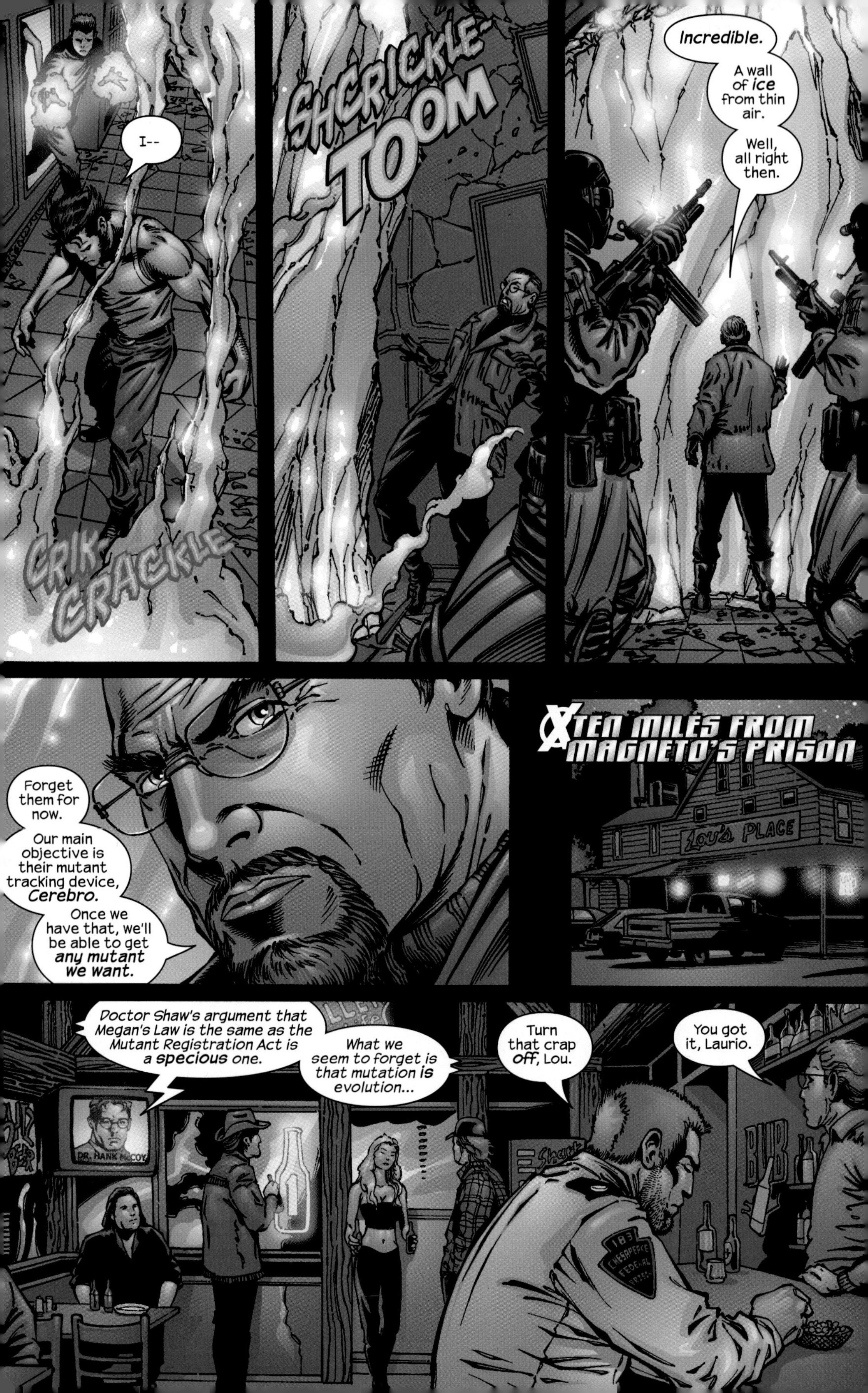
I--
CRIK-CRACKLE
SHCRICKLE-TOOM
Incredible.
A wall of ice from thin air.
Well, all right then.
Forget them for now.
Our main objective is their mutant tracking device, Cerebro.
Once we have that, we'll be able to get any mutant we want.
TEN MILES FROM MAGNETO'S PRISON
LOU'S PLACE
Doctor Shaw's argument that Megan's Law is the same as the Mutant Registration Act is a specious one.
What we seem to forget is that mutation is evolution...
DR. HANK McCOY
Turn that crap off, Lou.
You got it, Laurio.

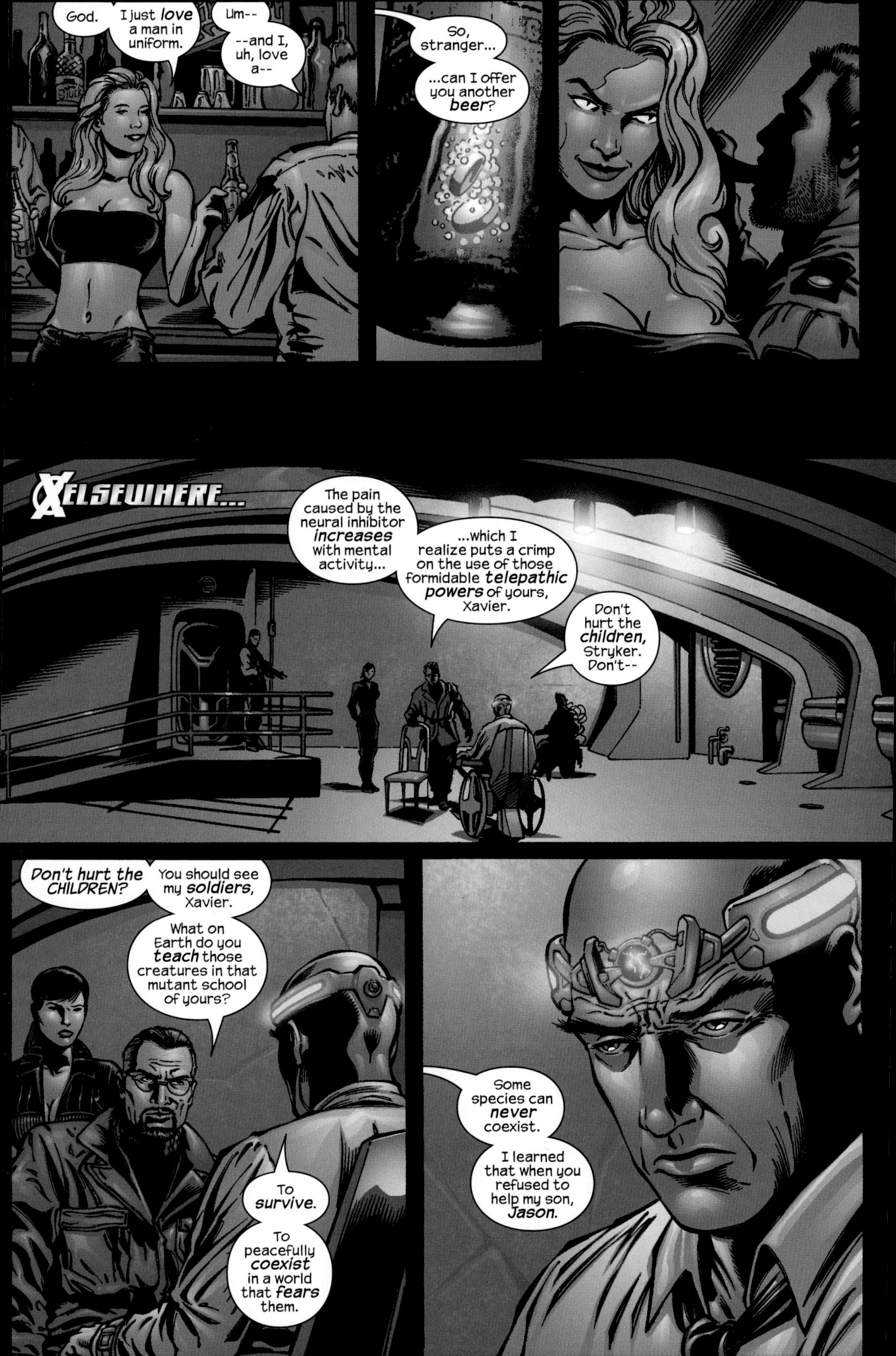
God.
I just love a man in uniform.
Um--
--and I, uh, love a--
So, stranger...
...can I offer you another beer?
ELSEWHERE...
The pain caused by the neural inhibitor increases with mental activity...
...which I realize puts a crimp on the use of those formidable telepathic powers of yours, Xavier.
Don't hurt the children, Stryker. Don't--
Don't hurt the CHILDREN?
You should see my soldiers, Xavier.
What on Earth do you teach those creatures in that mutant school of yours?
To survive.
To peacefully coexist in a world that fears them.
Some species can never coexist.
I learned that when you refused to help my son, Jason.

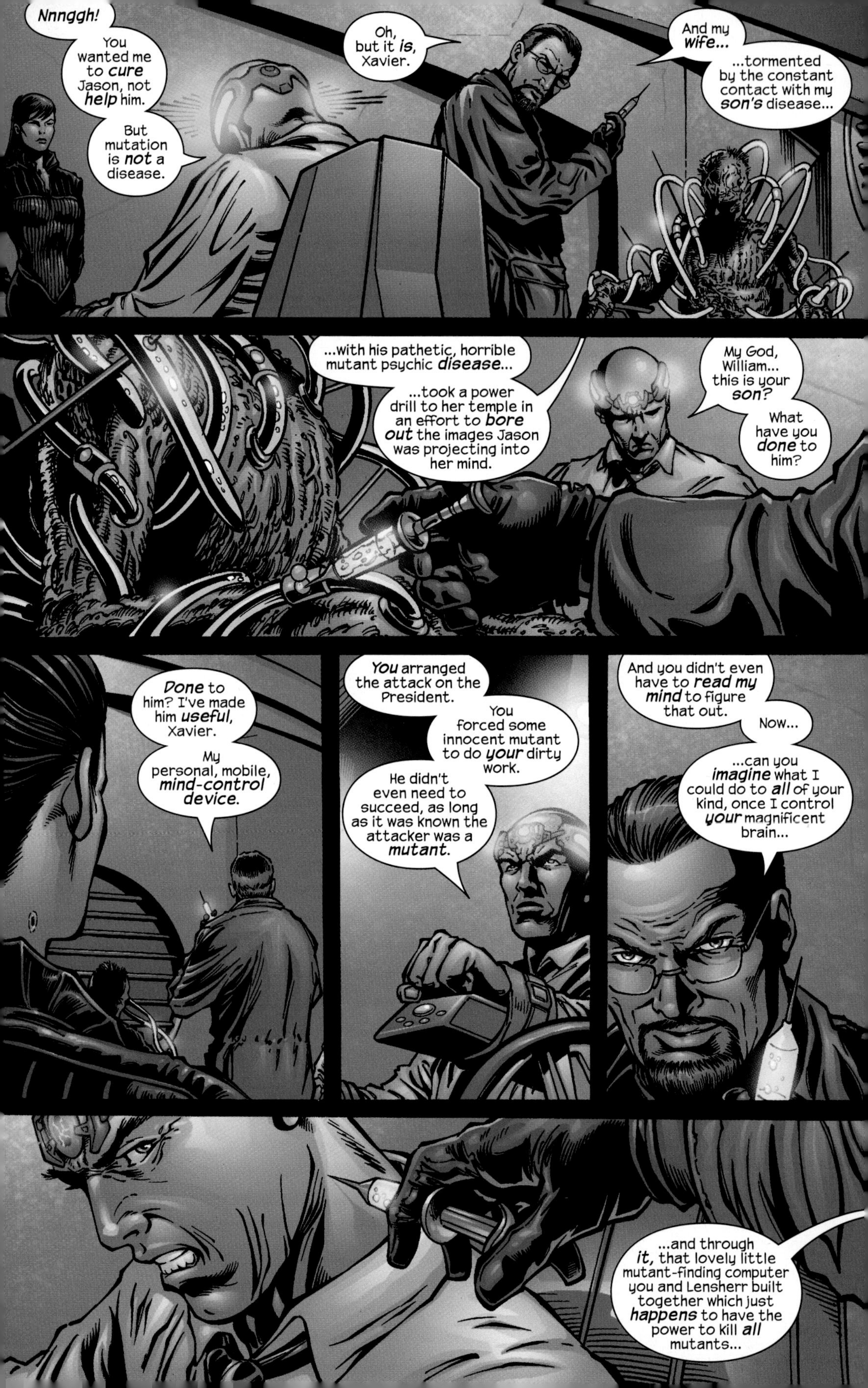

Nnngh!
You wanted me to *cure* Jason, not *help* him.
But mutation is *not* a disease.
Oh, but it *is*, Xavier.
And my *wife*...
...tormented by the constant contact with my *son's* disease...
...with his pathetic, horrible mutant psychic *disease*...
...took a power drill to her temple in an effort to *bore out* the images Jason was projecting into her mind.
My God, William... this is your *son?*
What have you *done* to him?
Done to him? I've made him *useful*, Xavier.
My personal, mobile, *mind-control device*.
You arranged the attack on the President.
You forced some innocent mutant to do *your* dirty work.
He didn't even need to succeed, as long as it was known the attacker was a *mutant*.
And you didn't even have to *read my mind* to figure that out.
Now...
...can you *imagine* what I could do to *all* of your kind, once I control *your* magnificent brain...
...and through *it*, that lovely little mutant-finding computer you and Lensherr built together which just *happens* to have the power to kill *all* mutants...

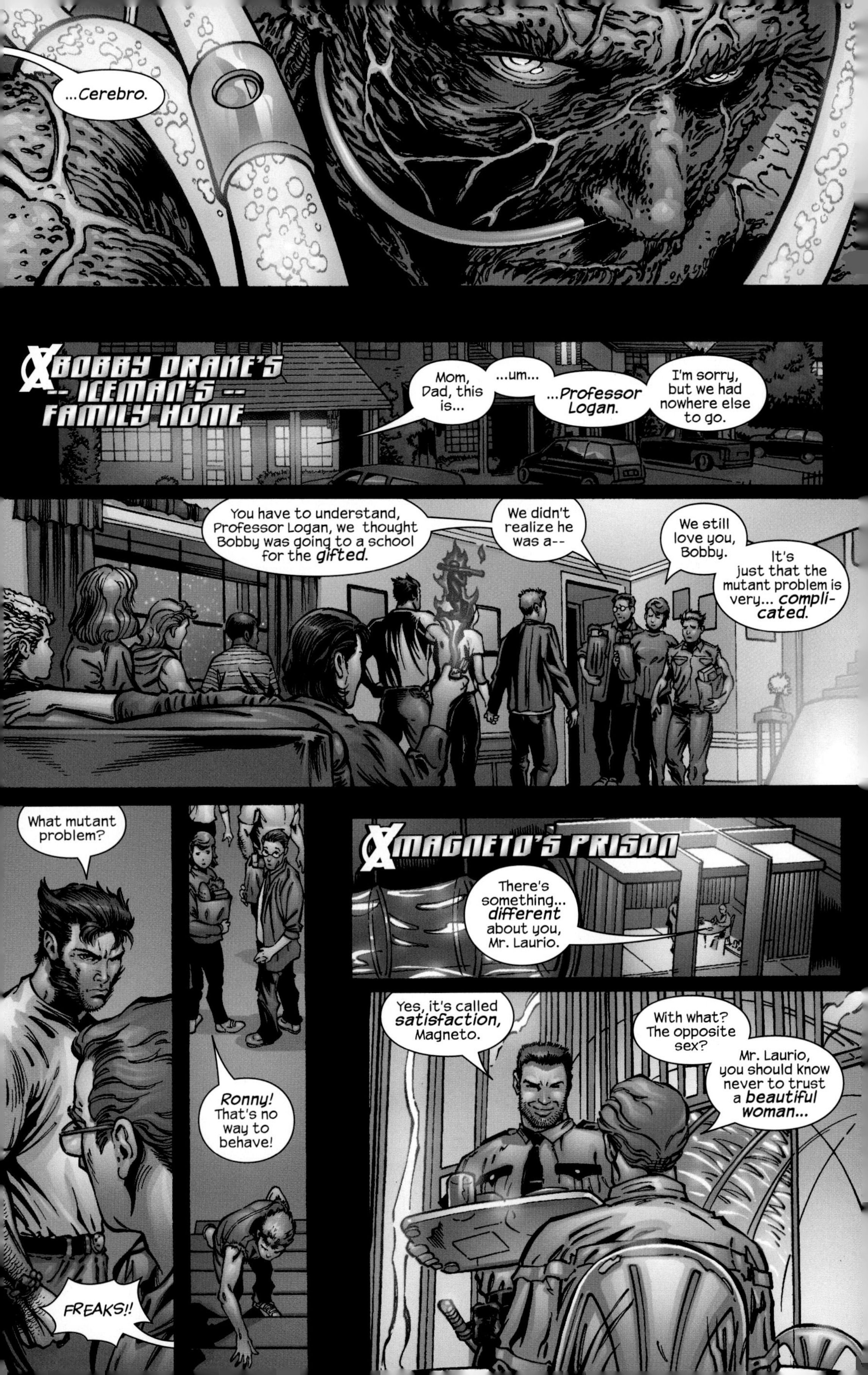

...Cerebro.
BOBBY DRAKE'S -- ICEMAN'S -- FAMILY HOME
Mom, Dad, this is...
...um...
...Professor Logan.
I'm sorry, but we had nowhere else to go.
You have to understand, Professor Logan, we thought Bobby was going to a school for the gifted.
We didn't realize he was a--
We still love you, Bobby.
It's just that the mutant problem is very... compli-cated.
What mutant problem?
Ronny! That's no way to behave!
FREAKS!!
MAGNETO'S PRISON
There's something... different about you, Mr. Laurio.
Yes, it's called satisfaction, Magneto.
With what? The opposite sex?
Mr. Laurio, you should know never to trust a beautiful woman...

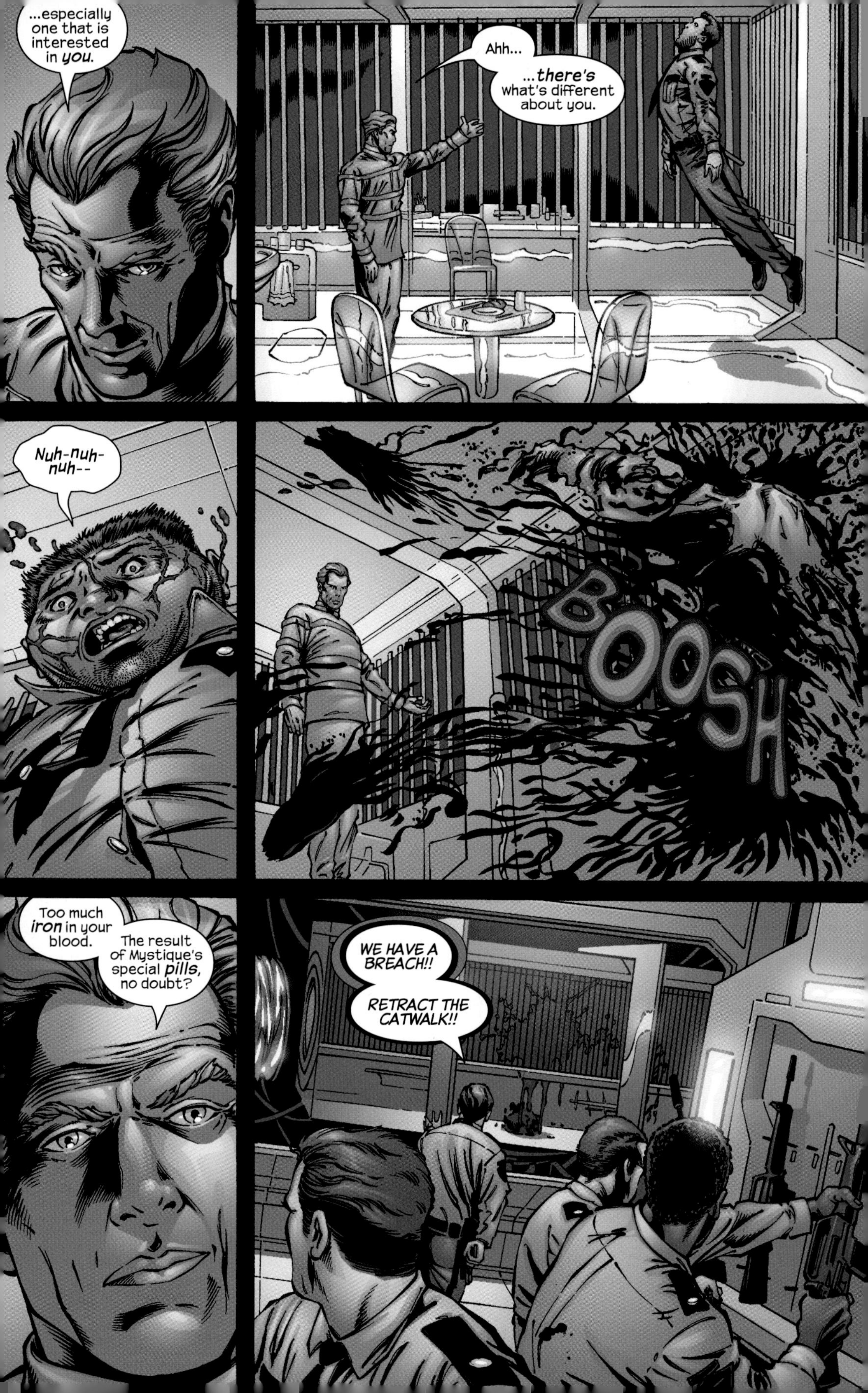
...especially one that is interested in *you*.
Ahh...
...*there's* what's different about you.
Nuh-nuh-nuh--
BOOSH
Too much *iron* in your blood.
The result of Mystique's special *pills*, no doubt?
WE HAVE A BREACH!!
RETRACT THE CATWALK!!

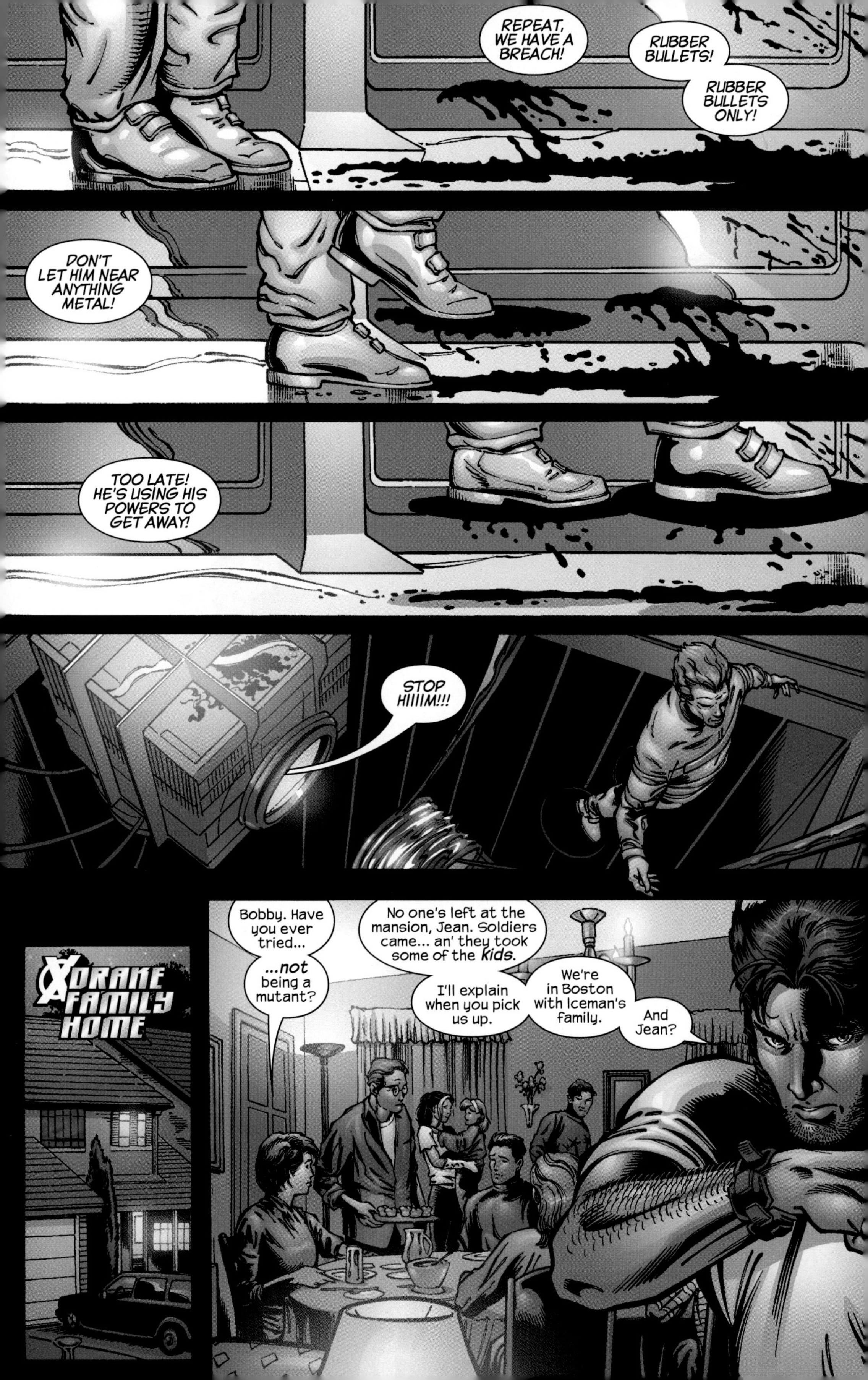
REPEAT, WE HAVE A BREACH!
RUBBER BULLETS!
RUBBER BULLETS ONLY!
DON'T LET HIM NEAR ANYTHING METAL!
TOO LATE! HE'S USING HIS POWERS TO GET AWAY!
STOP HIIIIM!!!
DRAKE FAMILY HOME
Bobby. Have you ever tried...
...not being a mutant?
No one's left at the mansion, Jean. Soldiers came... an' they took some of the kids.
I'll explain when you pick us up.
We're in Boston with Iceman's family.
And Jean?

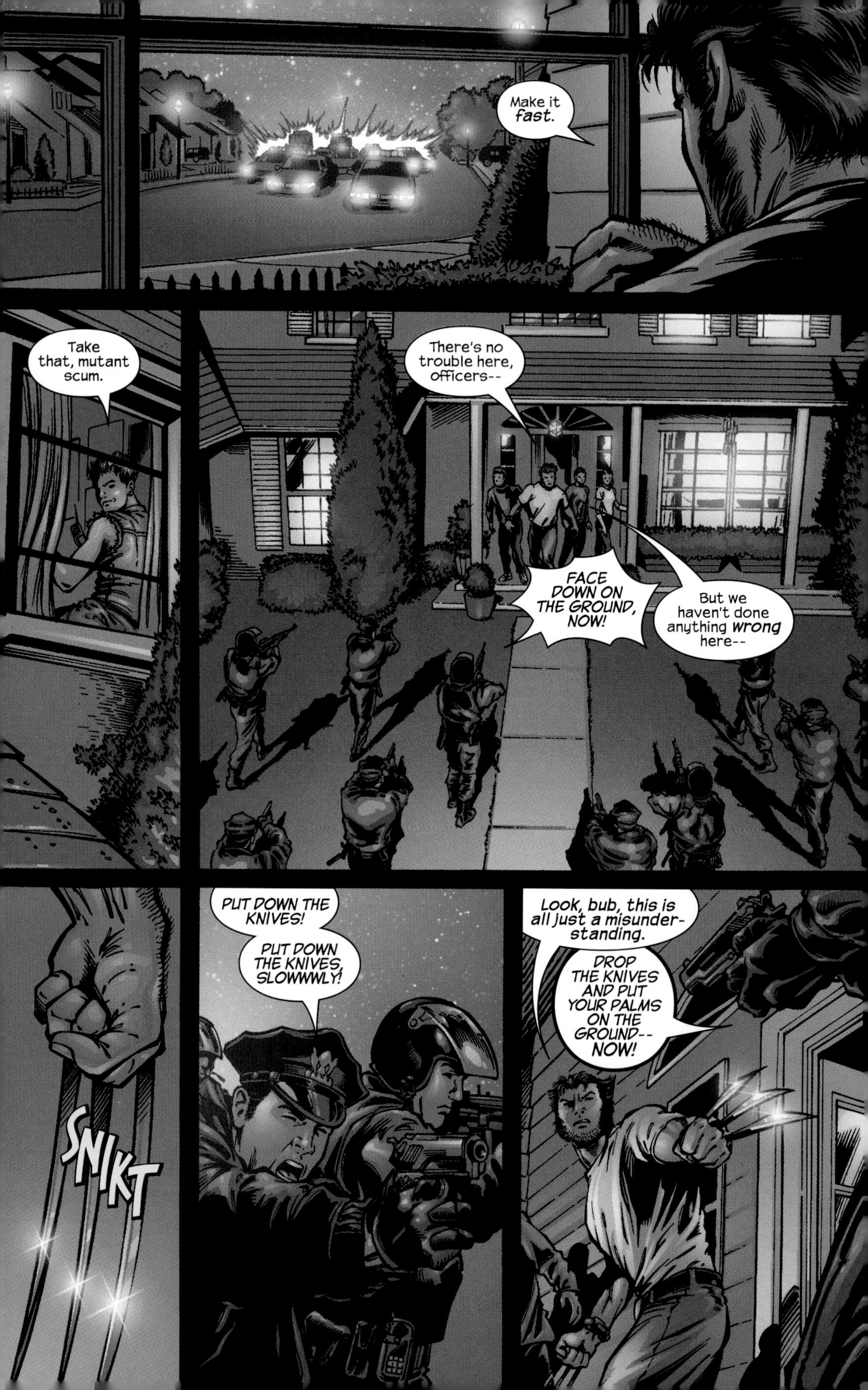
Make it *fast*.
Take that, mutant scum.
There's no trouble here, officers--
FACE DOWN ON THE GROUND, NOW!
But we haven't done anything *wrong* here--
SNIKT
PUT DOWN THE KNIVES!
PUT DOWN THE KNIVES, SLOWWWLY!
Look, bub, this is all just a misunder-standing.
DROP THE KNIVES AND PUT YOUR PALMS ON THE GROUND-- NOW!

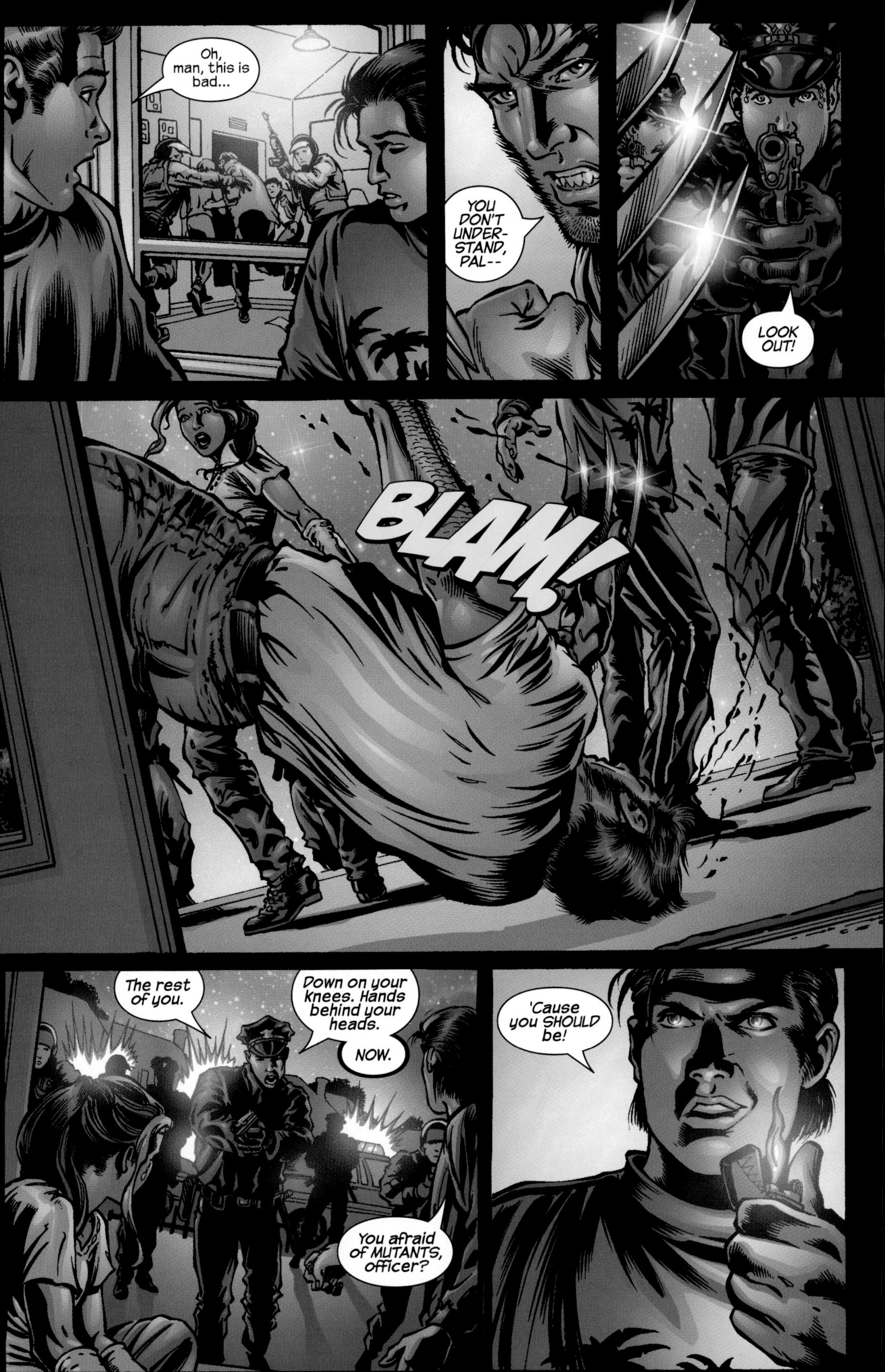
Oh, man, this is bad...
YOU DON'T UNDER-STAND, PAL--
LOOK OUT!
BLAM!
The rest of you.
Down on your knees. Hands behind your heads.
NOW.
You afraid of MUTANTS, officer?
'Cause you SHOULD be!

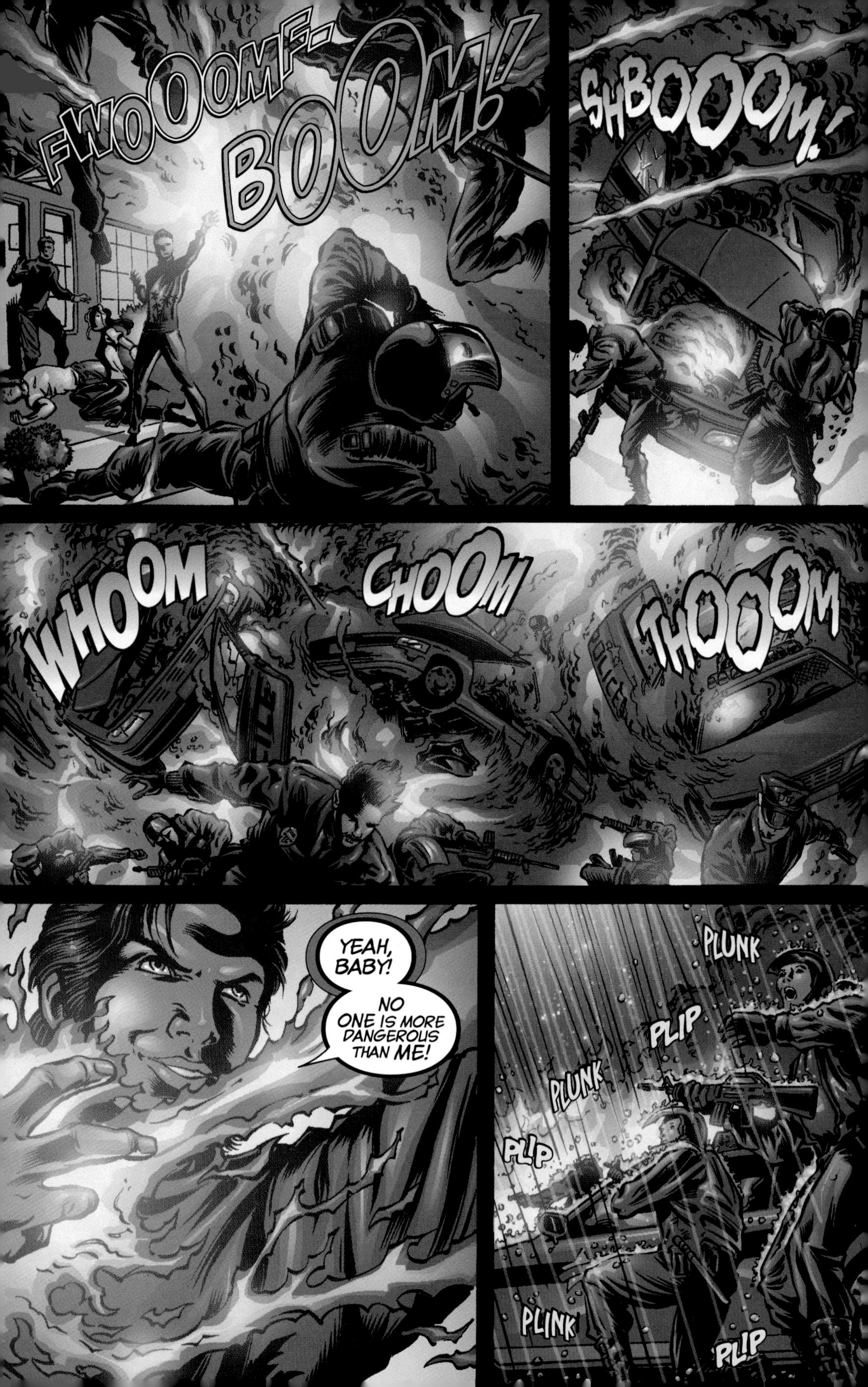
FWOOOMF-BOOM!
SHBOOOM!
WHOOM
CHOOM
THOOOM
YEAH, BABY!
NO ONE IS MORE DANGEROUS THAN ME!
PLUNK
PLIP
PLUNK
PLIP
PLINK
PLIP

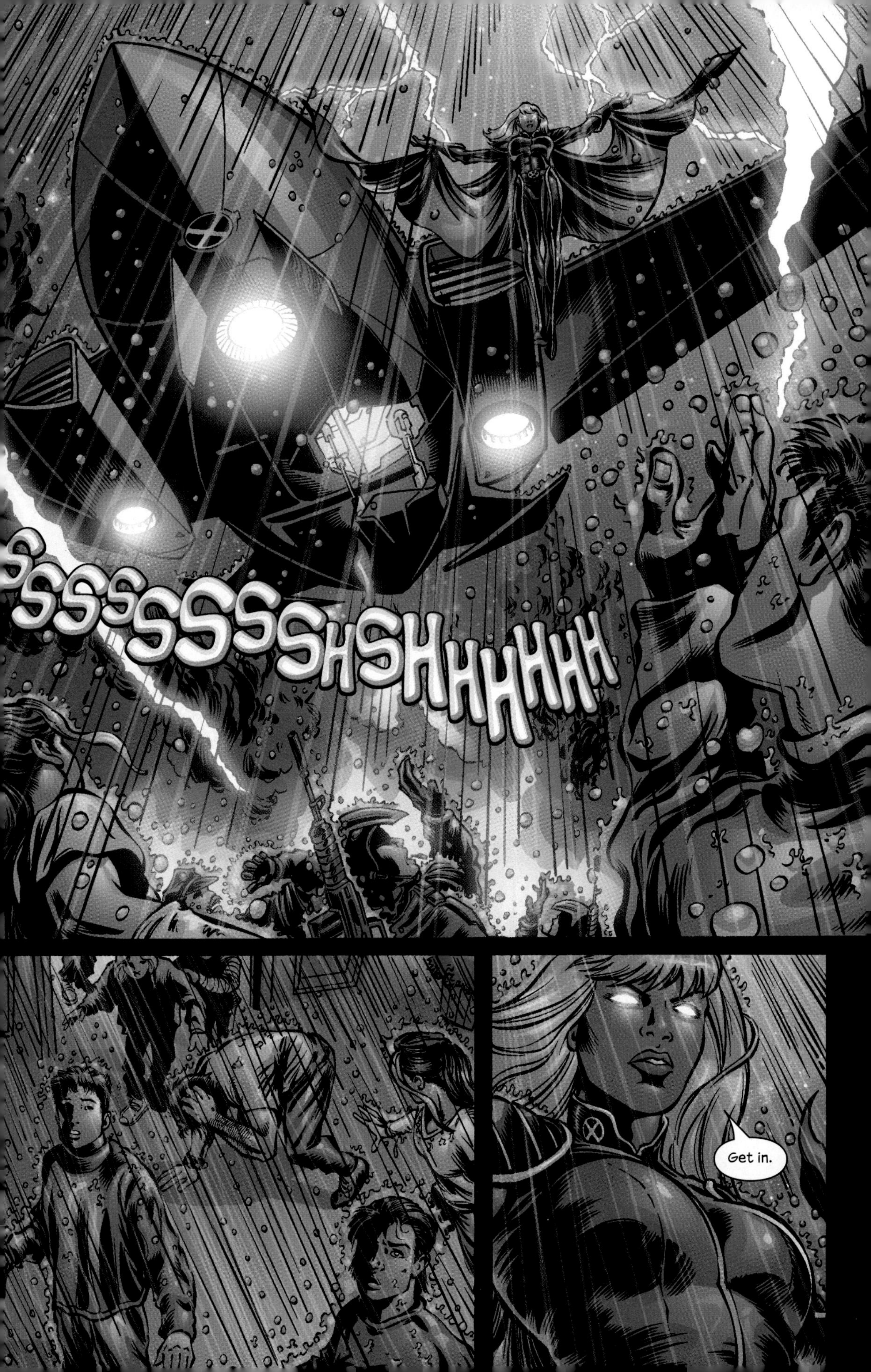
SSSSSSSSHSHHHHHH
Get in.

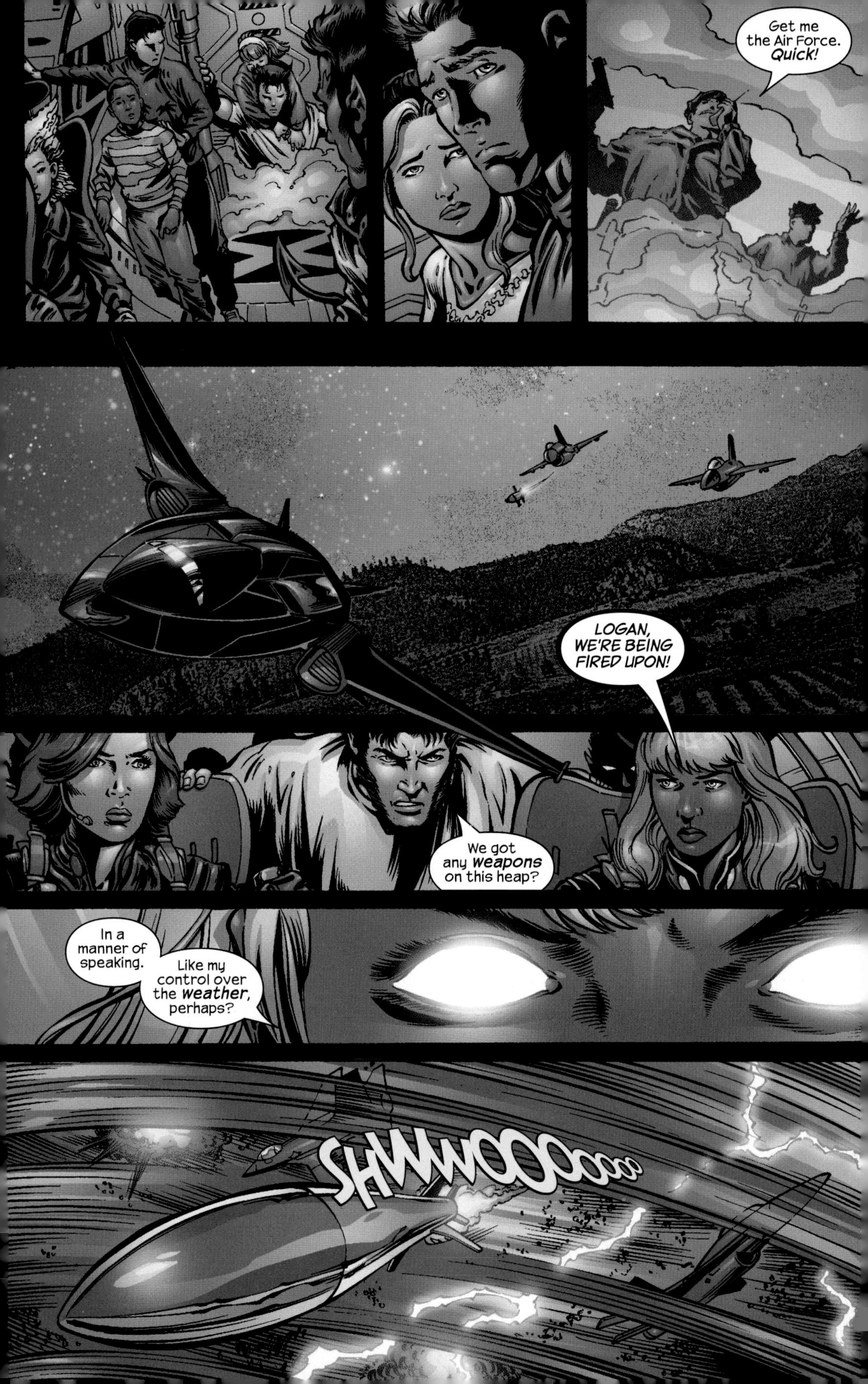

Get me the Air Force. *Quick!*
LOGAN, WE'RE BEING FIRED UPON!
We got any *weapons* on this heap?
In a manner of speaking.
Like my control over the *weather*, perhaps?
SHWWOOOOooo

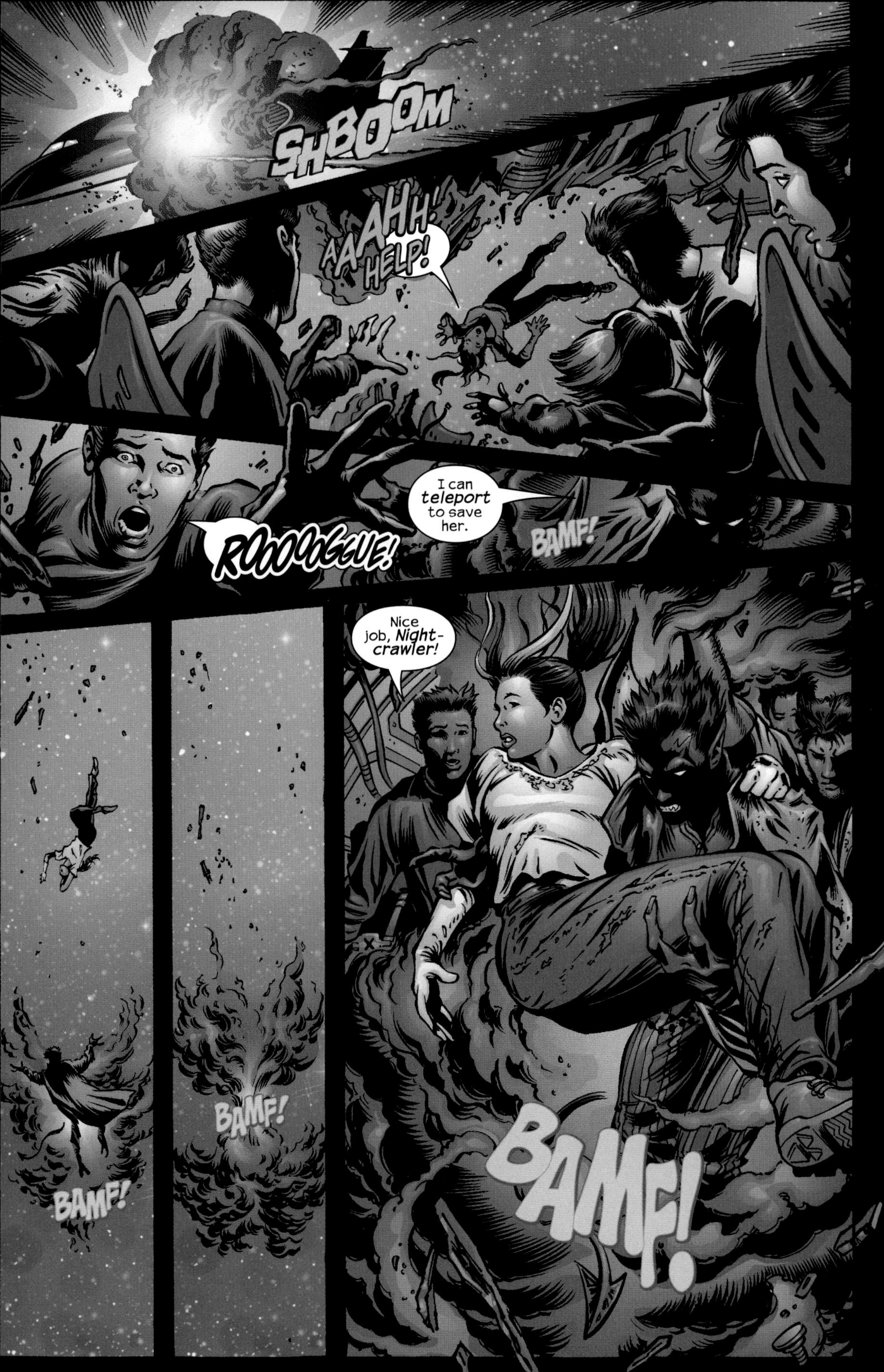
SHBOOM
AAAHH! HELP!
ROOOOOGGUE!
I can *teleport* to save her.
BAMF!
BAMF!
BAMF!
Nice job, *Night-crawler!*
BAMF!

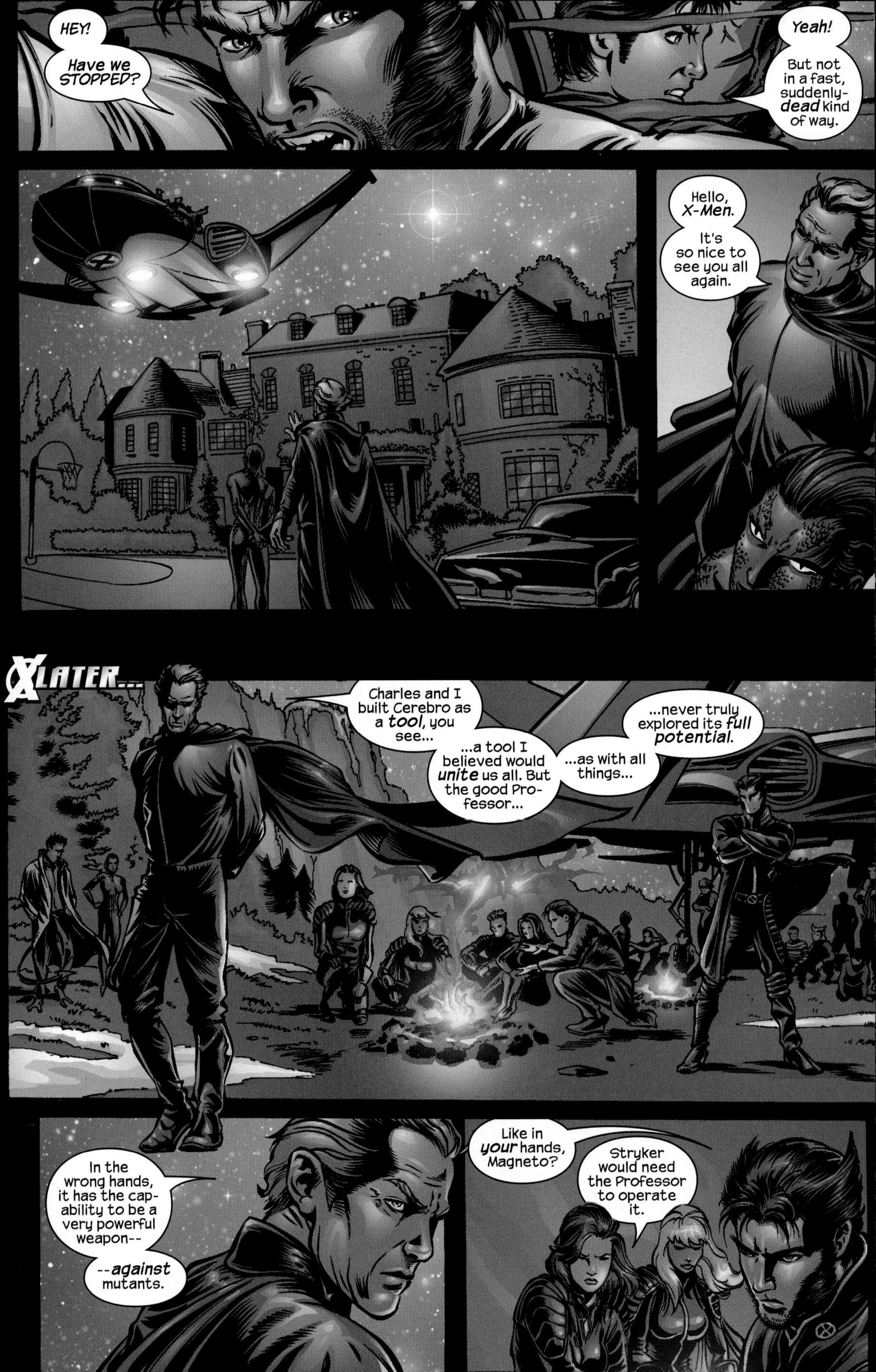
HEY!
Have we STOPPED?
Yeah!
But not in a fast, suddenly-dead kind of way.
Hello, X-Men.
It's so nice to see you all again.
LATER...
Charles and I built Cerebro as a tool, you see...
...a tool I believed would unite us all. But the good Professor...
...as with all things...
...never truly explored its full potential.
In the wrong hands, it has the capability to be a very powerful weapon--
--against mutants.
Like in your hands, Magneto?
Stryker would need the Professor to operate it.

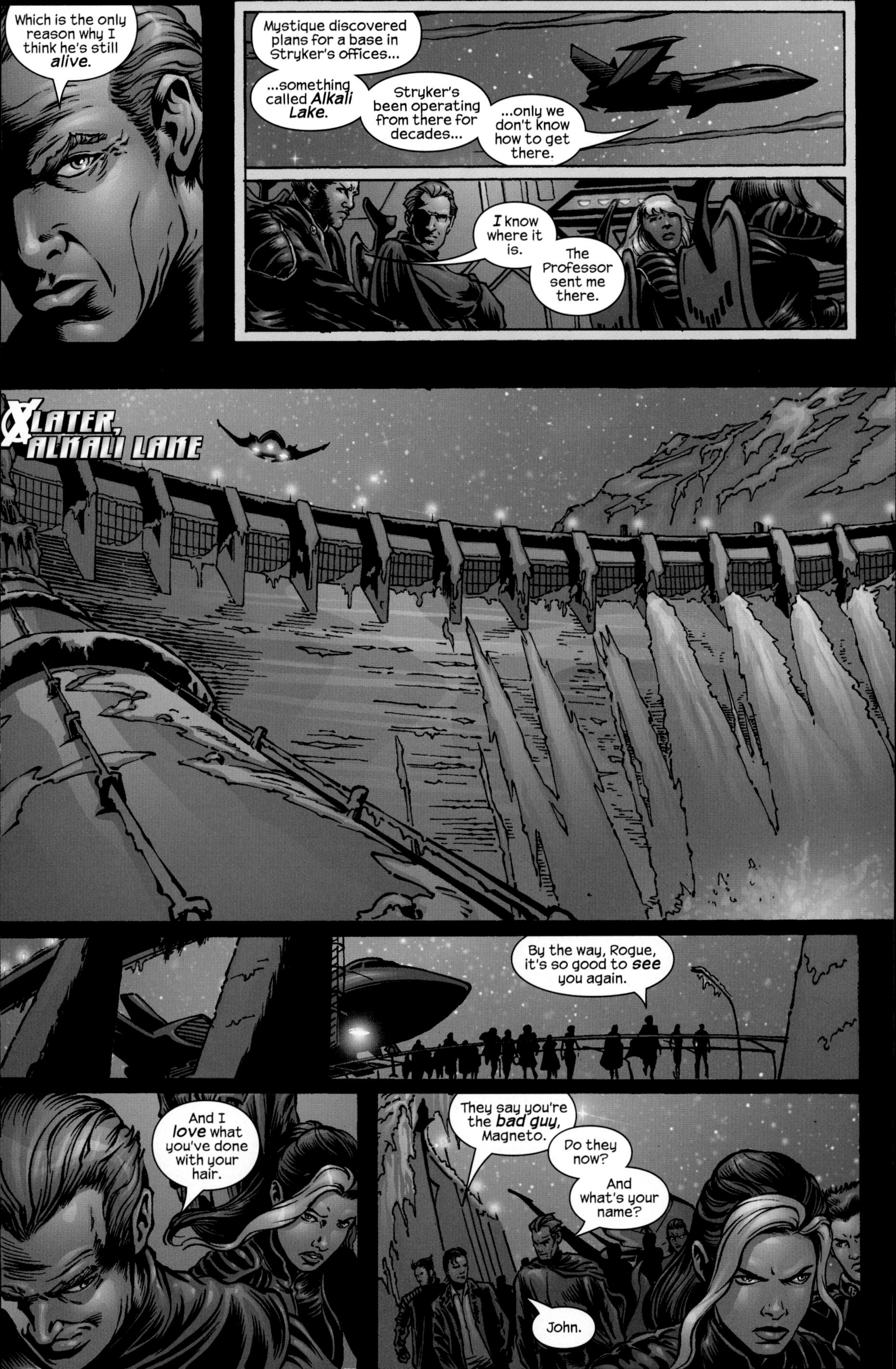
Which is the only reason why I think he's still *alive*.
Mystique discovered plans for a base in Stryker's offices...
...something called *Alkali Lake*.
Stryker's been operating from there for decades...
...only we don't know how to get there.
I know where it is.
The Professor sent me there.
LATER, ALKALI LAKE
By the way, Rogue, it's so good to *see* you again.
And I *love* what you've done with your hair.
They say you're the *bad guy*, Magneto.
Do they now?
And what's your name?
John.

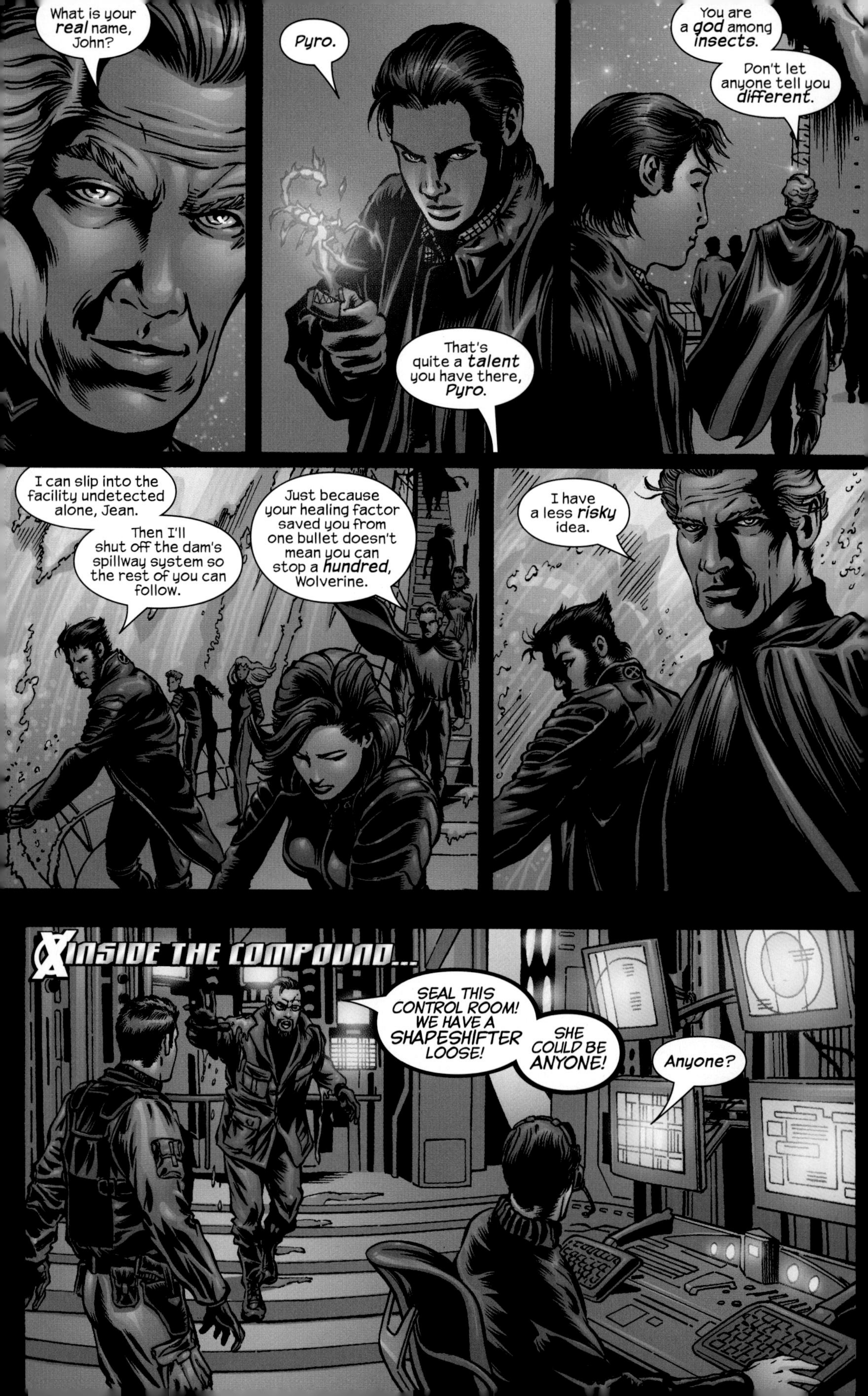

What is your real name, John?
Pyro.
That's quite a talent you have there, Pyro.
You are a god among insects.
Don't let anyone tell you different.
I can slip into the facility undetected alone, Jean.
Then I'll shut off the dam's spillway system so the rest of you can follow.
Just because your healing factor saved you from one bullet doesn't mean you can stop a hundred, Wolverine.
I have a less risky idea.
INSIDE THE COMPOUND...
SEAL THIS CONTROL ROOM! WE HAVE A SHAPESHIFTER LOOSE!
SHE COULD BE ANYONE!
Anyone?

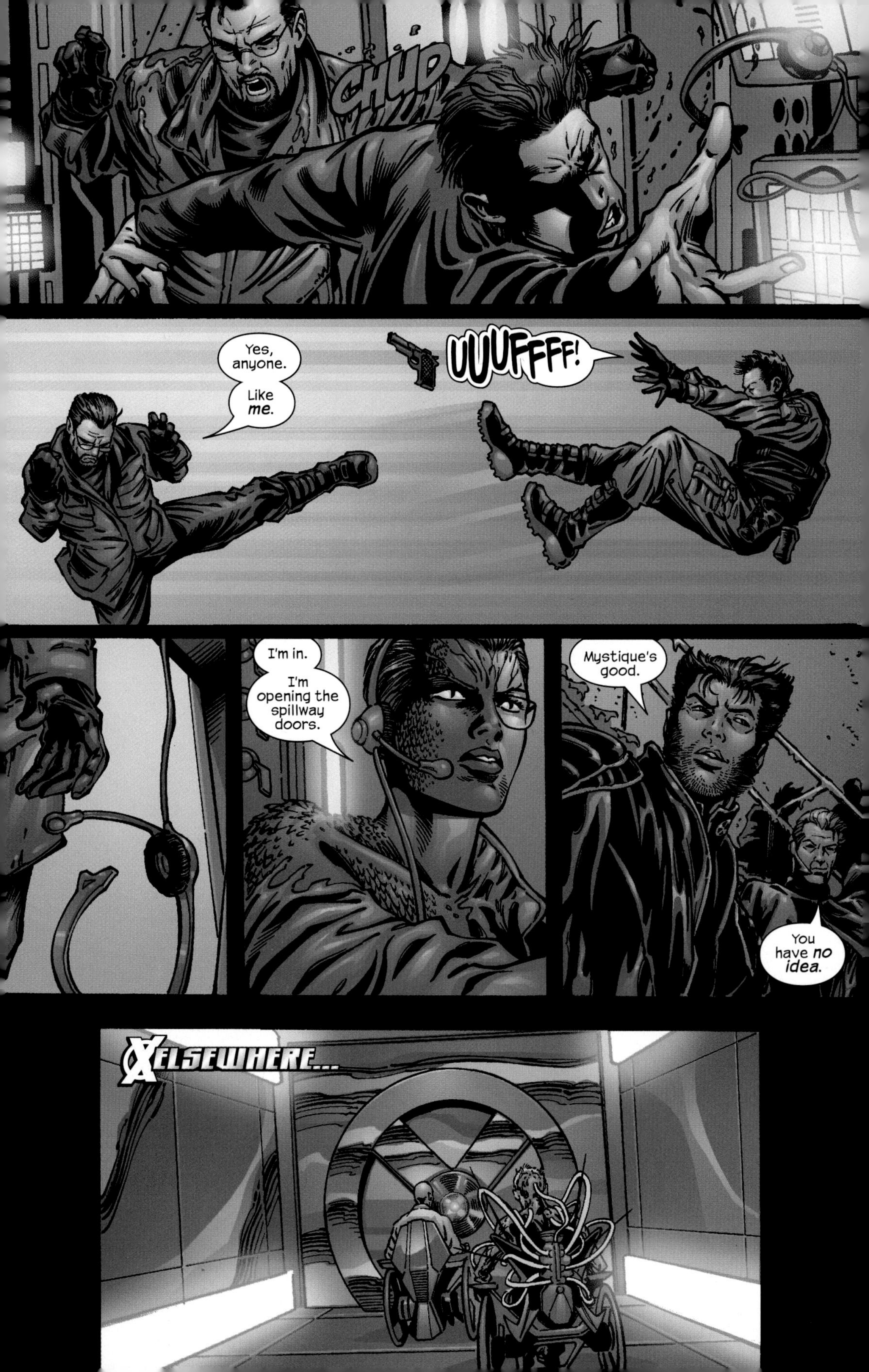

CHUD
Yes, anyone.
Like *me*.
UUUFFFF!
I'm in.
I'm opening the spillway doors.
Mystique's good.
You have *no idea*.
ELSEWHERE...

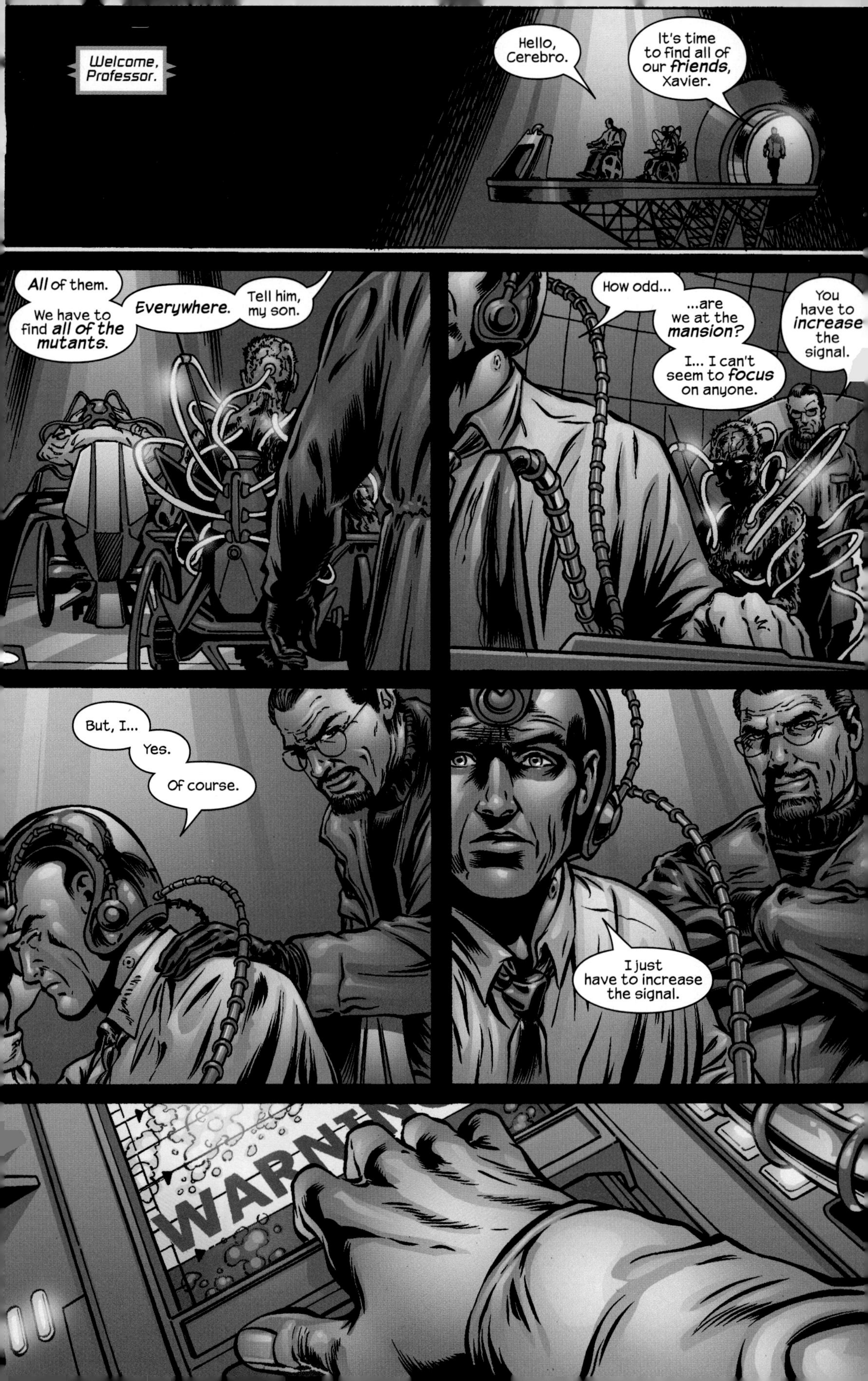
Welcome, Professor.
Hello, Cerebro.
It's time to find all of our friends, Xavier.
All of them.
We have to find all of the mutants.
Everywhere.
Tell him, my son.
How odd...
...are we at the mansion?
I... I can't seem to focus on anyone.
You have to increase the signal.
But, I...
Yes.
Of course.
I just have to increase the signal.
WARN

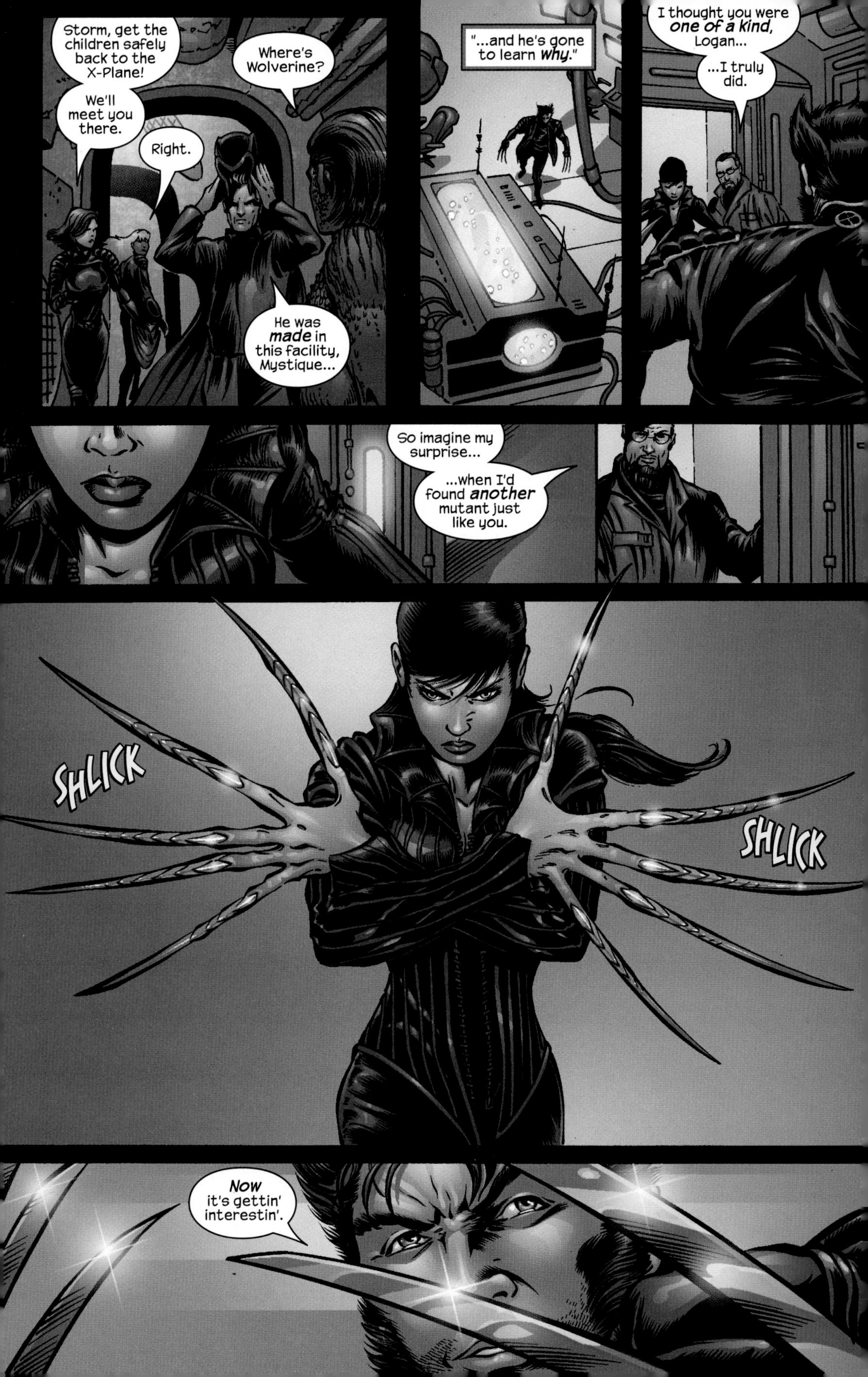
Storm, get the children safely back to the X-Plane!
We'll meet you there.
Right.
Where's Wolverine?
He was *made* in this facility, Mystique...
"...and he's gone to learn *why*."
I thought you were *one of a kind*, Logan...
...I truly did.
So imagine my surprise...
...when I'd found *another* mutant just like you.
SHLICK
SHLICK
Now it's gettin' interestin'.

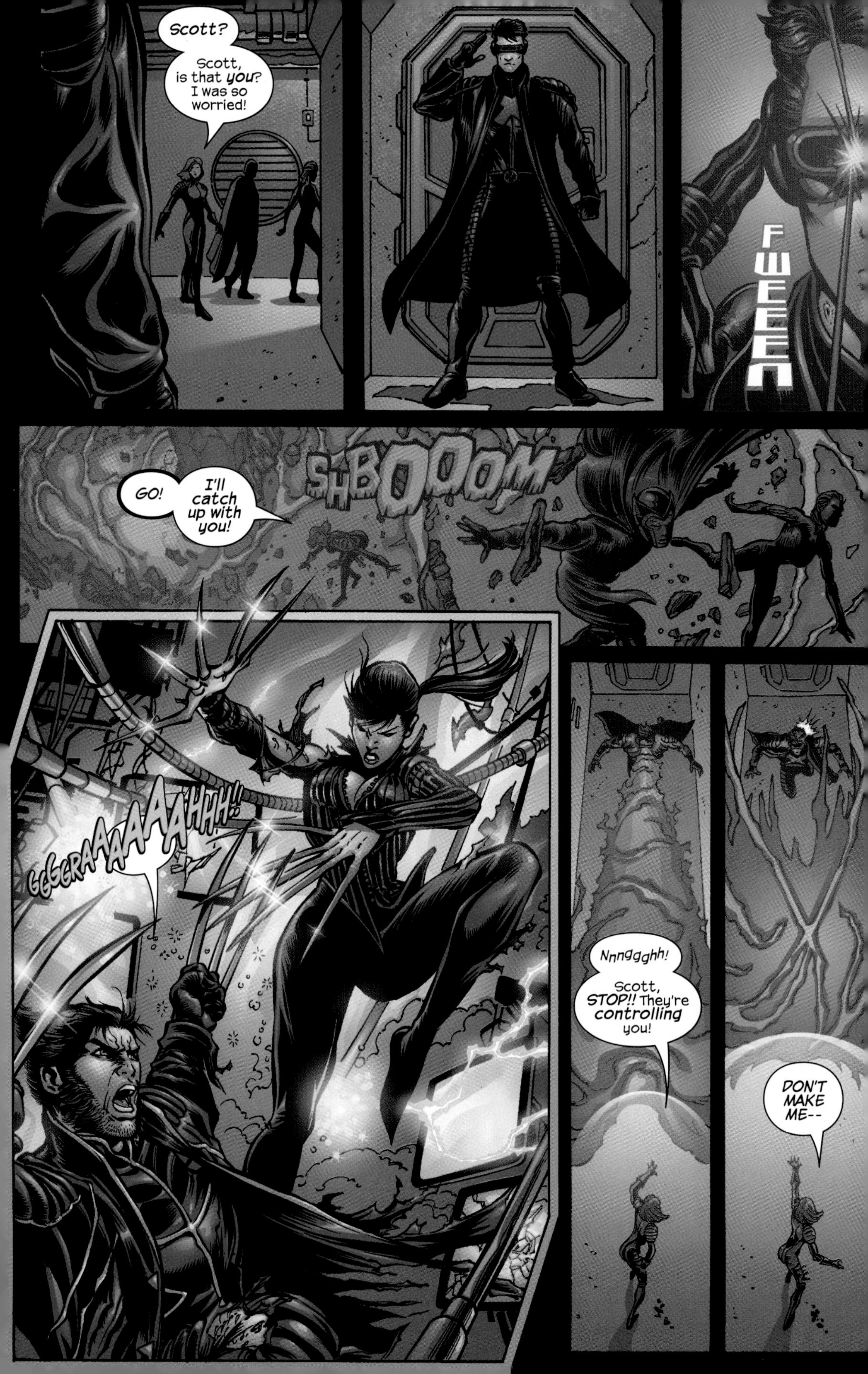
Scott?
Scott, is that you? I was so worried!
FWEEEN
SHBOOOM
GO!
I'll catch up with you!
GGGRAAAAAAHHH!!
Nnngghh!
Scott, STOP!! They're controlling you!
DON'T MAKE ME--

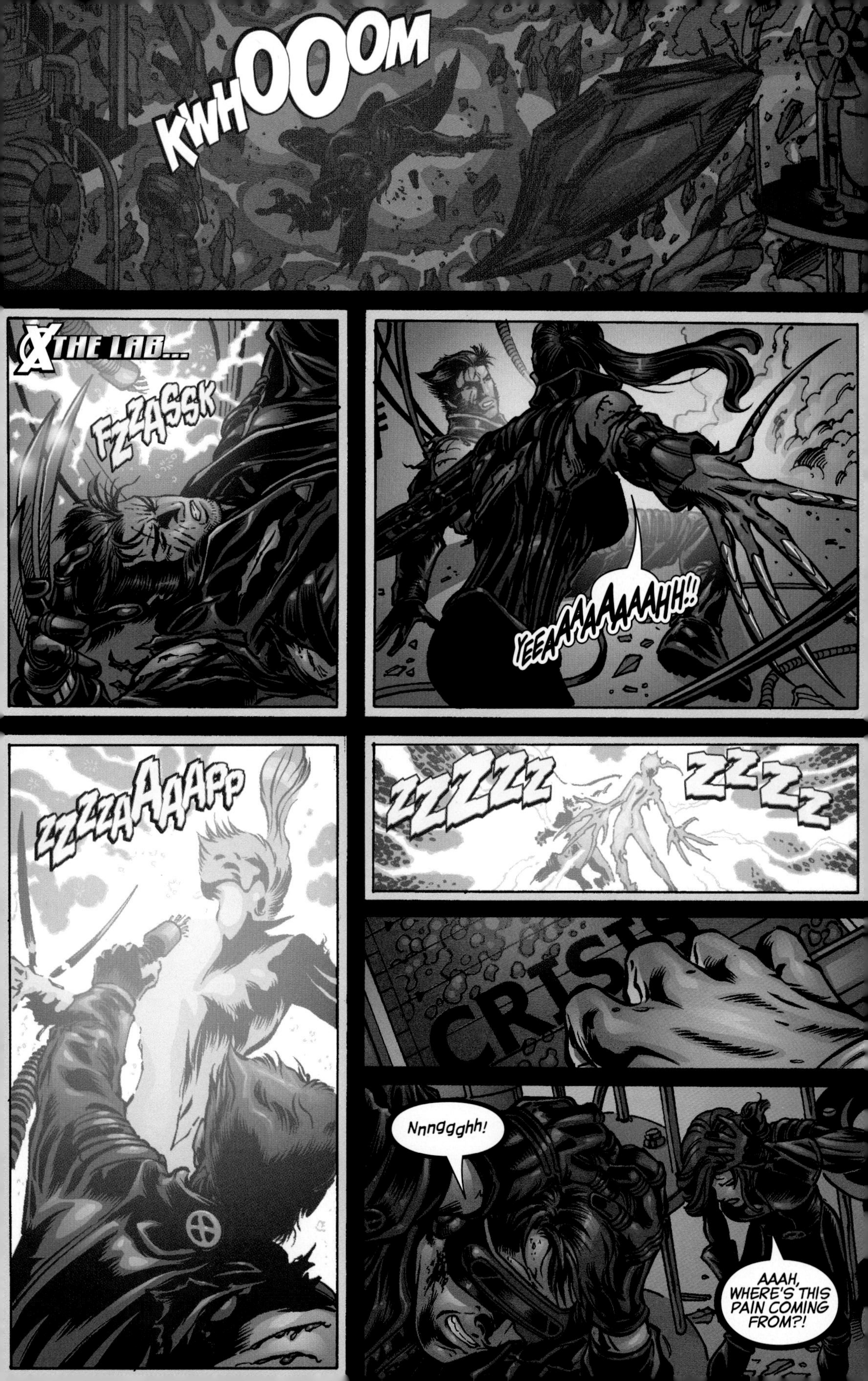
KWHOOOOM
THE LAB...
FZZASSK
YEEAAAAAAAAHH!!
ZZZZAAAAPP
ZZZZZ
ZZZZ
CRISTS
Nnngggh!
AAAH, WHERE'S THIS PAIN COMING FROM?!

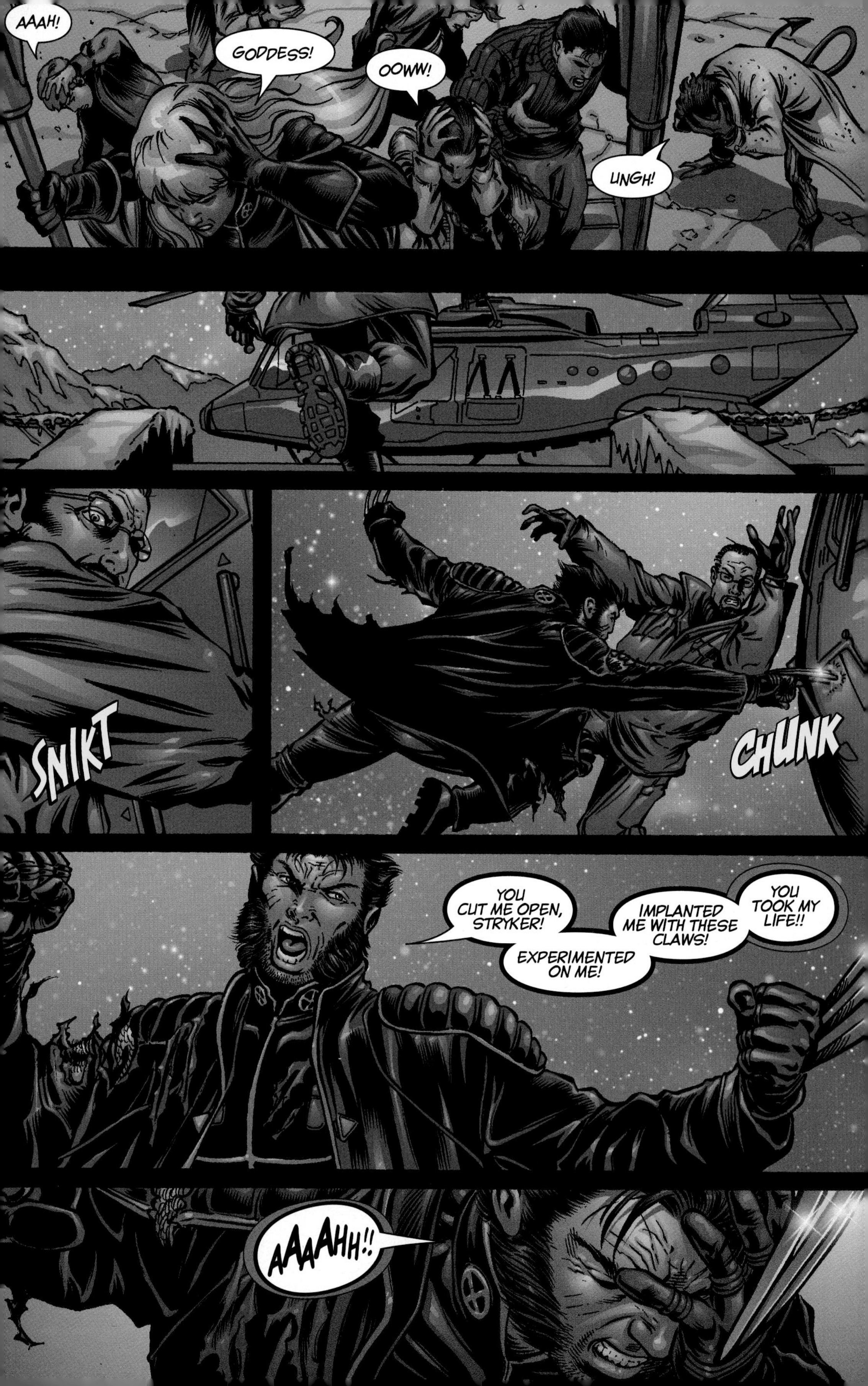
AAAH!
GODDESS!
OOWW!
UNGH!
SNIKT
CHUNK
YOU CUT ME OPEN, STRYKER!
EXPERIMENTED ON ME!
IMPLANTED ME WITH THESE CLAWS!
YOU TOOK MY LIFE!!
AAAAHH!!

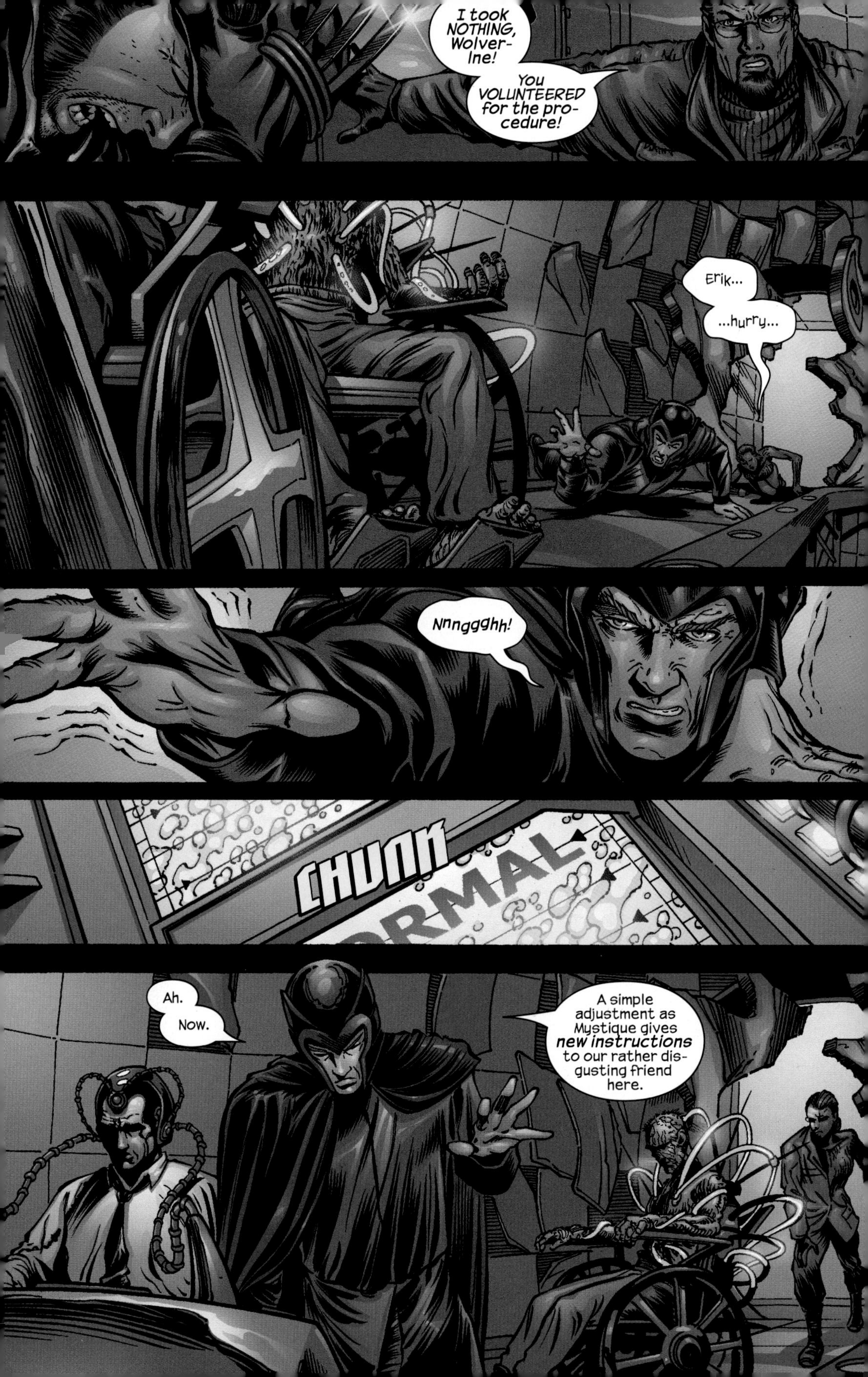
I took NOTHING, Wolver-ine!
You VOLUNTEERED for the pro-cedure!
Erik...
...hurry...
Nnngghh!
CHUNK
ORMAL
Ah.
Now.
A simple adjustment as Mystique gives *new instructions* to our rather dis-gusting friend here.

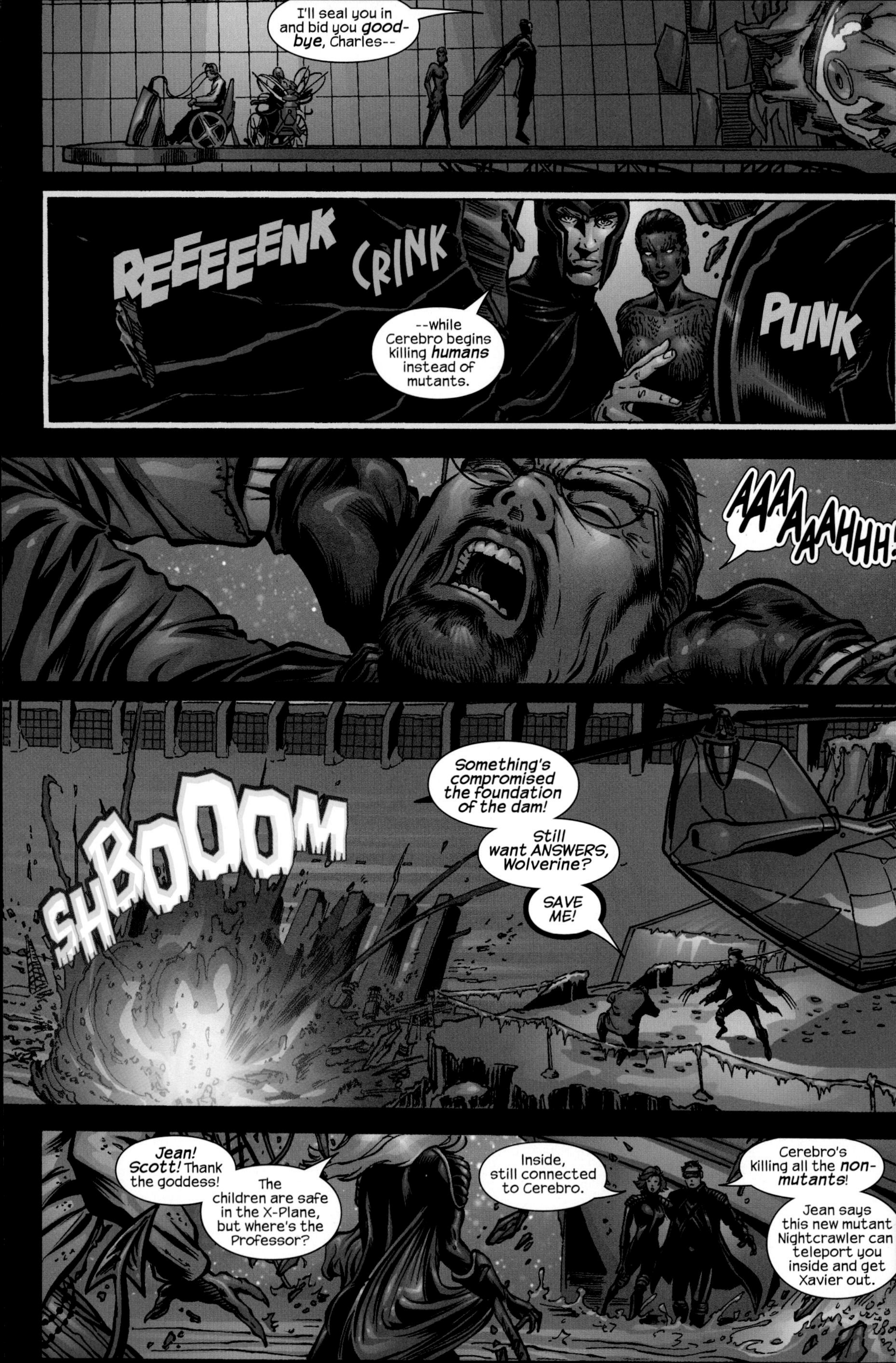
I'll seal you in and bid you good-bye, Charles--
REEEEEENK
CRINK
--while Cerebro begins killing humans instead of mutants.
PUNK
AAAAAAHHH!
SHBOOOM
Something's compromised the foundation of the dam!
Still want ANSWERS, Wolverine?
SAVE ME!
Jean! Scott! Thank the goddess!
The children are safe in the X-Plane, but where's the Professor?
Inside, still connected to Cerebro.
Cerebro's killing all the non-mutants!
Jean says this new mutant Nightcrawler can teleport you inside and get Xavier out.

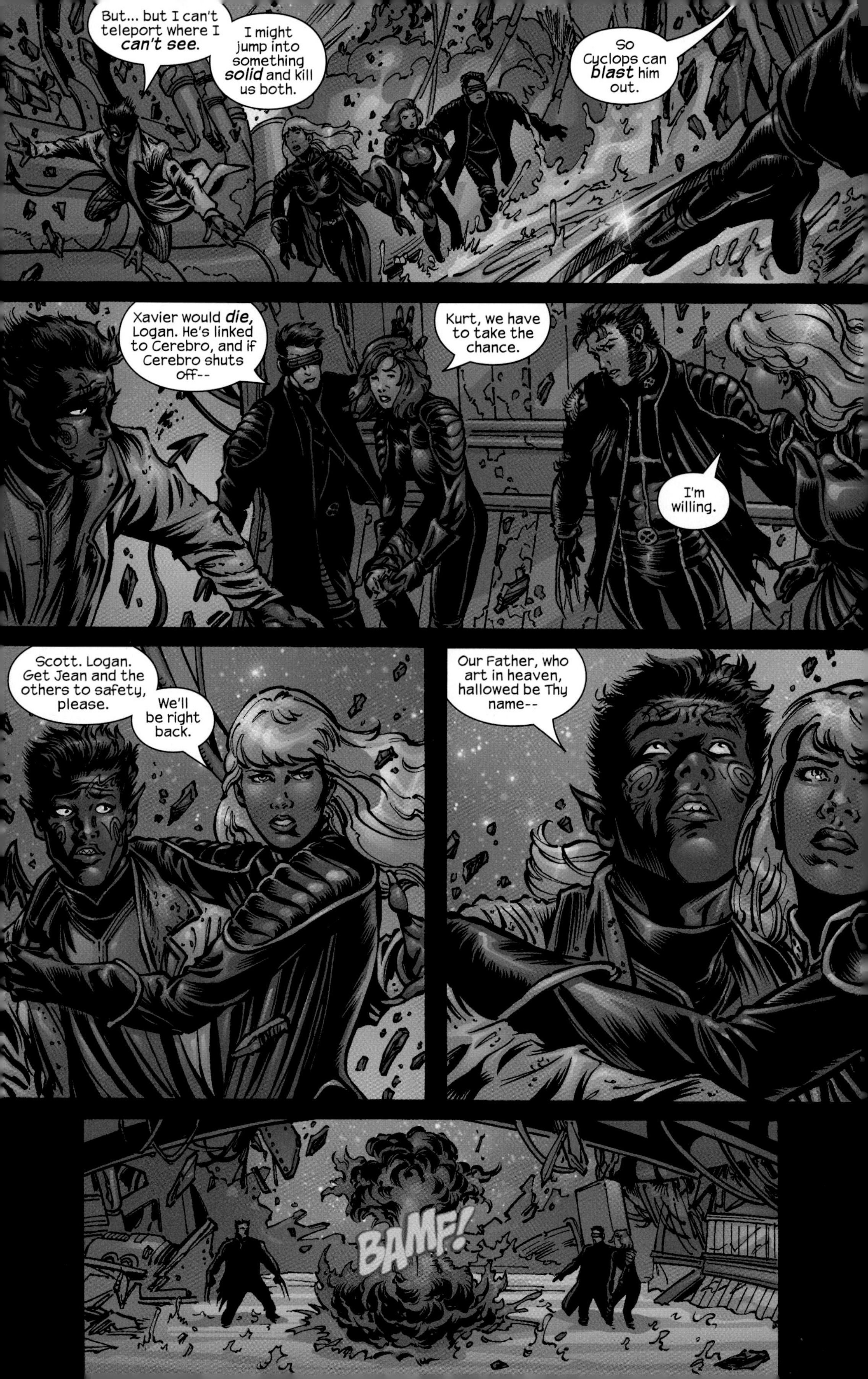
But... but I can't teleport where I *can't see*.
I might jump into something *solid* and kill us both.
So Cyclops can *blast* him out.
Xavier would *die,* Logan. He's linked to Cerebro, and if Cerebro shuts off--
Kurt, we have to take the chance.
I'm willing.
Scott. Logan. Get Jean and the others to safety, please.
We'll be right back.
Our Father, who art in heaven, hallowed be Thy name--
BAMF!

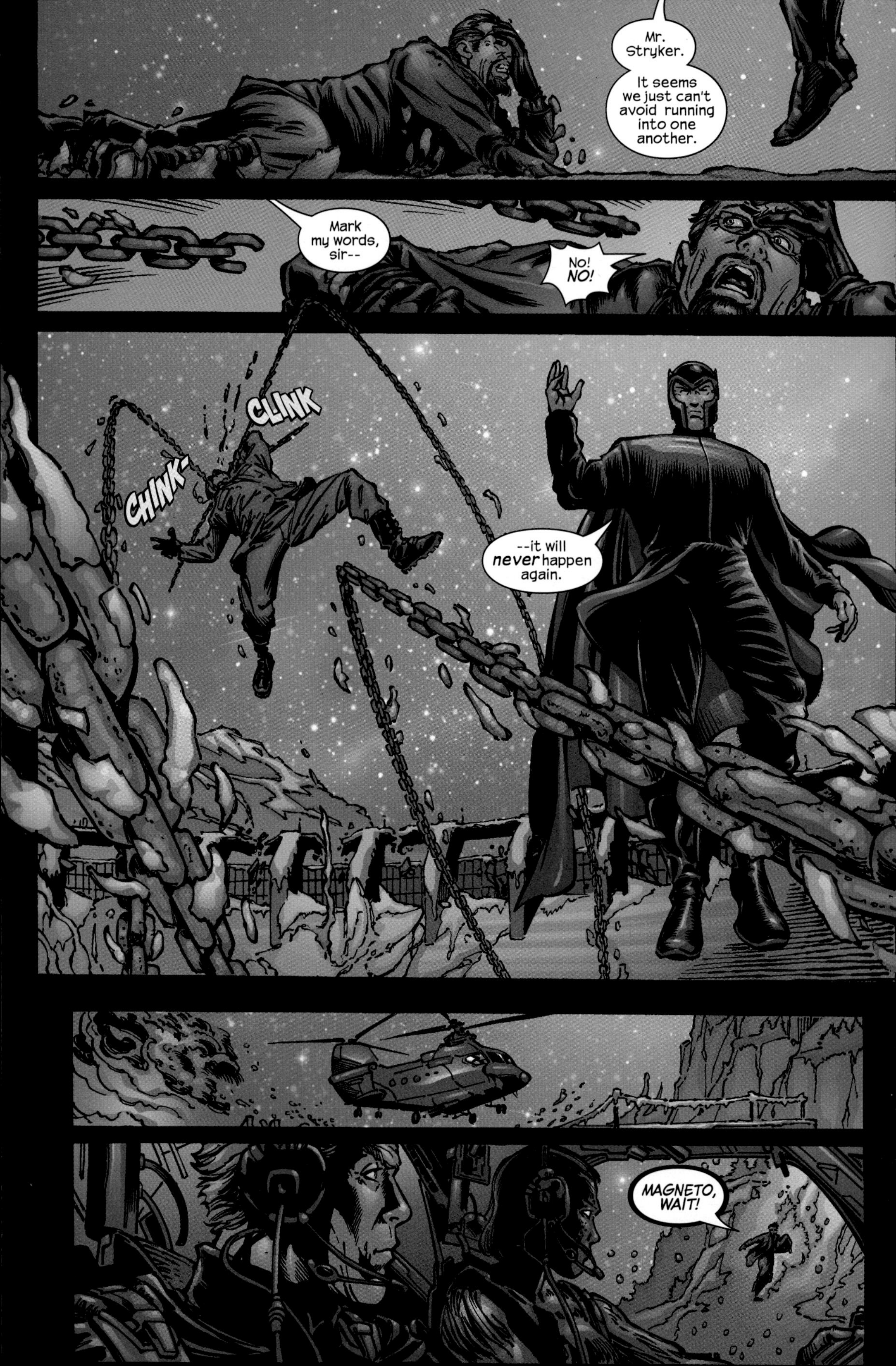
Mr. Stryker.
It seems we just can't avoid running into one another.
Mark my words, sir--
No! NO!
CHINK-
CLINK
--it will never happen again.
MAGNETO, WAIT!

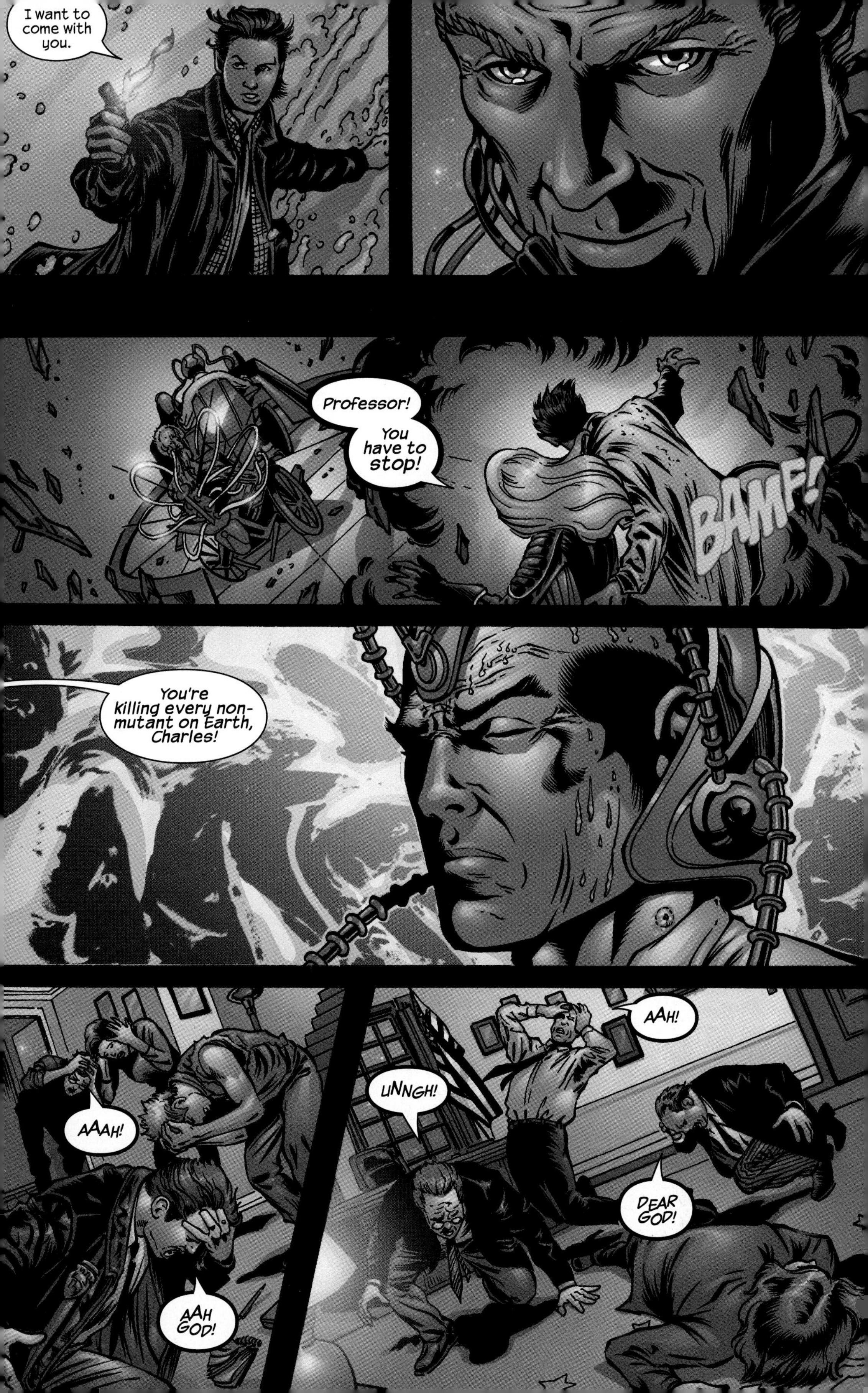
I want to come with you.
Professor!
You have to stop!
BAMF!
You're killing every non-mutant on Earth, Charles!
AAAH!
AAH GOD!
UNNGH!
AAH!
DEAR GOD!

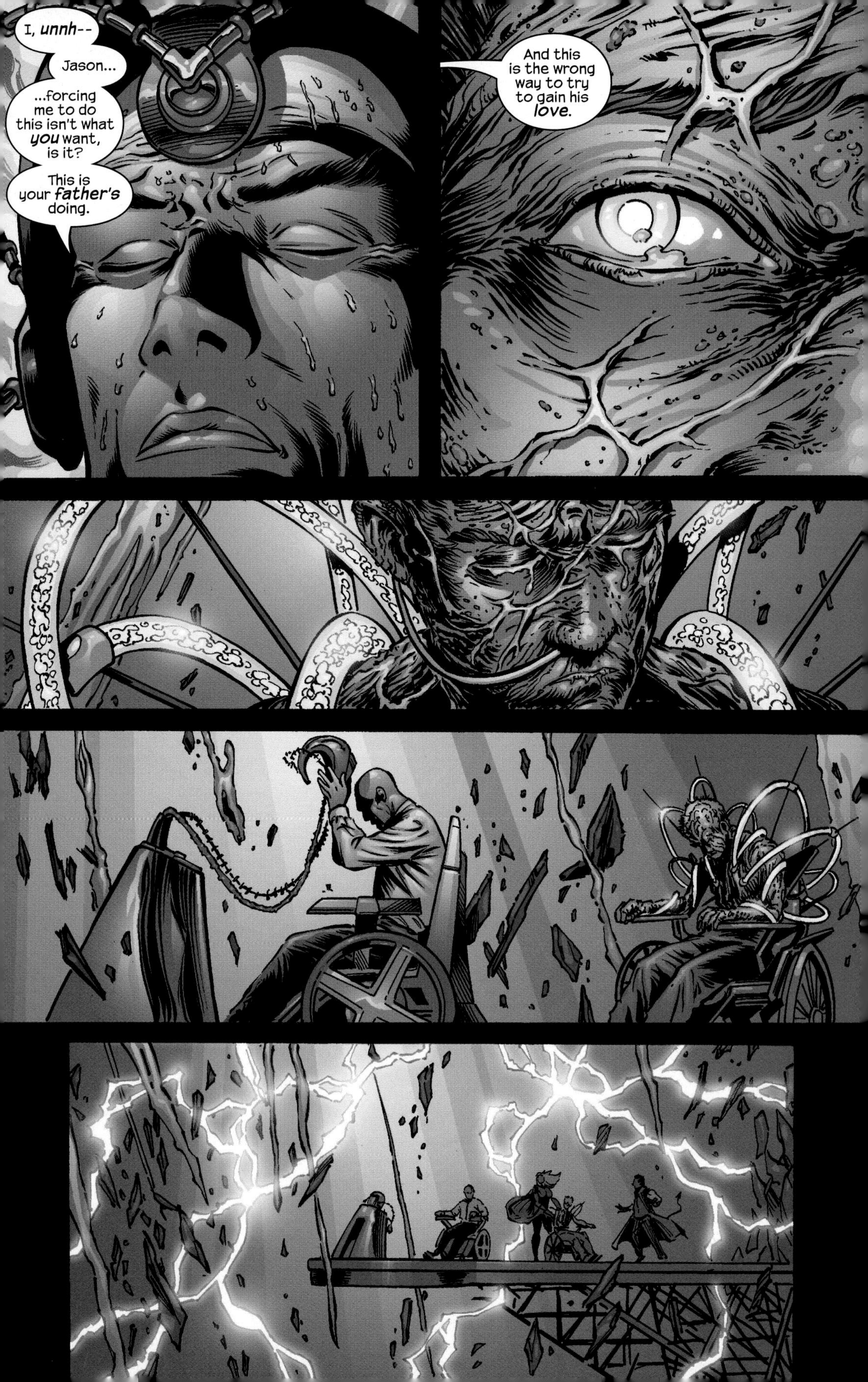
I, *unnh*--
Jason...
...forcing me to do this isn't what *you* want, is it?
This is your *father's* doing.
And this is the wrong way to try to gain his *love*.

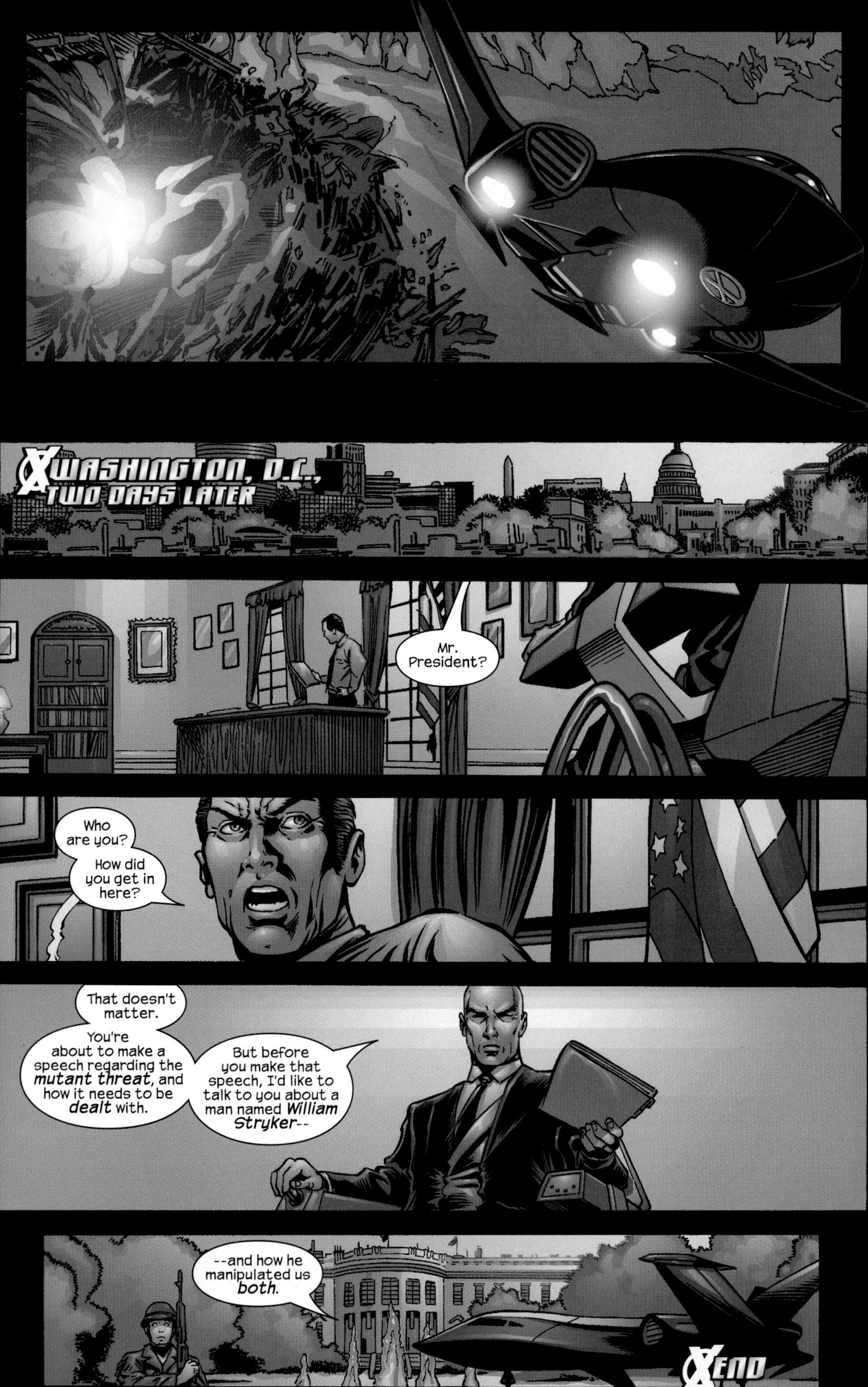
WASHINGTON, D.C., TWO DAYS LATER
Mr. President?
Who are you?
How did you get in here?
That doesn't matter.
You're about to make a speech regarding the *mutant threat*, and how it needs to be *dealt* with.
But before you make that speech, I'd like to talk to you about a man named *William Stryker*--
--and how he manipulated us *both*.
END

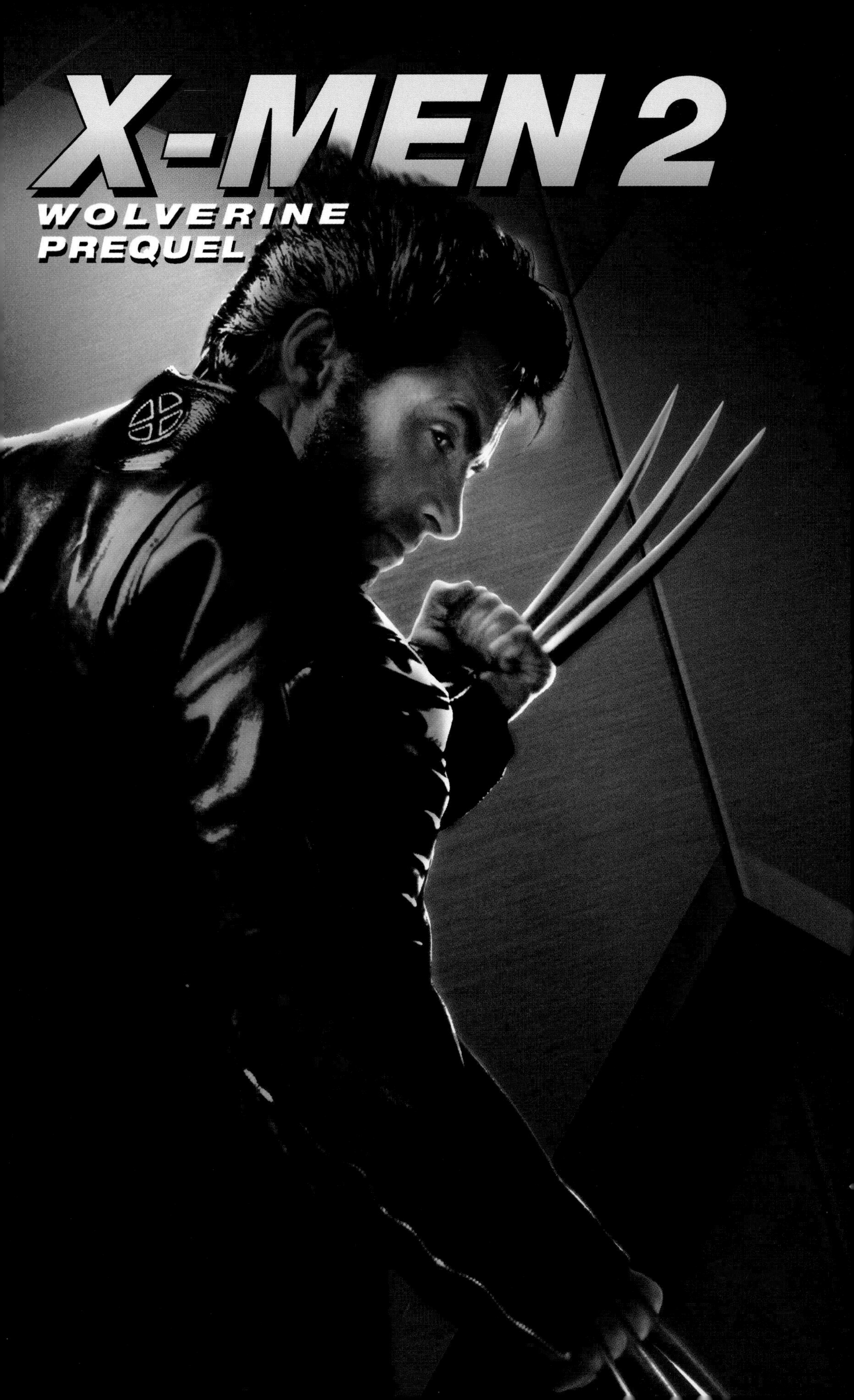
X-MEN 2
WOLVERINE
PREQUEL

PREVIOUSLY IN X-MEN: THE MOVIE

The man known as Wolverine has long been searching for the truth about his mysterious past.

What he knows about himself is very little ... he knows he has unusually keen senses. He knows he has an enhanced healing factor that allows him to quickly recover from virtually any wound. He knows -- from distant memory -- that his name is Logan. And most disturbingly ... he knows he has razor-sharp claws that extend from his hands.

But why can't he remember anything about his past? Where did he get his amazing claws from? How did his skeleton become laced with a rare and powerful metal called adamantium that makes his bones unbreakable? And who gave him the dog tag he still carries that identifies him as WOLVERINE?

Recently, Professor Charles Xavier, the powerful telepath and founder of the X-MEN, discovered Wolverine on a routine search in Alberta, Canada. Through Professor Xavier, Wolverine learned that his incredible powers made him a mutant, like Professor Xavier's team of X-Men -- super heroes born with extraordinary powers that set them apart from humankind.

When Professor Xavier's enemy Magneto and his henchman Sabretooth planned to attack humanity in New York City, Professor Xavier asked for Wolverine's help. In exchange, he made Wolverine a promise -- that he would do whatever it took to uncover Wolverine's secret past.

In New York City, Wolverine joined the X-Men and tracked Magneto and his Brotherhood of Mutants to the Statue of Liberty. Things got personal when Wolverine's young mutant friend Rogue was captured, but Wolverine was able to save Rogue and, along with the X-Men, thwart Magneto's plan.

Now, with Magneto in prison, Wolverine thinks his time with the X-Men may be over. He is still filled with questions about his past. Who is he? Did someone tamper with his memory? Was his body experimented on to make him more powerful than he previously was?

With Professor Xavier's help, Wolverine may finally be able to learn the truth...

WOLVERINE   PROF. X   SABRETOOTH   ROGUE   MAGNETO

BRIAN K. VAUGHAN
writer

TOM MANDRAKE
artist

PAUL TUTRONE
letterer

DAN BROWN
colorist

MIKE RAICHT & NOVA REN SUMA
assistant editors

MIKE MARTS
editor

JOE QUESADA
editor in chief

BILL JEMAS
president

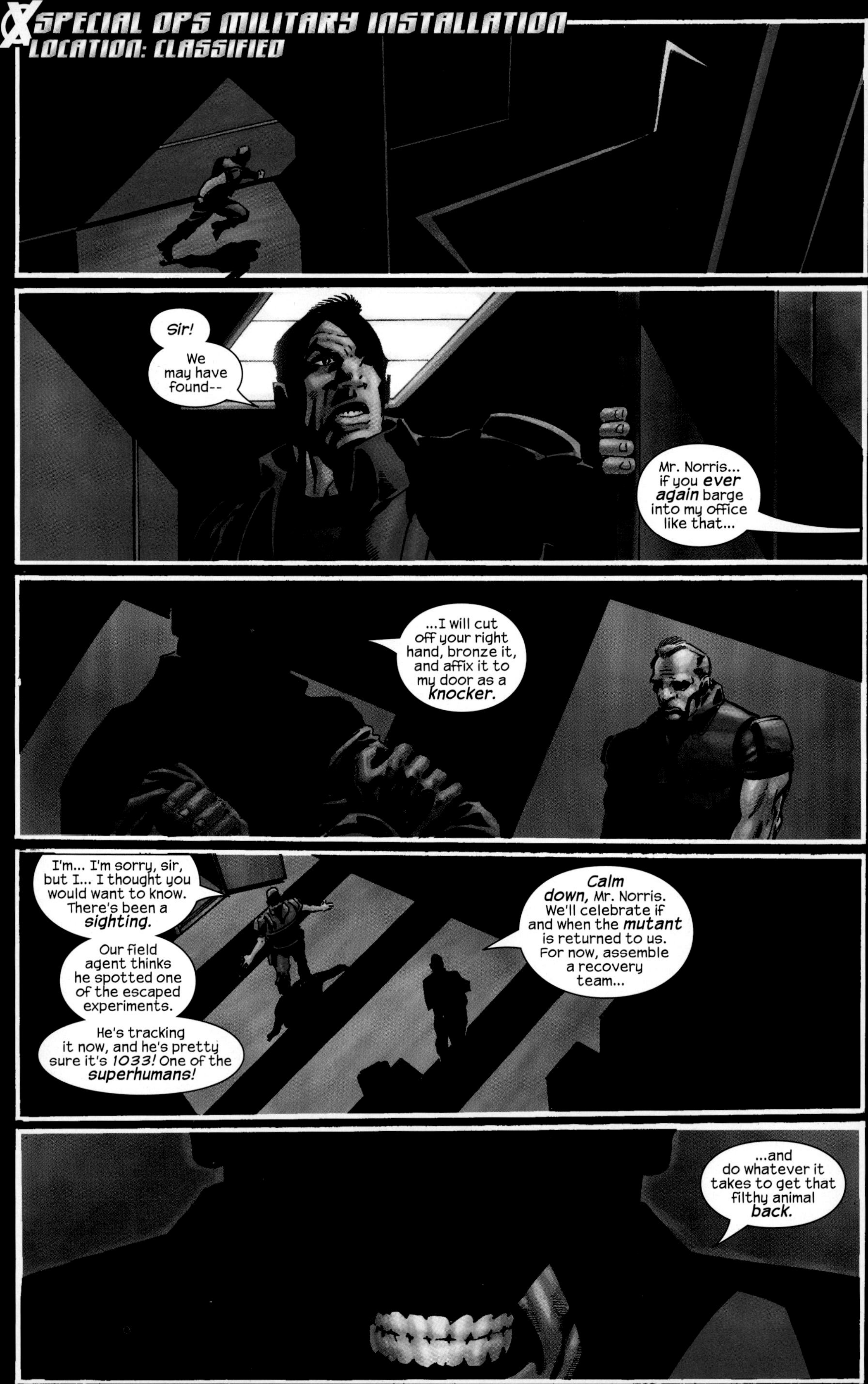
SPECIAL OPS MILITARY INSTALLATION
LOCATION: CLASSIFIED
Sir!
We may have found--
Mr. Norris... if you ever again barge into my office like that...
...I will cut off your right hand, bronze it, and affix it to my door as a knocker.
I'm... I'm sorry, sir, but I... I thought you would want to know. There's been a sighting.
Our field agent thinks he spotted one of the escaped experiments.
He's tracking it now, and he's pretty sure it's 1033! One of the superhumans!
Calm down, Mr. Norris. We'll celebrate if and when the mutant is returned to us. For now, assemble a recovery team...
...and do whatever it takes to get that filthy animal back.

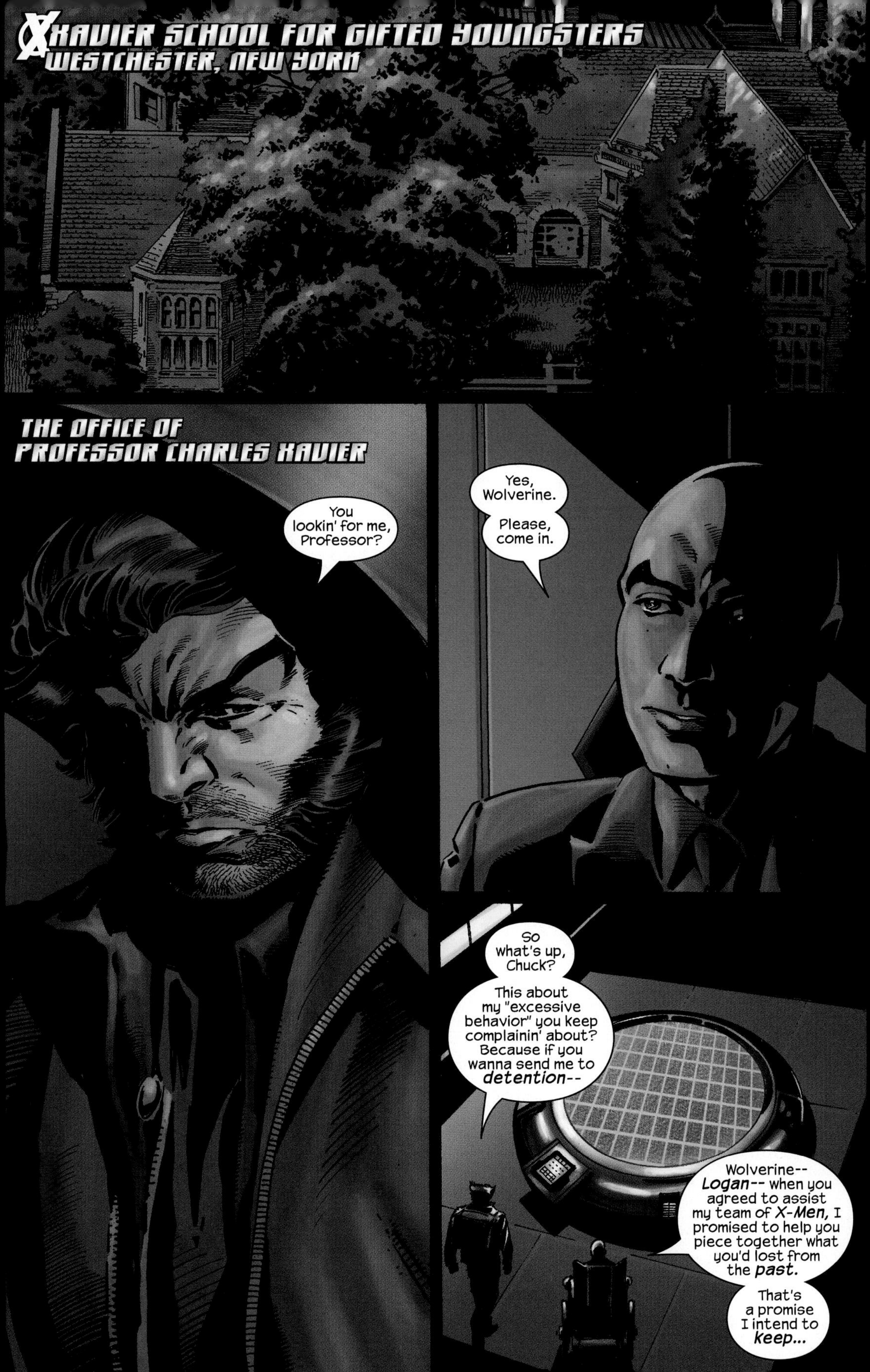

XAVIER SCHOOL FOR GIFTED YOUNGSTERS
WESTCHESTER, NEW YORK
THE OFFICE OF PROFESSOR CHARLES XAVIER
You lookin' for me, Professor?
Yes, Wolverine.
Please, come in.
So what's up, Chuck?
This about my "excessive behavior" you keep complainin' about? Because if you wanna send me to detention--
Wolverine-- Logan-- when you agreed to assist my team of X-Men, I promised to help you piece together what you'd lost from the past.
That's a promise I intend to keep...

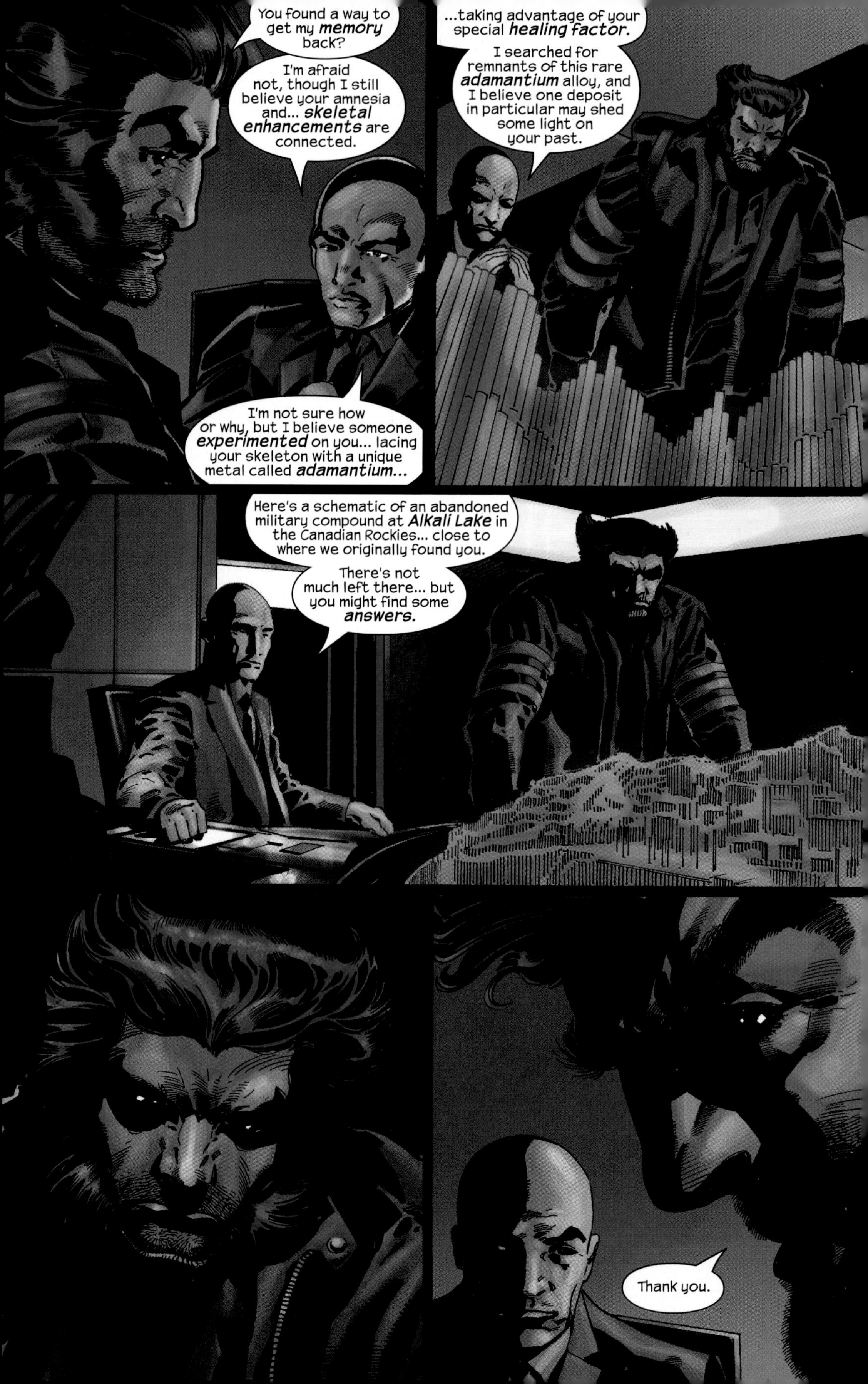

You found a way to get my memory back?
I'm afraid not, though I still believe your amnesia and... skeletal enhancements are connected.
I'm not sure how or why, but I believe someone experimented on you... lacing your skeleton with a unique metal called adamantium...
...taking advantage of your special healing factor.
I searched for remnants of this rare adamantium alloy, and I believe one deposit in particular may shed some light on your past.
Here's a schematic of an abandoned military compound at Alkali Lake in the Canadian Rockies... close to where we originally found you.
There's not much left there... but you might find some answers.
Thank you.

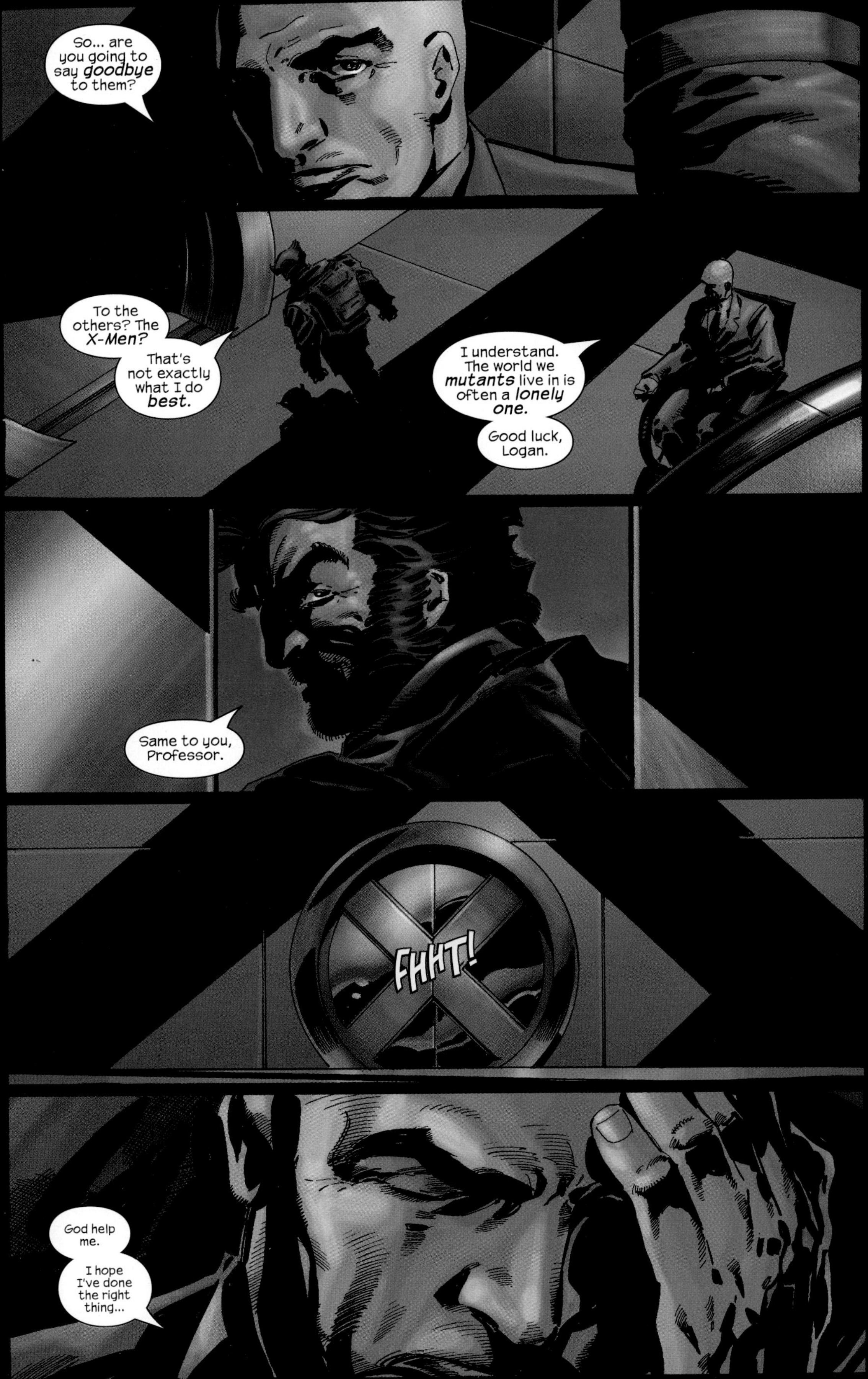

So... are you going to say *goodbye* to them?
To the others? The *X-Men?*
That's not exactly what I do *best.*
I understand. The world we *mutants* live in is often a *lonely one.*
Good luck, Logan.
Same to you, Professor.
FHHT!
God help me.
I hope I've done the right thing...

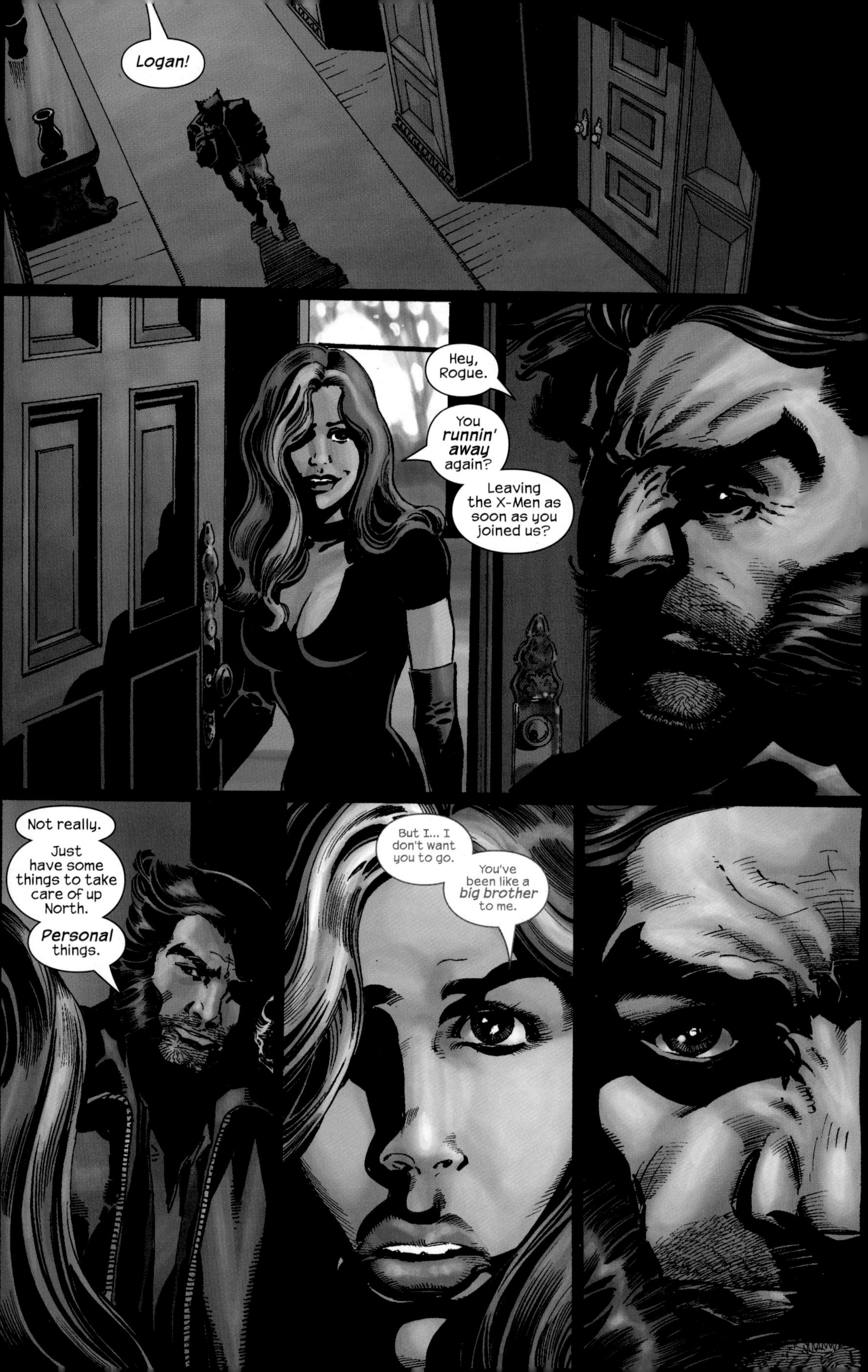
Logan!
Hey, Rogue.
You runnin' away again?
Leaving the X-Men as soon as you joined us?
Not really.
Just have some things to take care of up North.
Personal things.
But I... I don't want you to go.
You've been like a big brother to me.

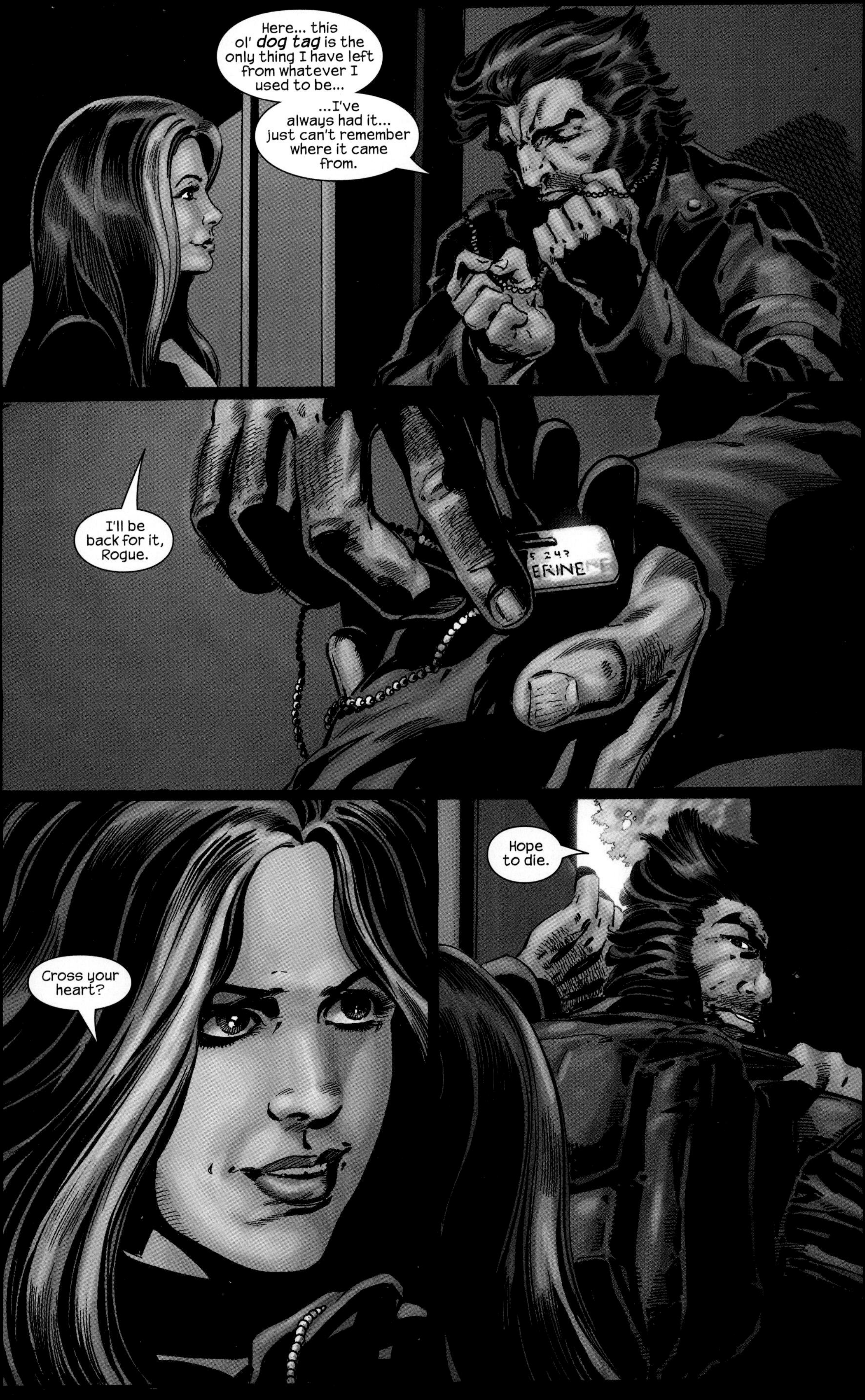
Here... this ol' *dog tag* is the only thing I have left from whatever I used to be...
...I've always had it... just can't remember where it came from.
I'll be back for it, Rogue.
Cross your heart?
Hope to die.

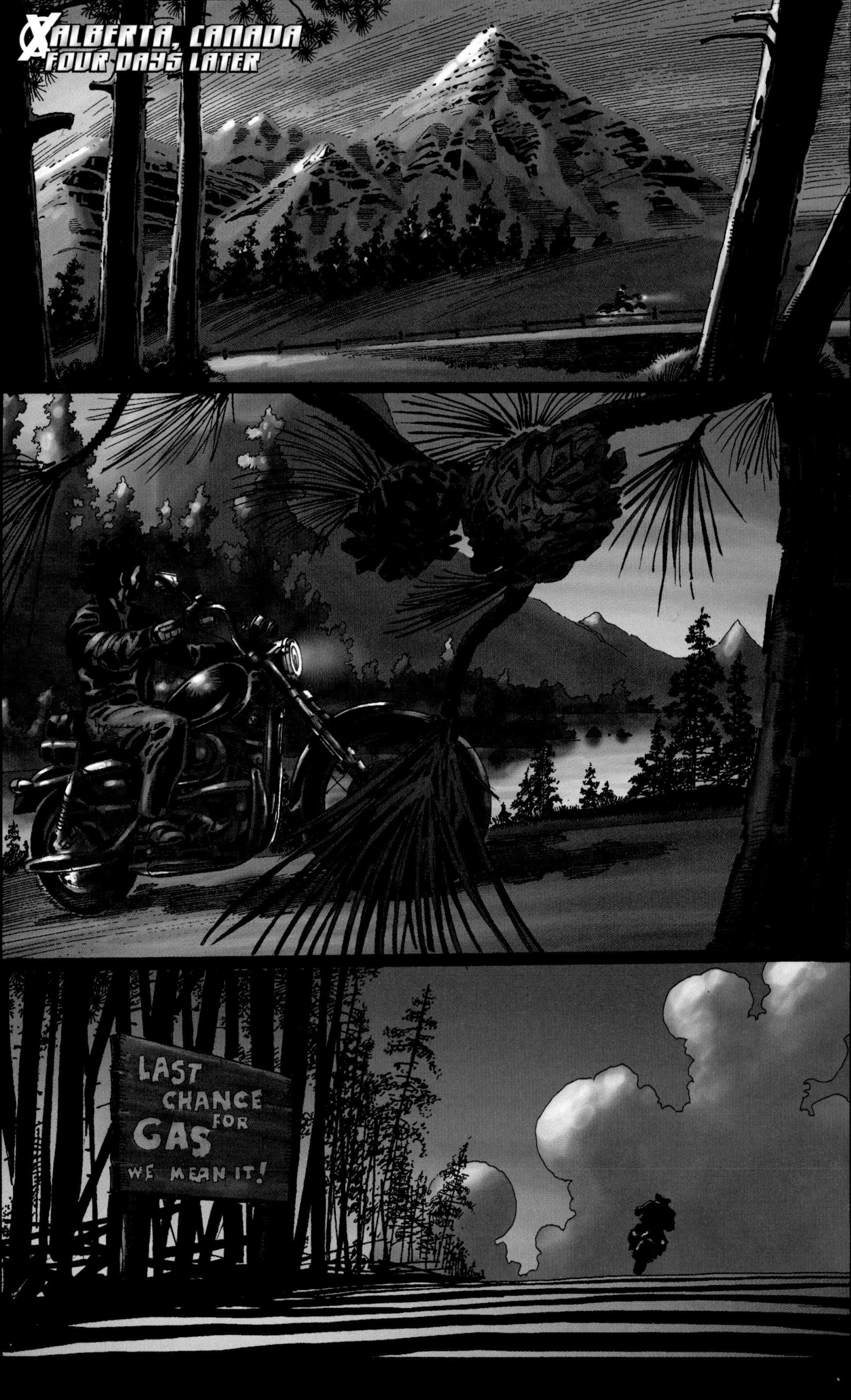
ALBERTA, CANADA
FOUR DAYS LATER
LAST CHANCE FOR GAS
WE MEAN IT!

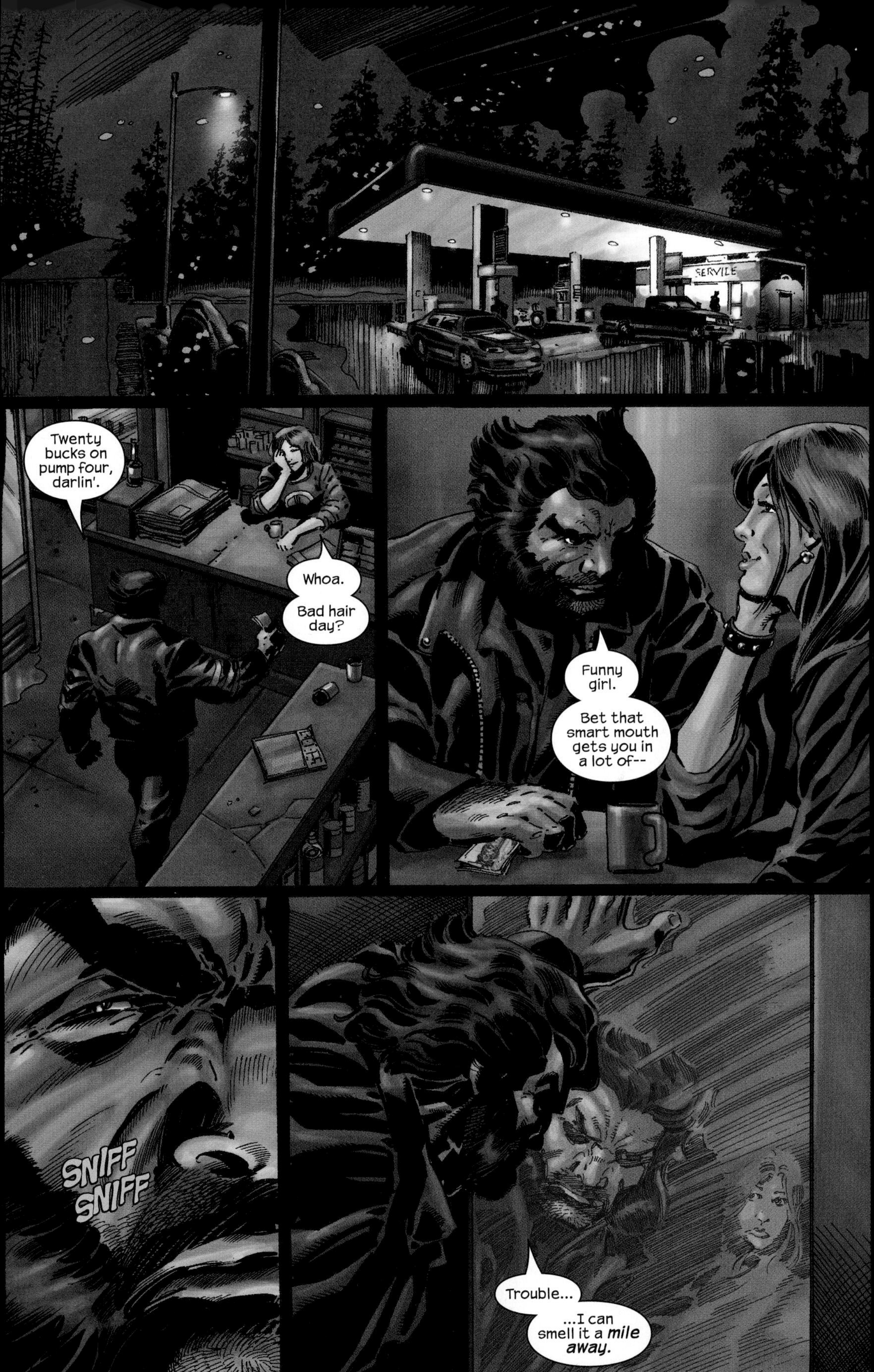
SERVICE
Twenty bucks on pump four, darlin'.
Whoa.
Bad hair day?
Funny girl.
Bet that smart mouth gets you in a lot of--
SNIFF SNIFF
Trouble...
...I can smell it a *mile away.*

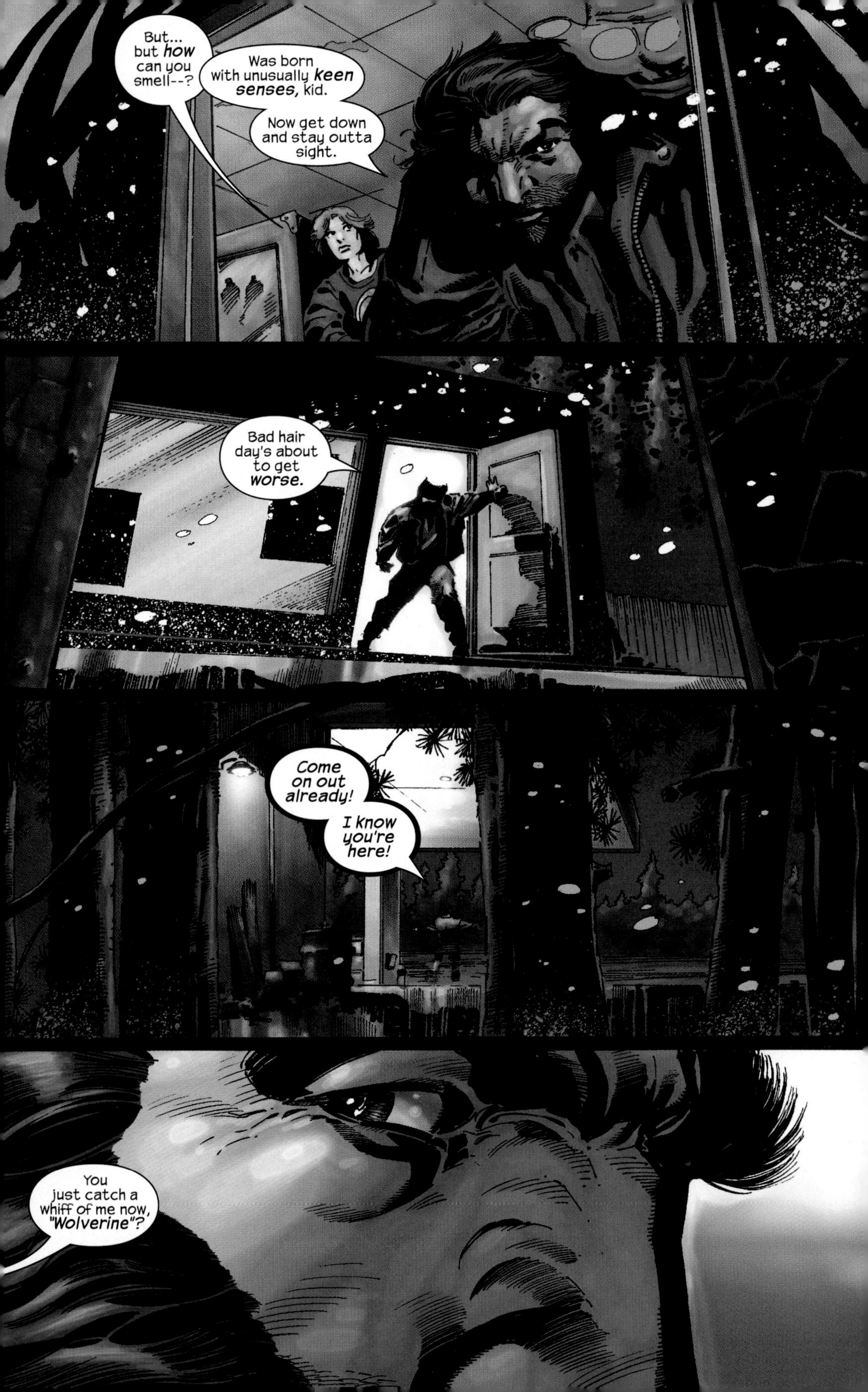
But... but *how* can you smell--?
Was born with unusually ***keen senses,*** kid.
Now get down and stay outta sight.
Bad hair day's about to get ***worse.***
Come on out already!
I know you're here!
You just catch a whiff of me now, ***"Wolverine"?***

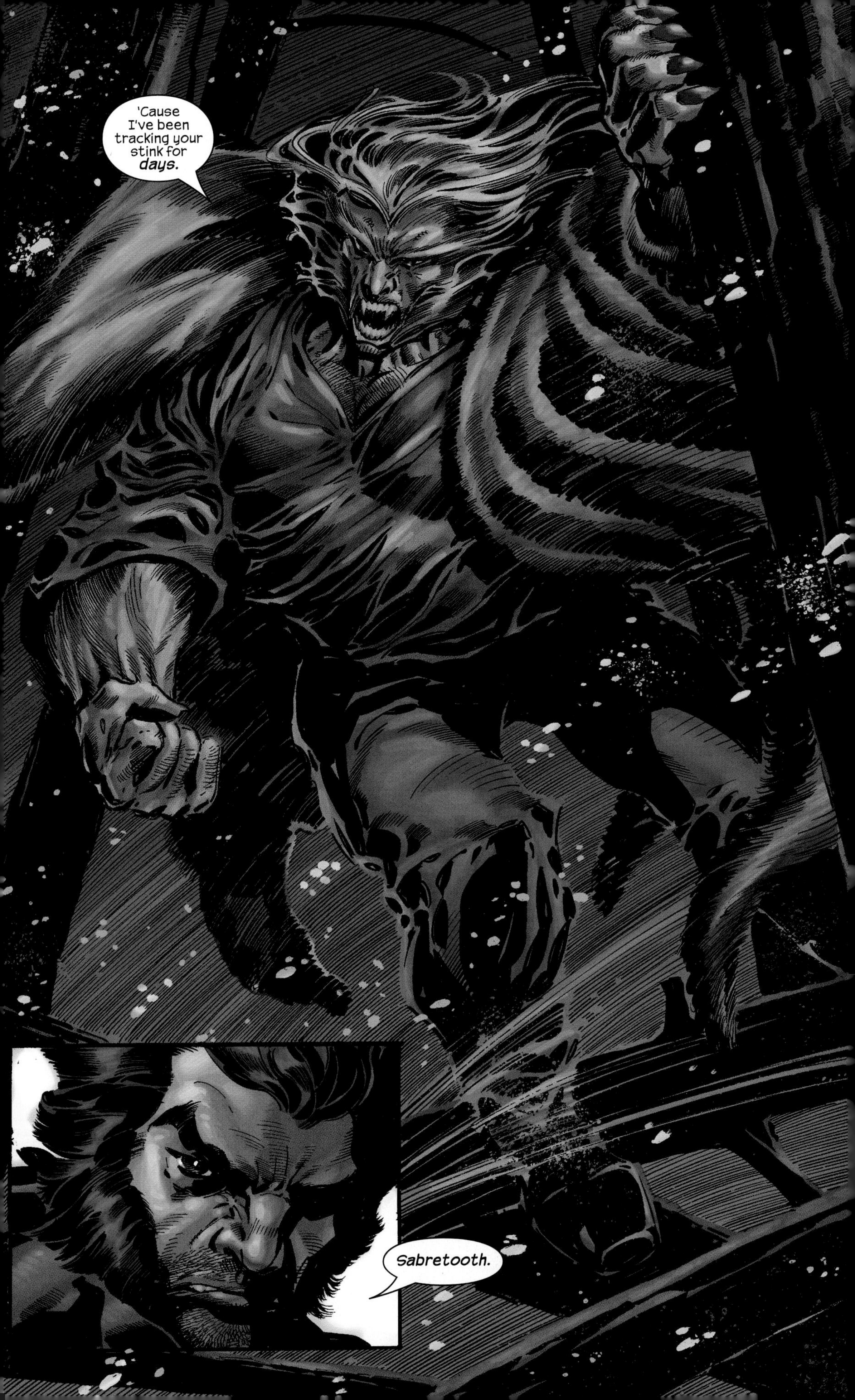
'Cause I've been tracking your stink for *days.*
Sabretooth.

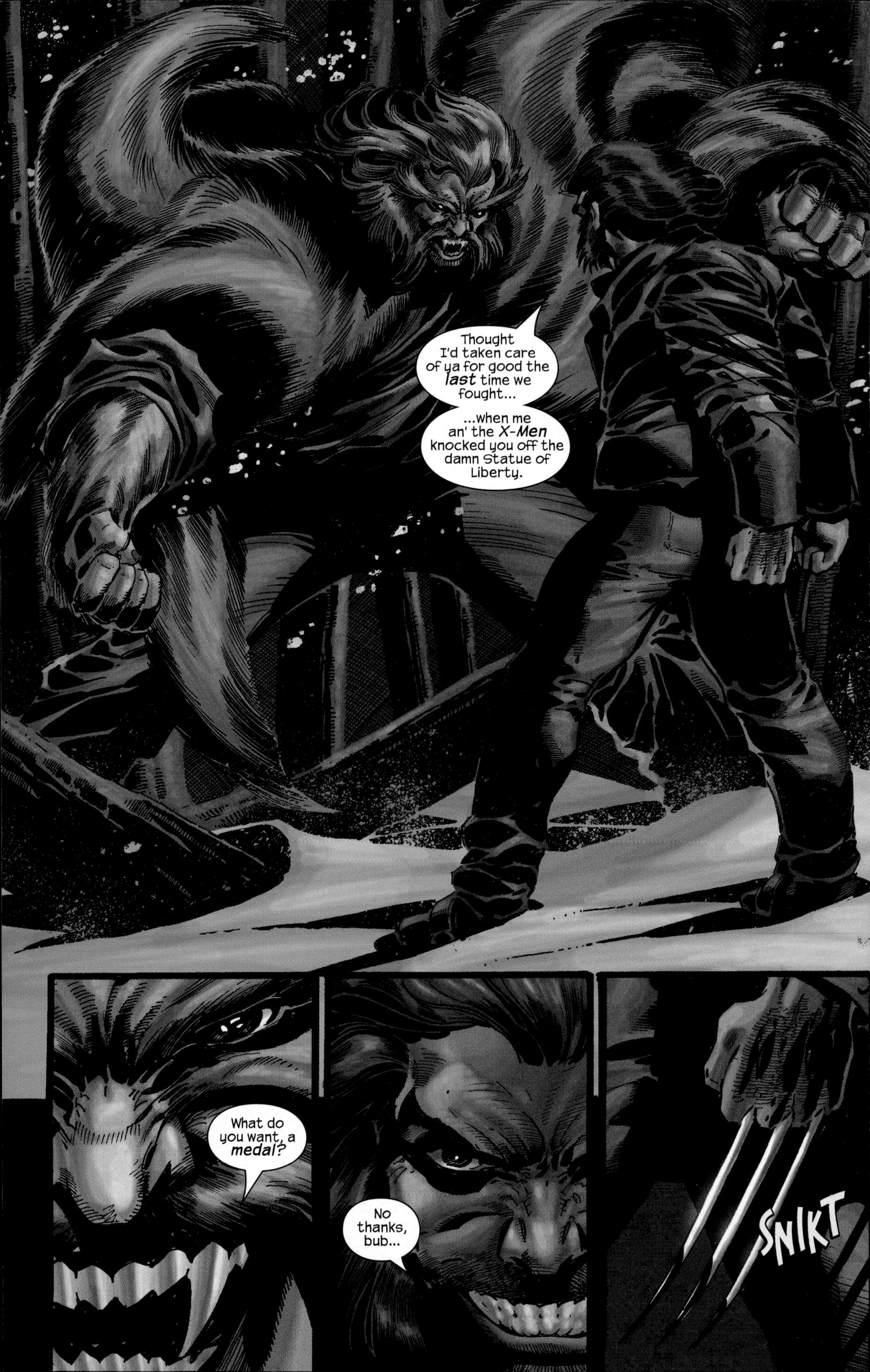
Thought I'd taken care of ya for good the *last* time we fought...
...when me an' the *X-Men* knocked you off the damn Statue of Liberty.
What do you want, a *medal*?
No thanks, bub...
SNIKT

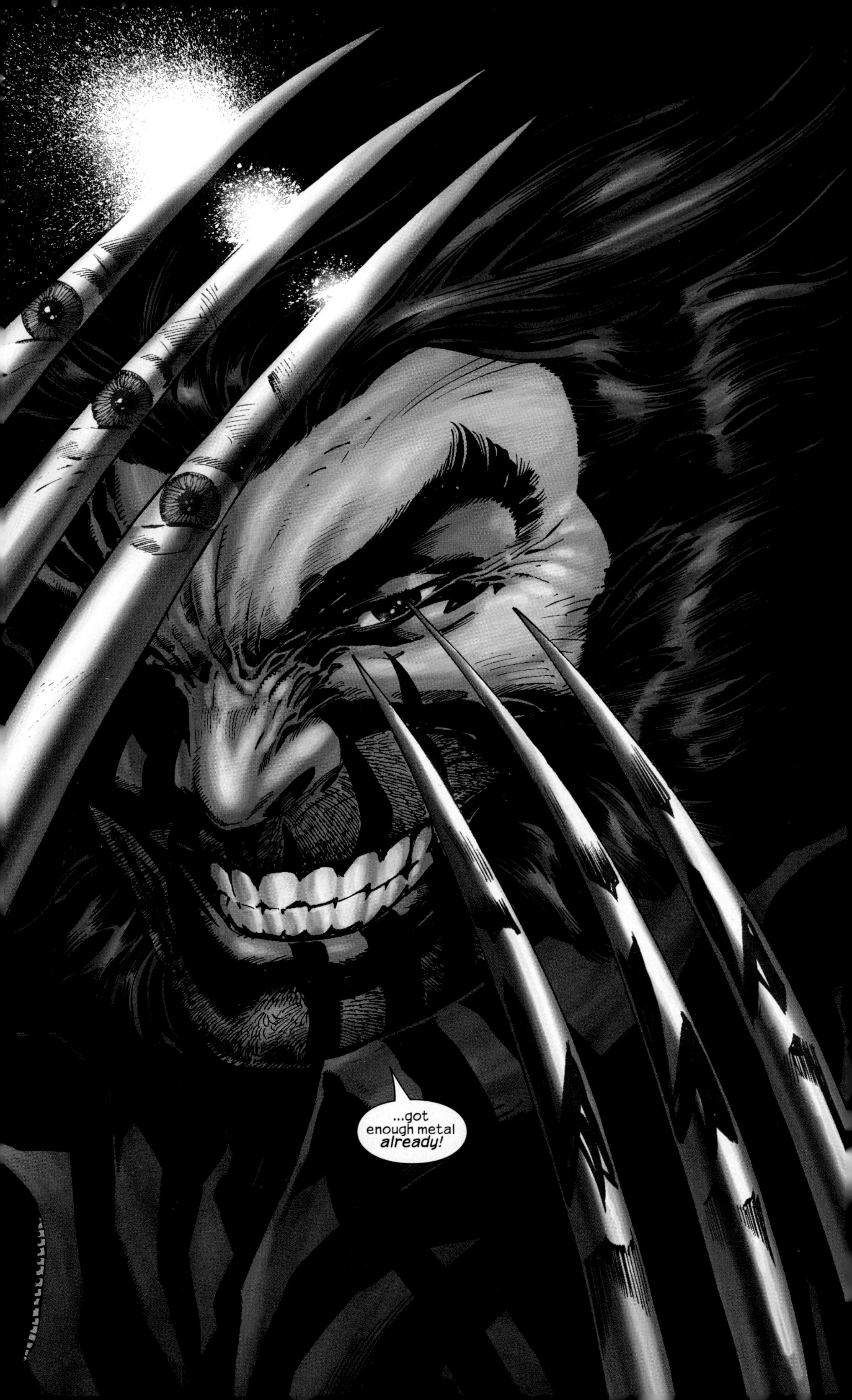
...got enough metal *already!*

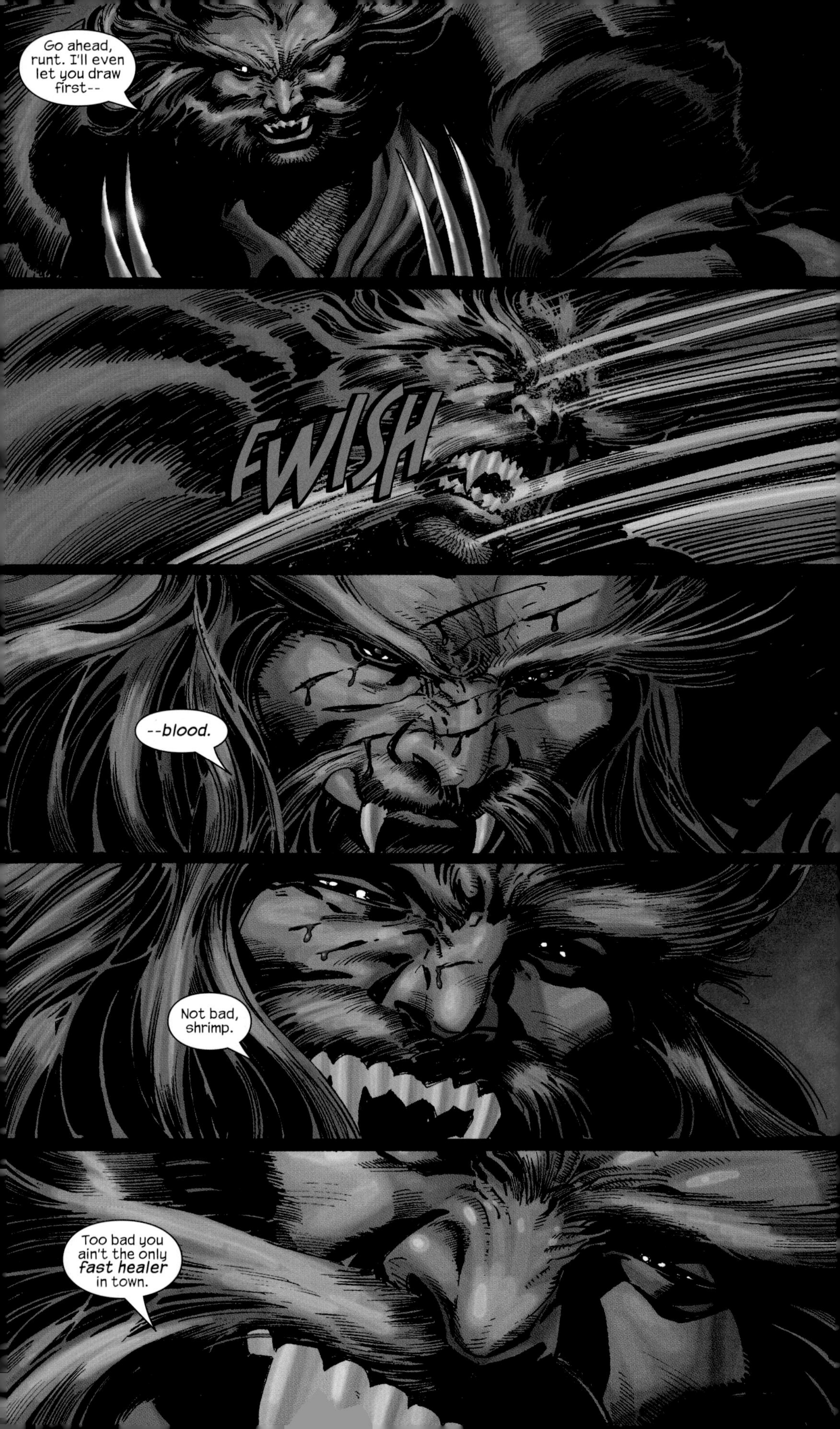

Go ahead, runt. I'll even let you draw first--
FWISH
--blood.
Not bad, shrimp.
Too bad you ain't the only *fast healer* in town.

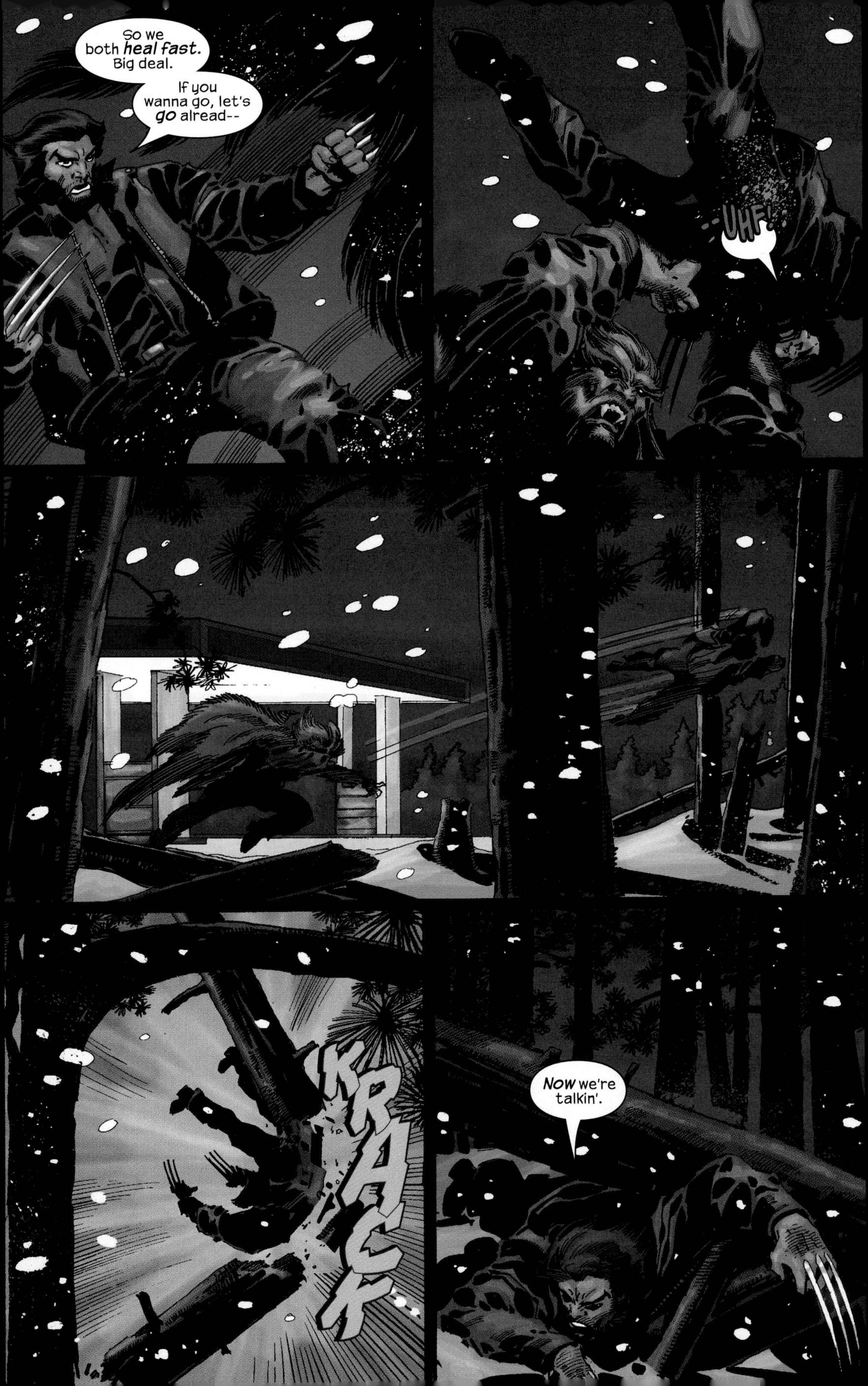
So we both heal fast. Big deal.
If you wanna go, let's go alread--
UHF!
KRACK
NOW we're talkin'.

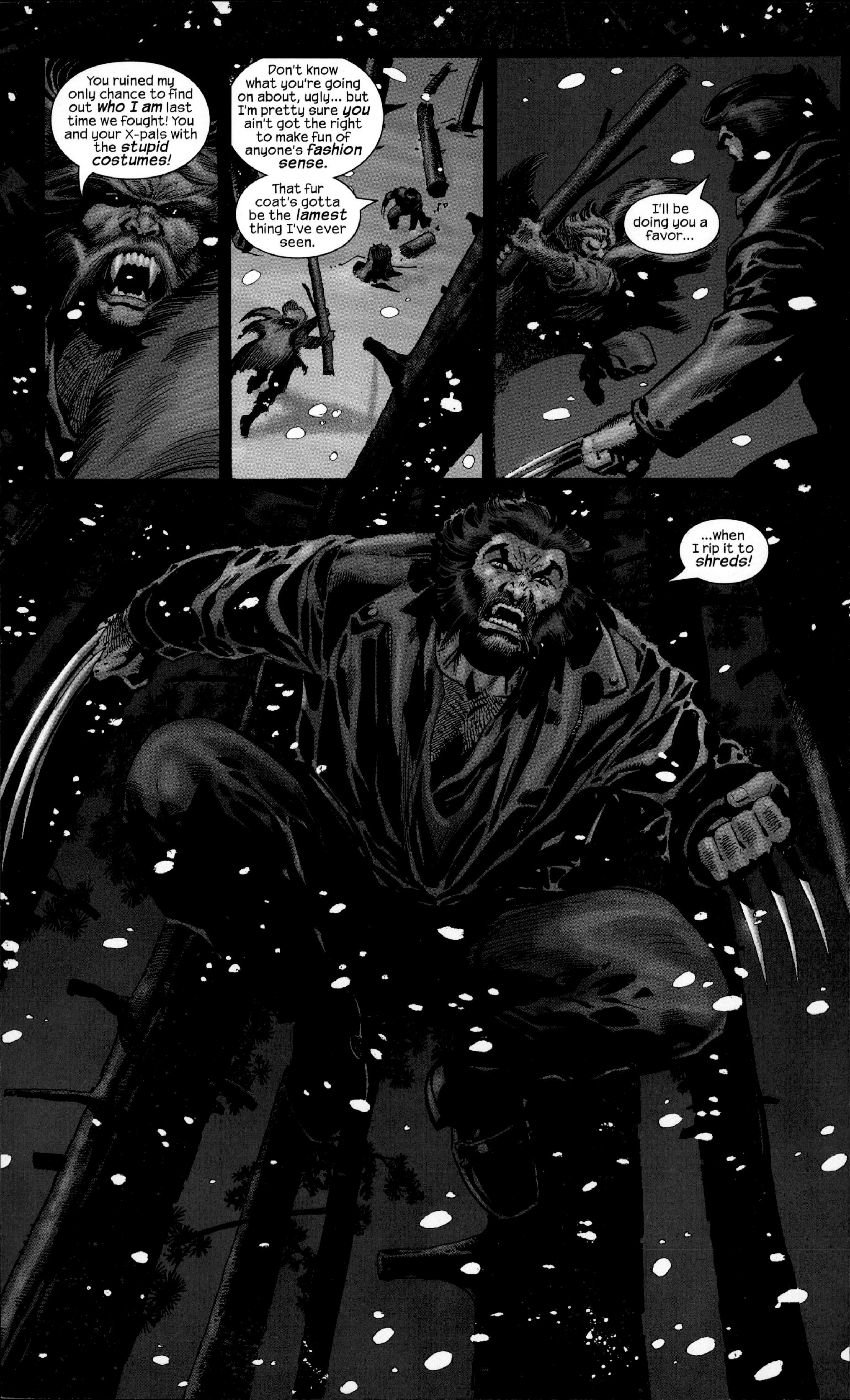

You ruined my only chance to find out **who I am** last time we fought! You and your X-pals with the **stupid costumes!**
Don't know what you're going on about, ugly... but I'm pretty sure **you** ain't got the right to make fun of anyone's **fashion sense.**
That fur coat's gotta be the **lamest** thing I've ever seen.
I'll be doing you a favor...
...when I rip it to **shreds!**

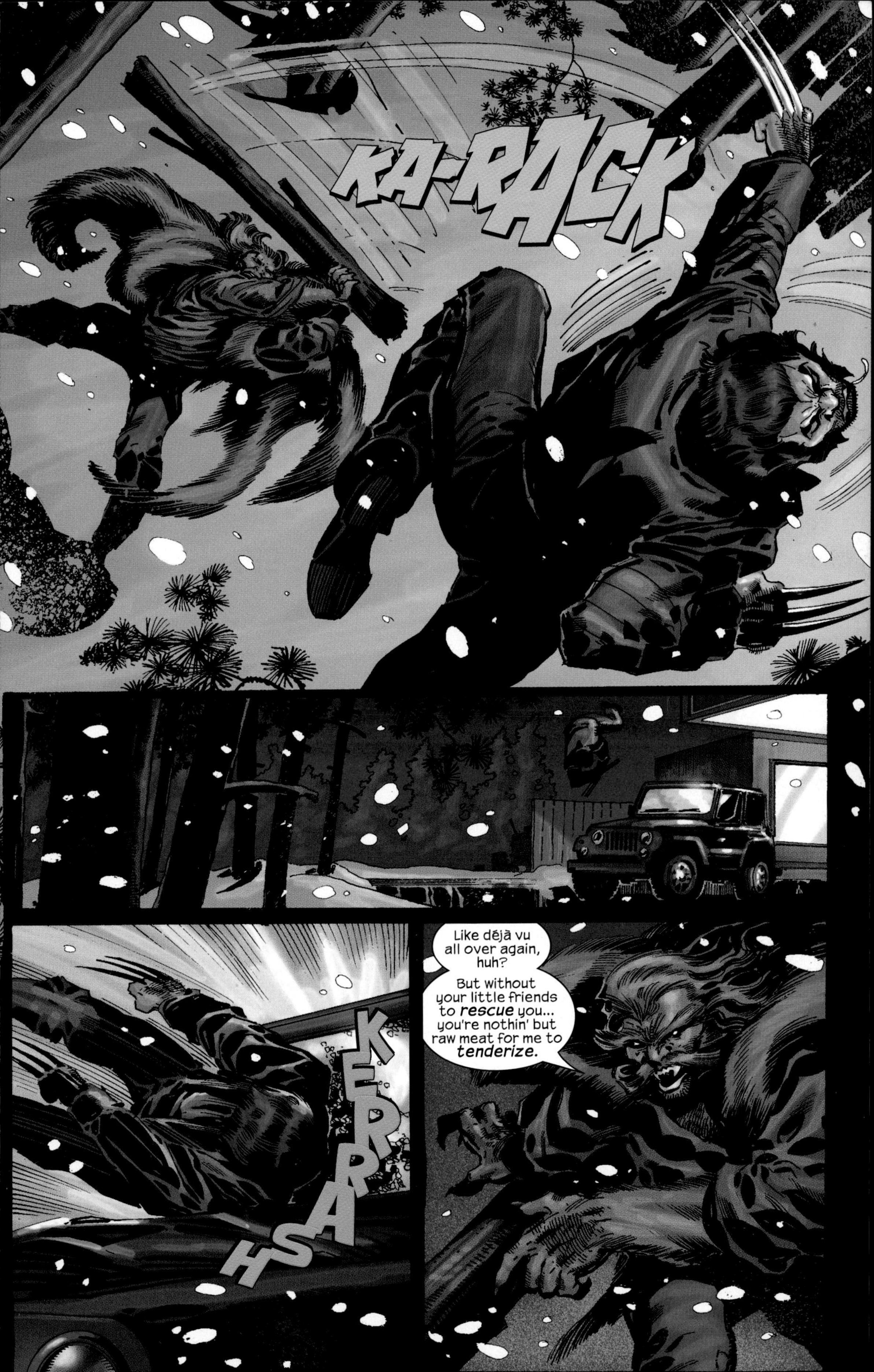

KA-RACK
KERRASH
Like déjà vu all over again, huh?
But without your little friends to *rescue* you... you're nothin' but raw meat for me to *tenderize.*

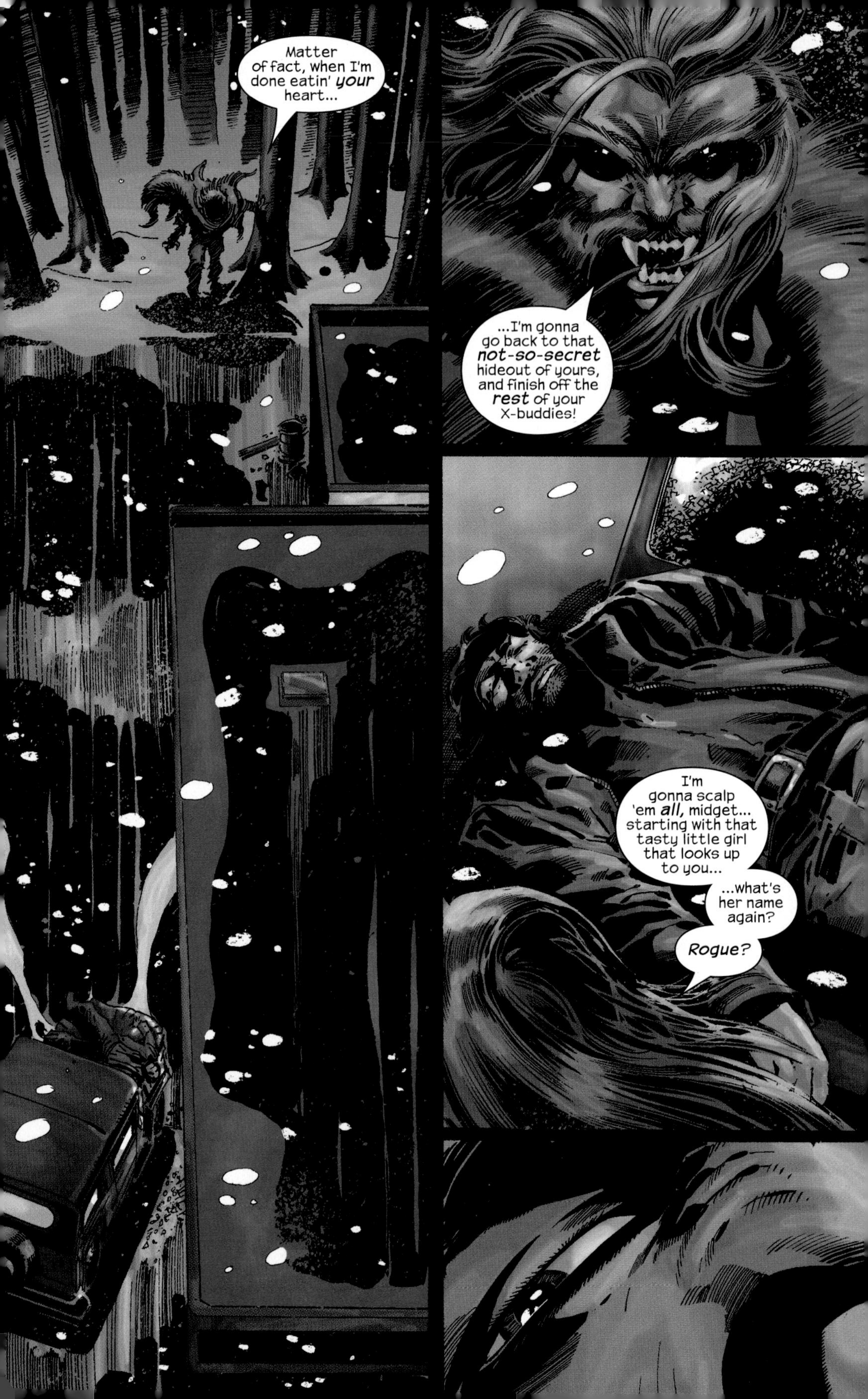
Matter of fact, when I'm done eatin' *your* heart...
...I'm gonna go back to that *not-so-secret* hideout of yours, and finish off the *rest* of your X-buddies!
I'm gonna scalp 'em *all*, midget... starting with that tasty little girl that looks up to you...
...what's her name again?
Rogue?

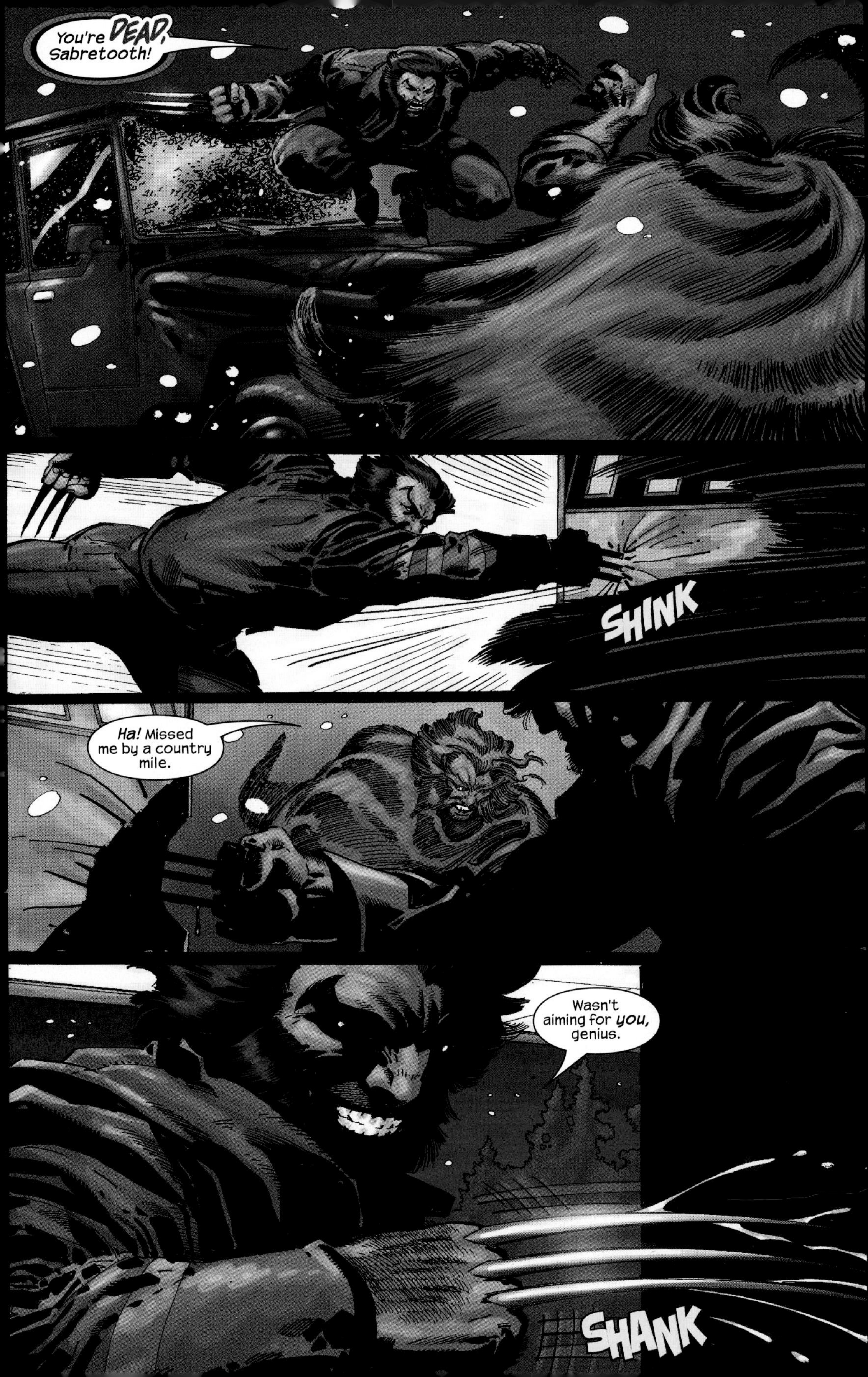
You're DEAD, Sabretooth!
SHINK
Ha! Missed me by a country mile.
Wasn't aiming for you, genius.
SHANK

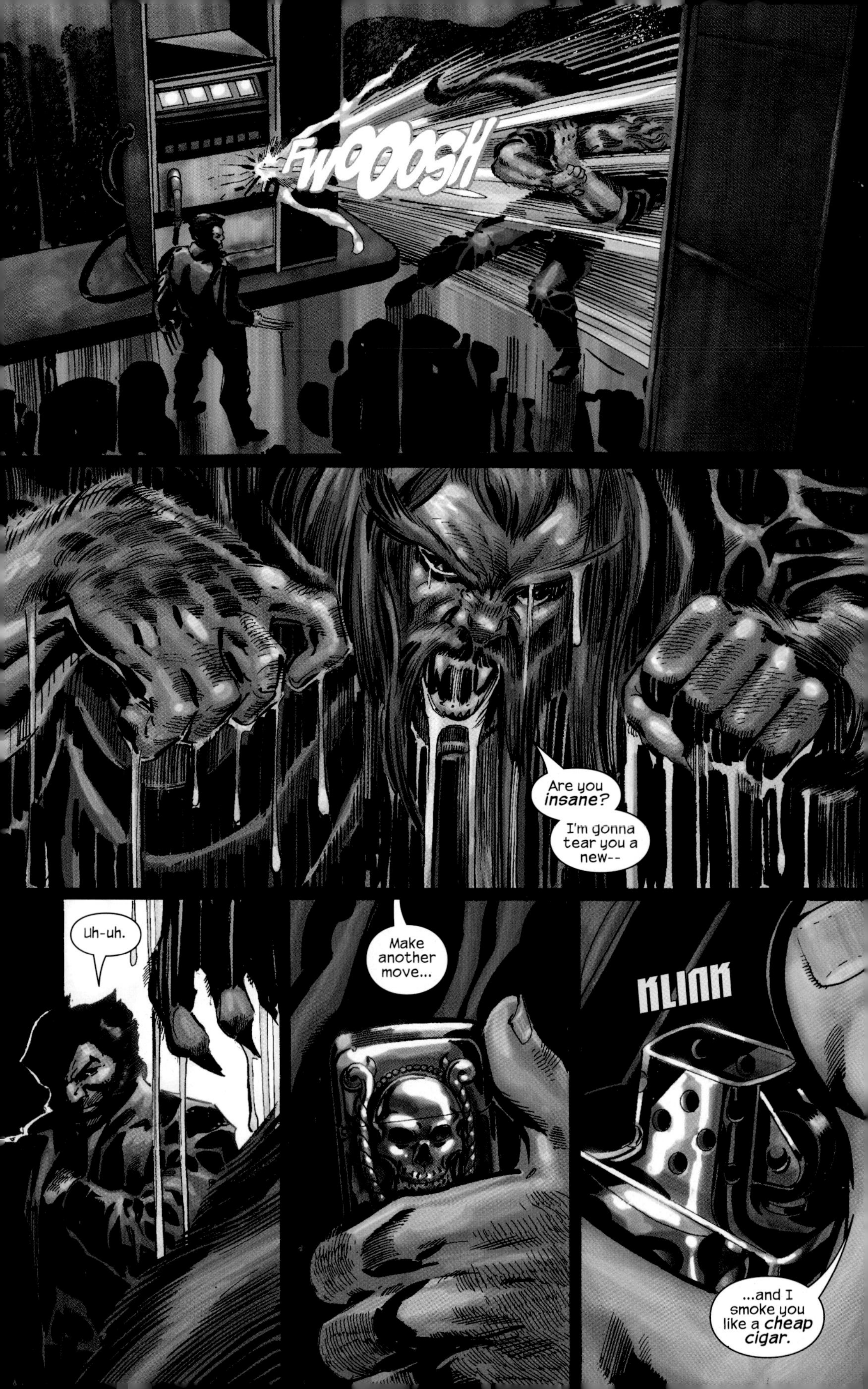
FWOOOSH
Are you *insane*?
I'm gonna tear you a new--
Uh-uh.
Make another move...
KLINK
...and I smoke you like a *cheap cigar*.

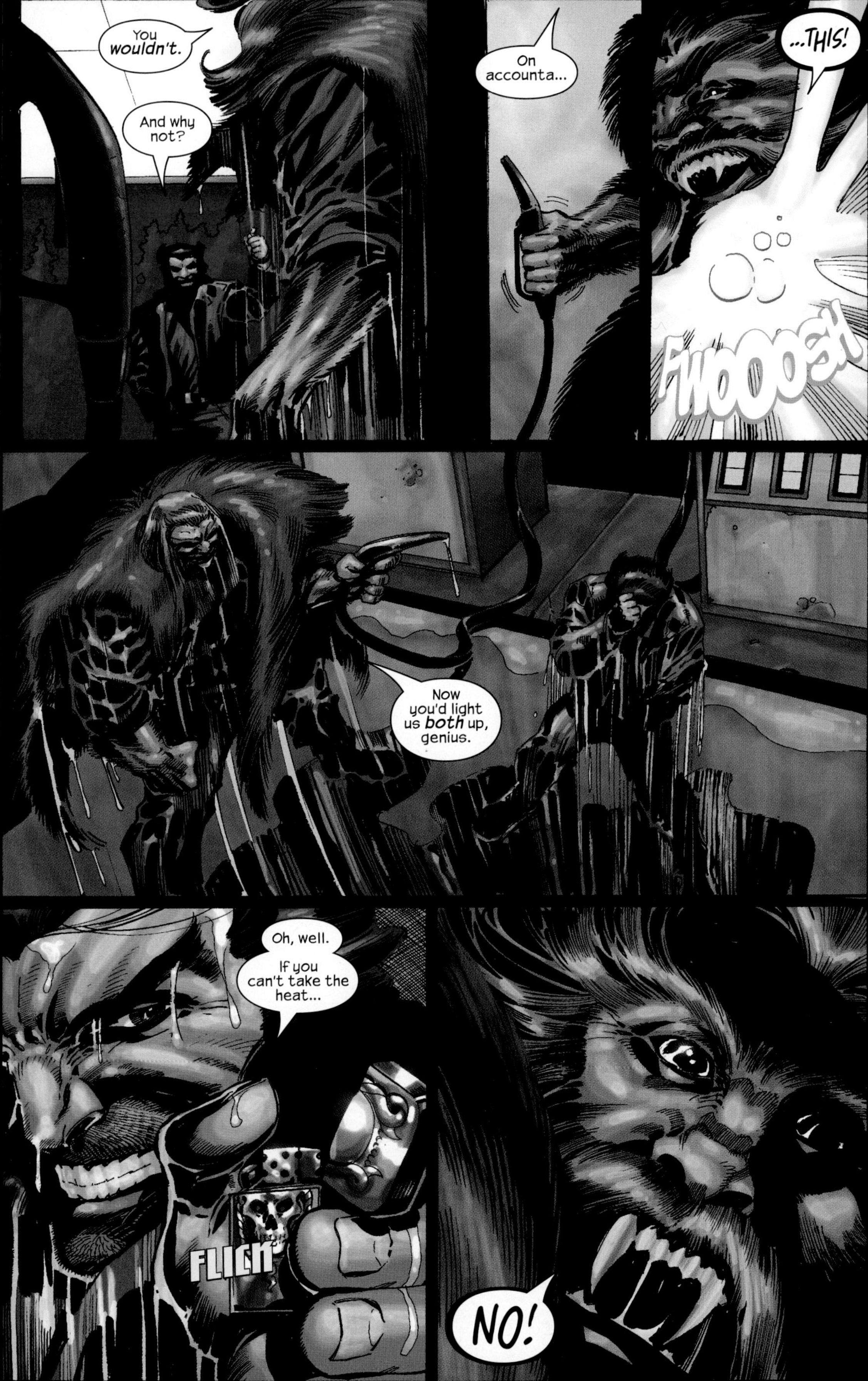

You *wouldn't.*
And why not?
On accounta...
...THIS!
FWOOOSH
Now you'd light us *both* up, genius.
Oh, well.
If you can't take the heat...
FLICK
NO!

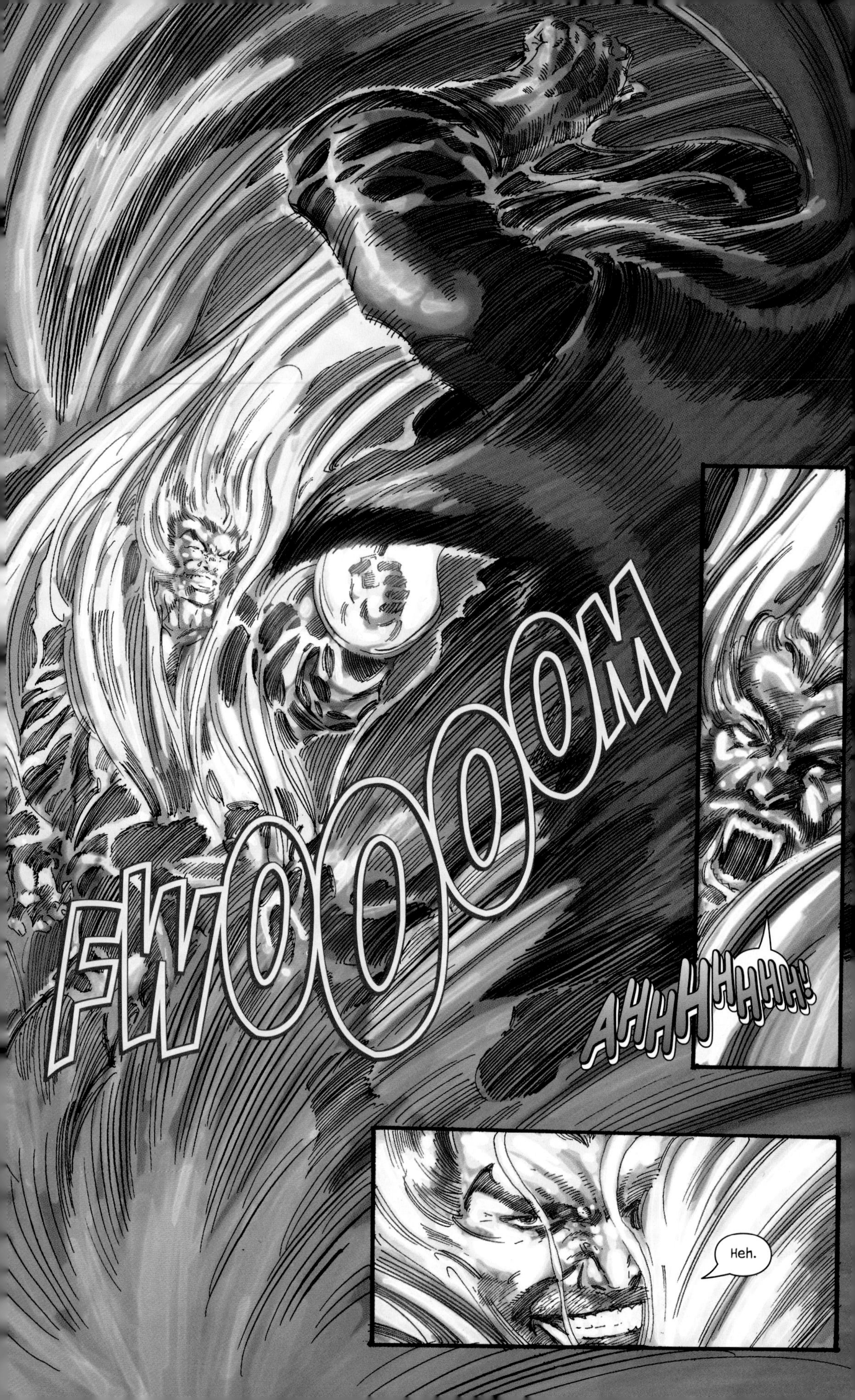
FWOOOOOOM
AHHHHHHHHH!
Heh.

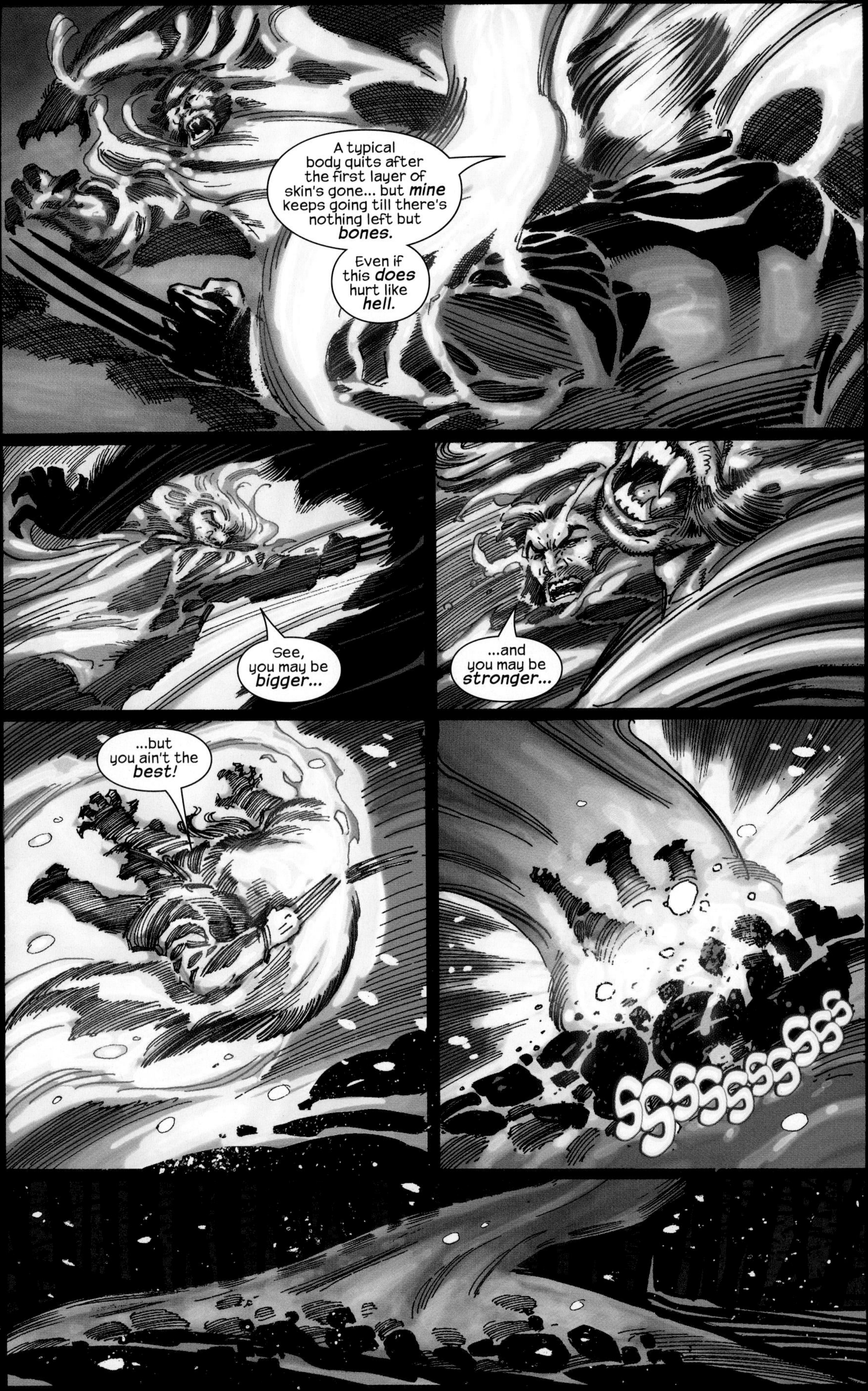
A typical body quits after the first layer of skin's gone... but *mine* keeps going till there's nothing left but *bones.*
Even if this *does* hurt like *hell.*
See, you may be *bigger...*
...and you may be *stronger...*
...but you ain't the *best!*
SSSSSSSSSS

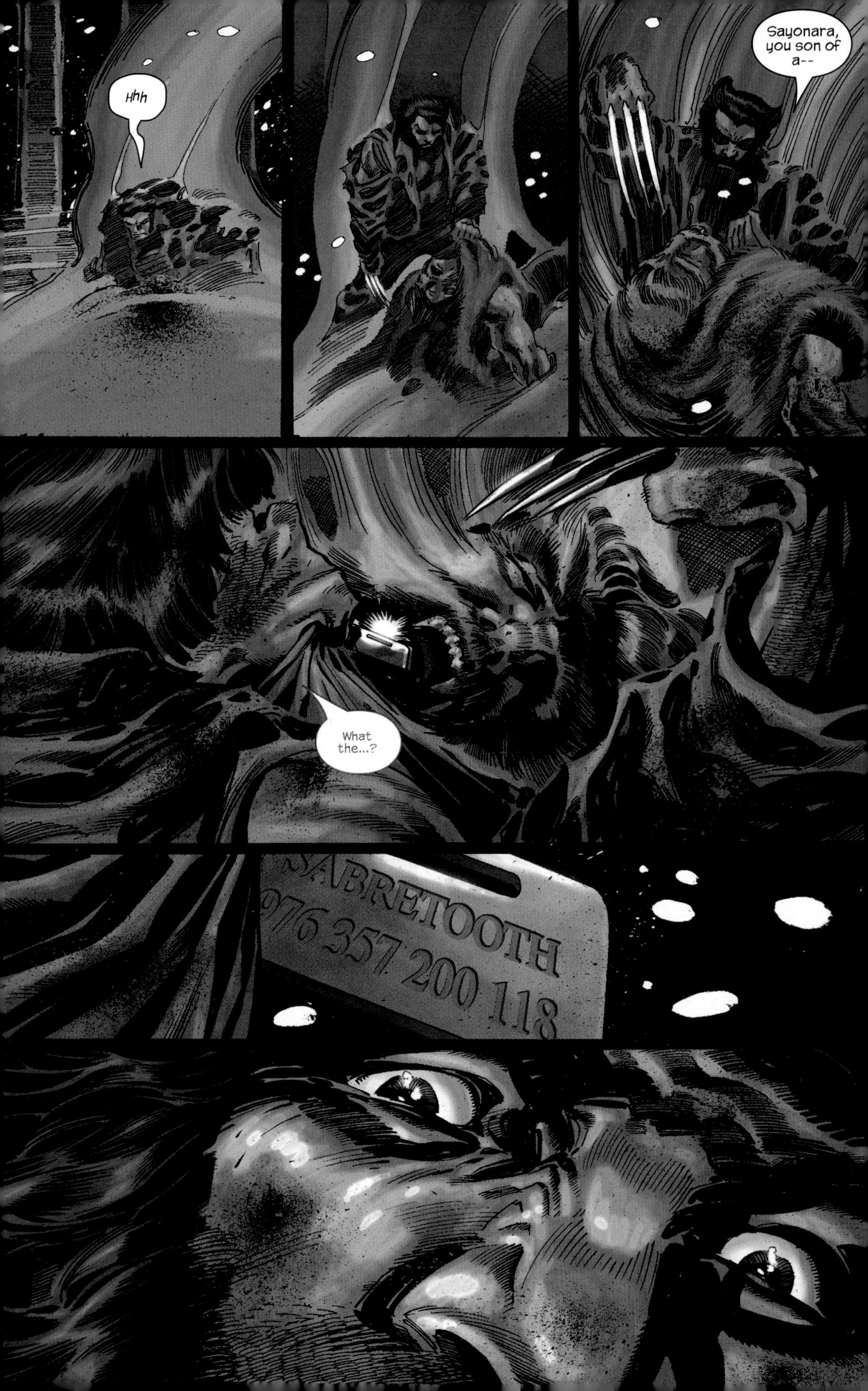
Hhh
Sayonara, you son of a--
What the...?
SABRETOOTH
976 357 200 118

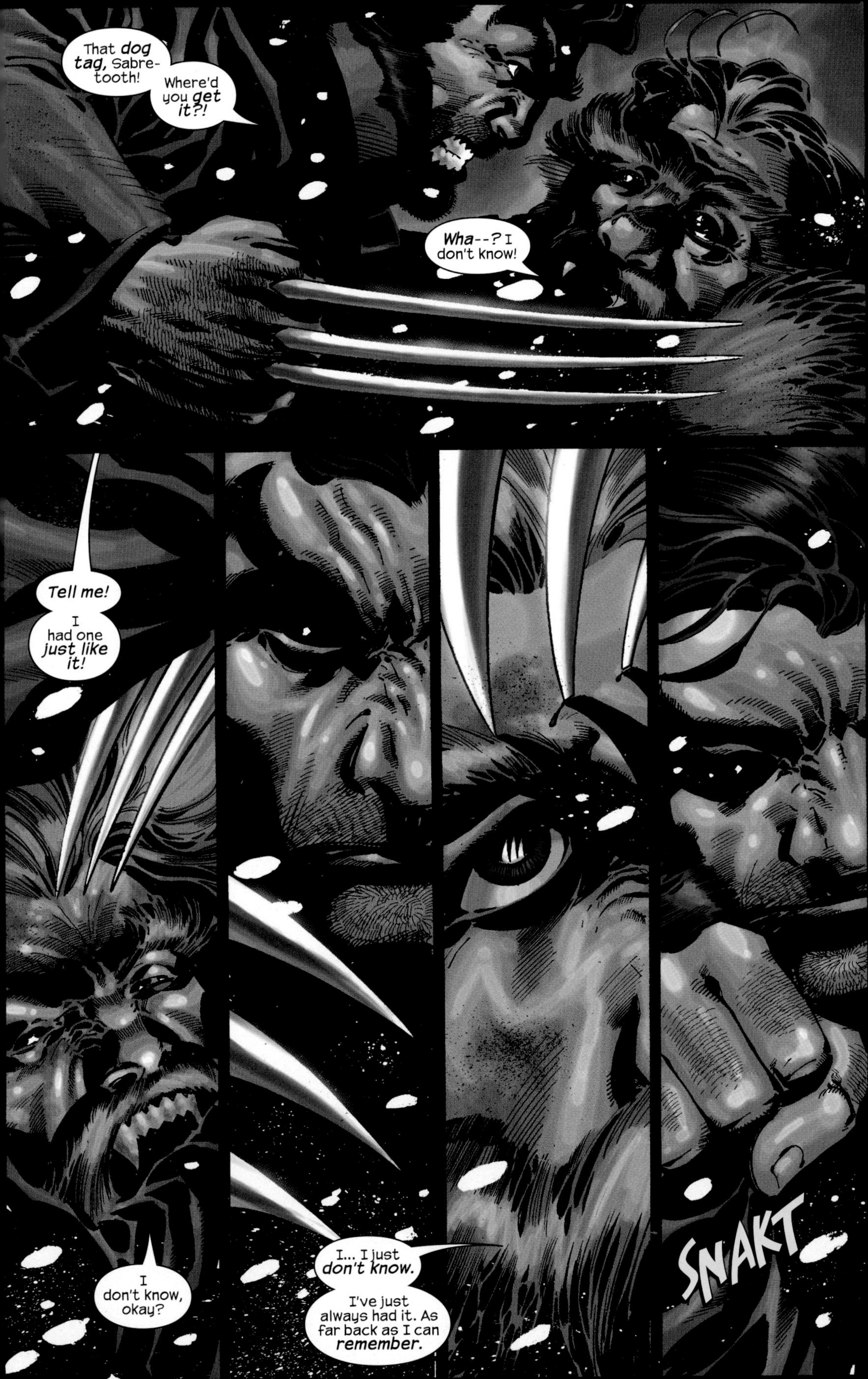
That dog tag, Sabretooth!
Where'd you get it?!
Wha--? I don't know!
Tell me!
I had one just like it!
I don't know, okay?
I... I just don't know.
I've just always had it. As far back as I can remember.
SNAKT

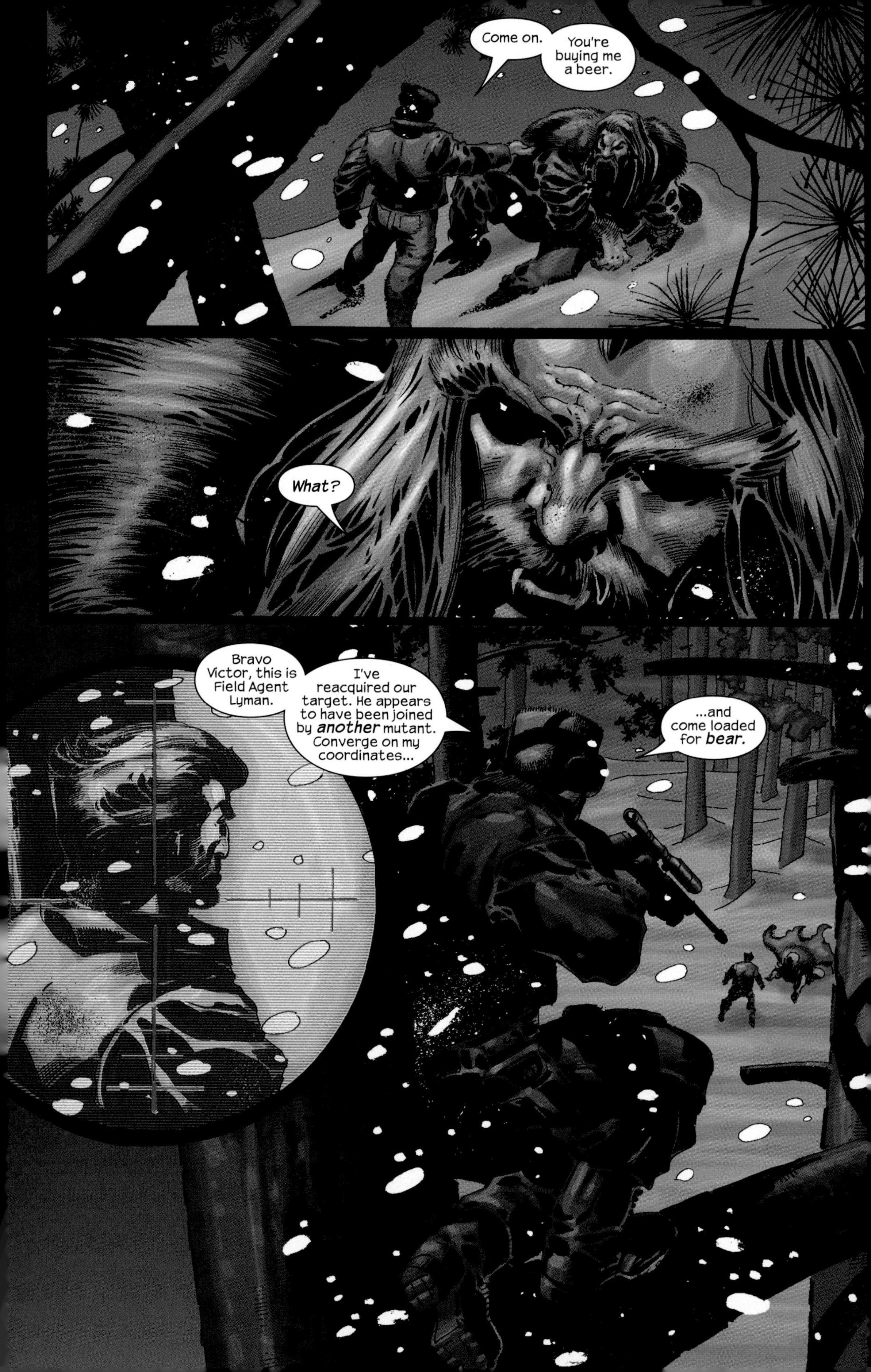
Come on.
You're buying me a beer.
What?
Bravo Victor, this is Field Agent Lyman.
I've reacquired our target. He appears to have been joined by another mutant. Converge on my coordinates...
...and come loaded for bear.

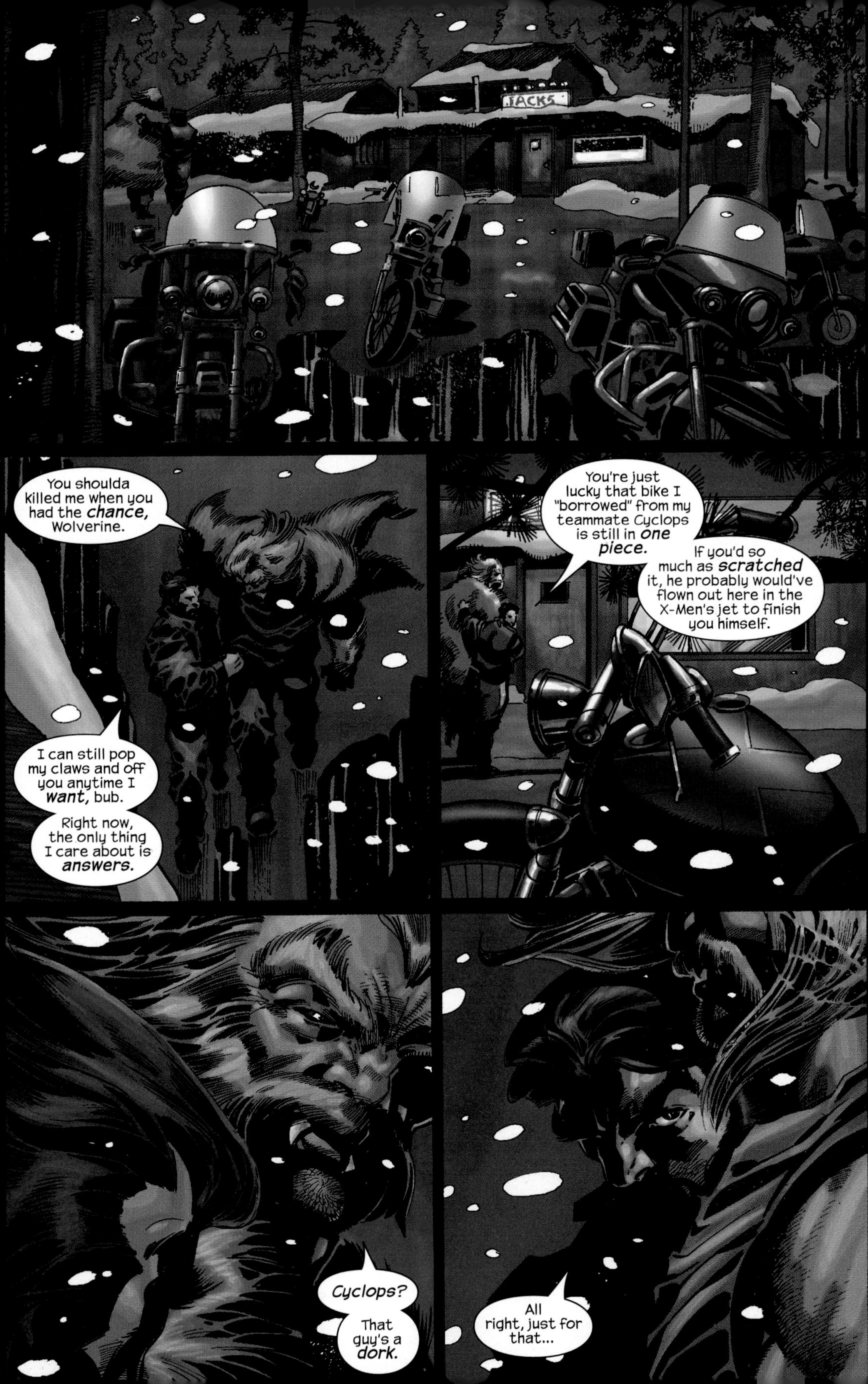
JACKS
You shoulda killed me when you had the *chance,* Wolverine.
I can still pop my claws and off you anytime I *want,* bub.
Right now, the only thing I care about is *answers.*
You're just lucky that bike I "borrowed" from my teammate Cyclops is still in *one piece.*
If you'd so much as *scratched* it, he probably would've flown out here in the X-Men's jet to finish you himself.
Cyclops?
That guy's a *dork.*
All right, just for that...

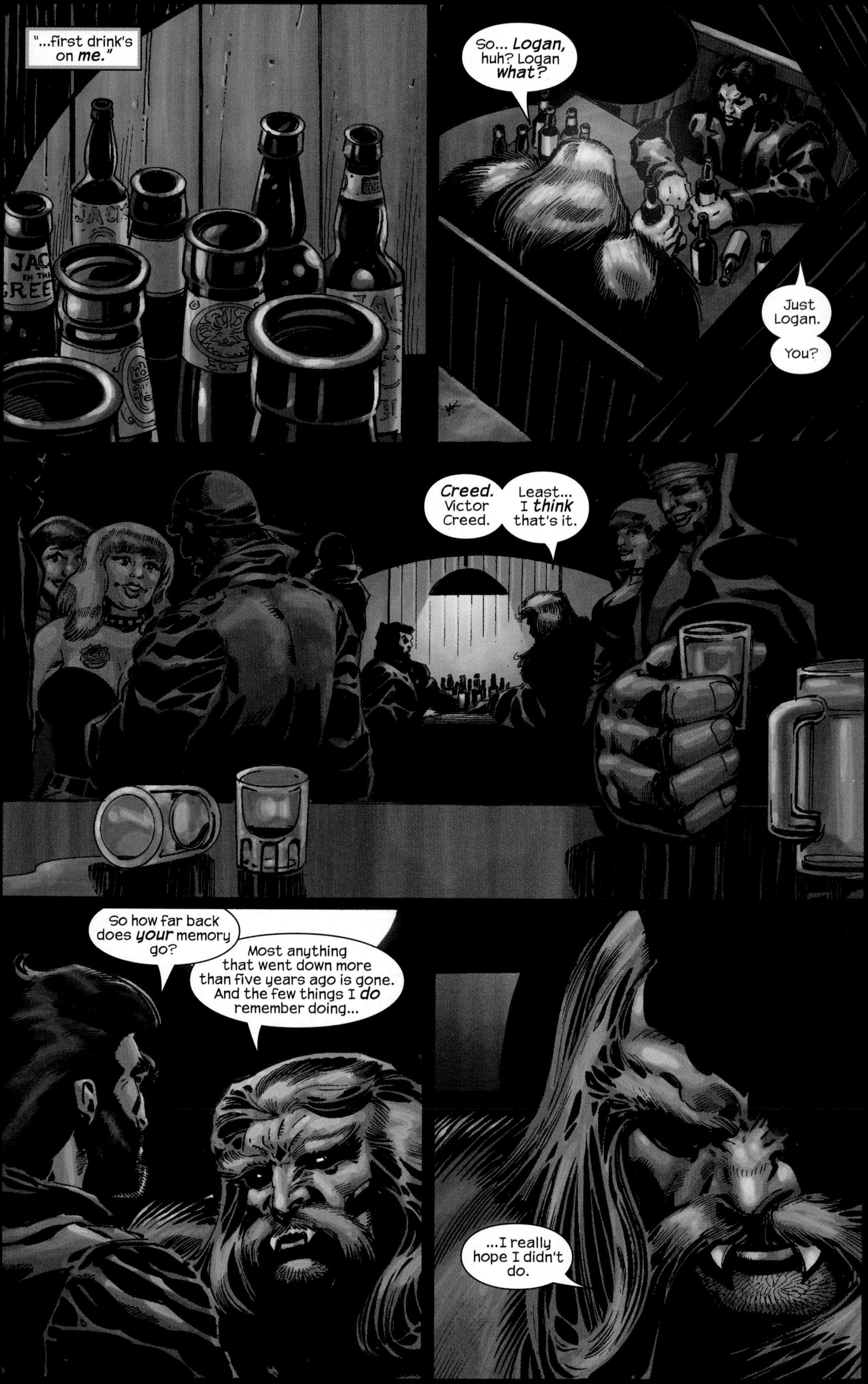
"...first drink's on *me.*"
So... *Logan,* huh? Logan *what?*
Just Logan.
You?
Creed. Victor Creed.
Least... I *think* that's it.
So how far back does *your* memory go?
Most anything that went down more than five years ago is gone. And the few things I *do* remember doing...
...I really hope I didn't do.

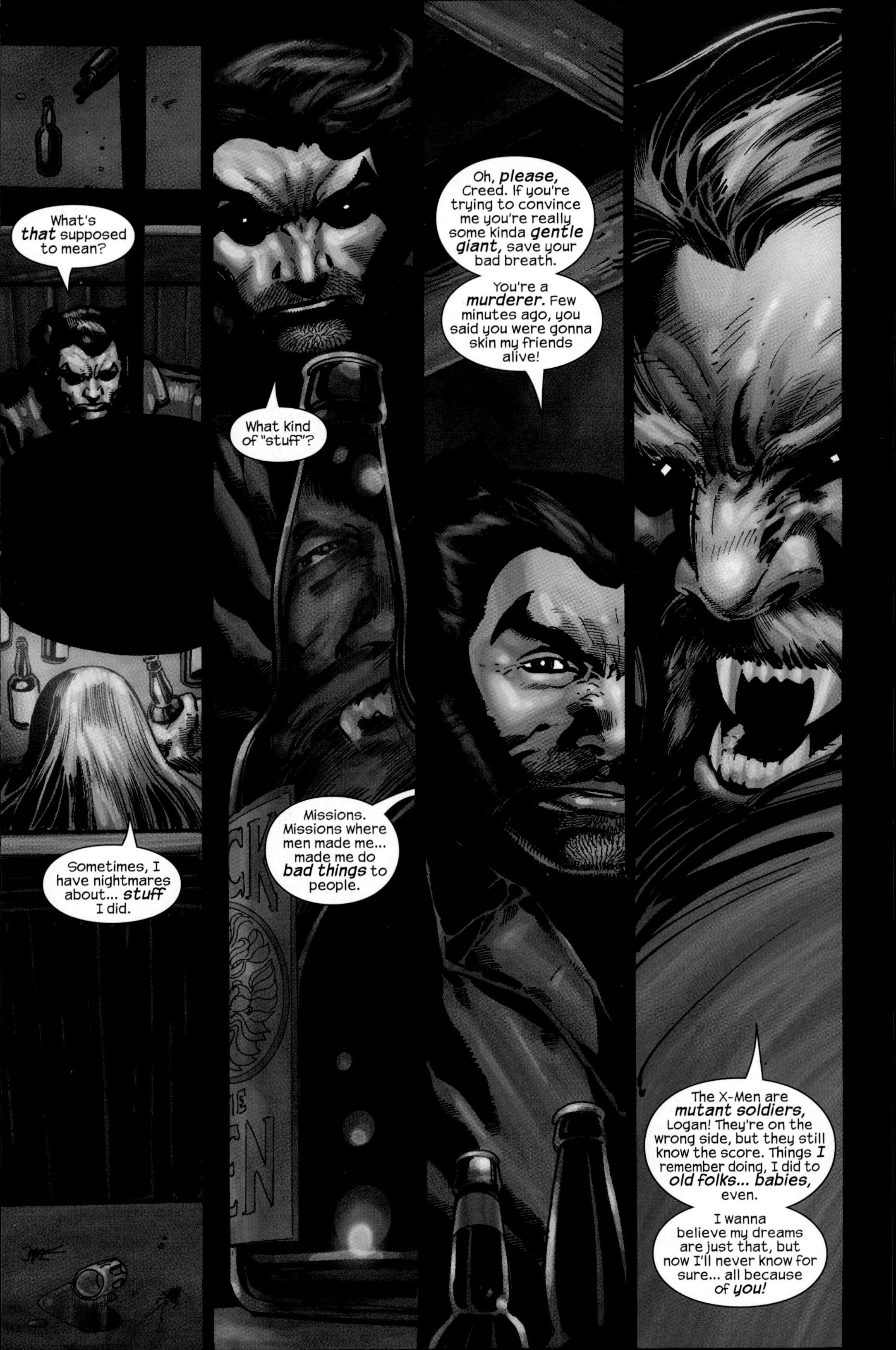
What's *that* supposed to mean?
Sometimes, I have nightmares about... *stuff* I did.
What kind of "stuff"?
Missions. Missions where men made me... made me do *bad things* to people.
Oh, *please,* Creed. If you're trying to convince me you're really some kinda *gentle giant,* save your bad breath.
You're a *murderer.* Few minutes ago, you said you were gonna skin my friends alive!
The X-Men are *mutant soldiers,* Logan! They're on the wrong side, but they still know the score. Things *I* remember doing, I did to *old folks... babies,* even.
I wanna believe my dreams are just that, but now I'll never know for sure... all because of *you!*

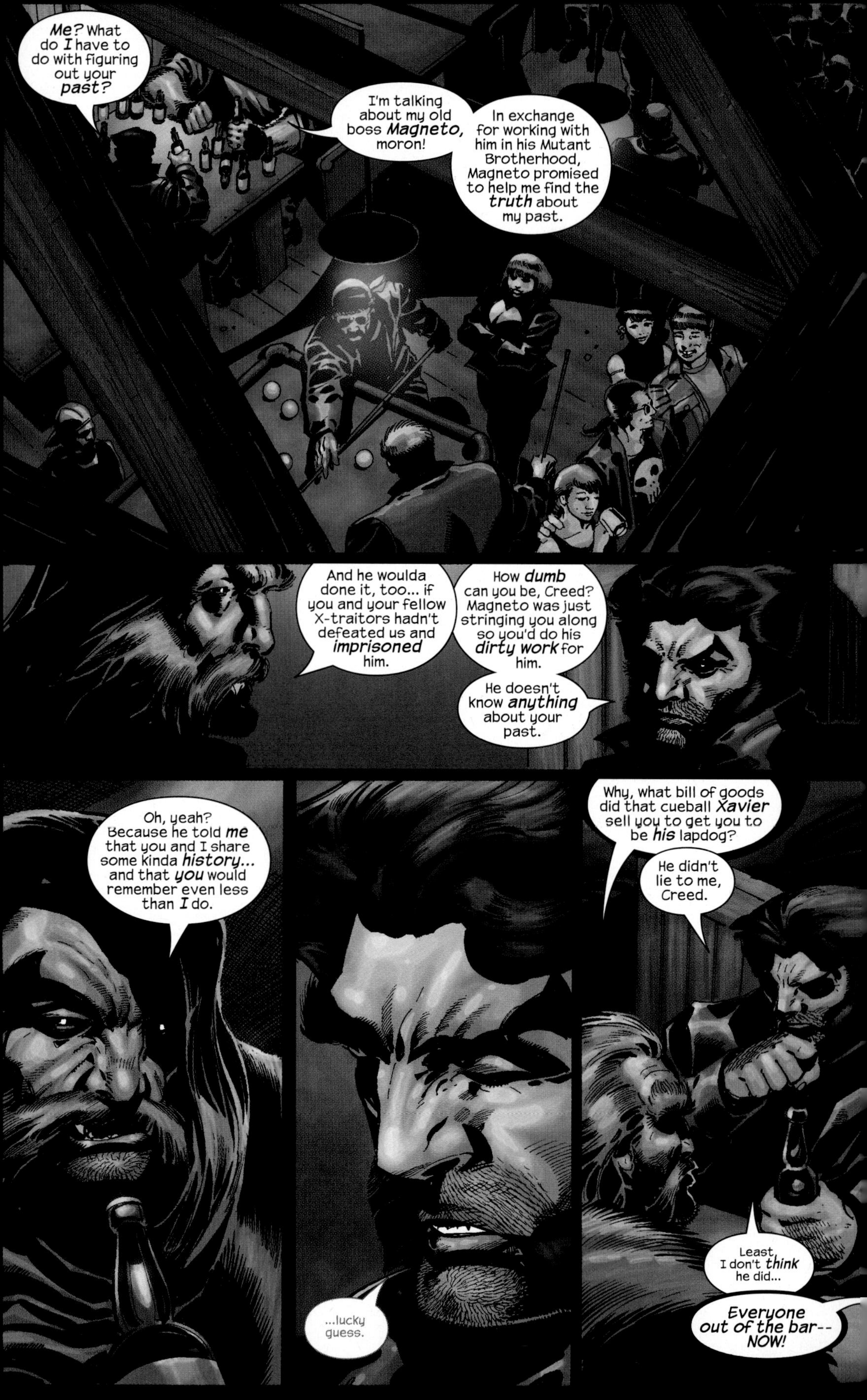
Me? What do I have to do with figuring out your past?
I'm talking about my old boss Magneto, moron!
In exchange for working with him in his Mutant Brotherhood, Magneto promised to help me find the truth about my past.
And he woulda done it, too... if you and your fellow X-traitors hadn't defeated us and imprisoned him.
How dumb can you be, Creed? Magneto was just stringing you along so you'd do his dirty work for him.
He doesn't know anything about your past.
Oh, yeah? Because he told me that you and I share some kinda history... and that you would remember even less than I do.
...lucky guess.
Why, what bill of goods did that cueball Xavier sell you to get you to be his lapdog?
He didn't lie to me, Creed.
Least, I don't think he did...
Everyone out of the bar--NOW!

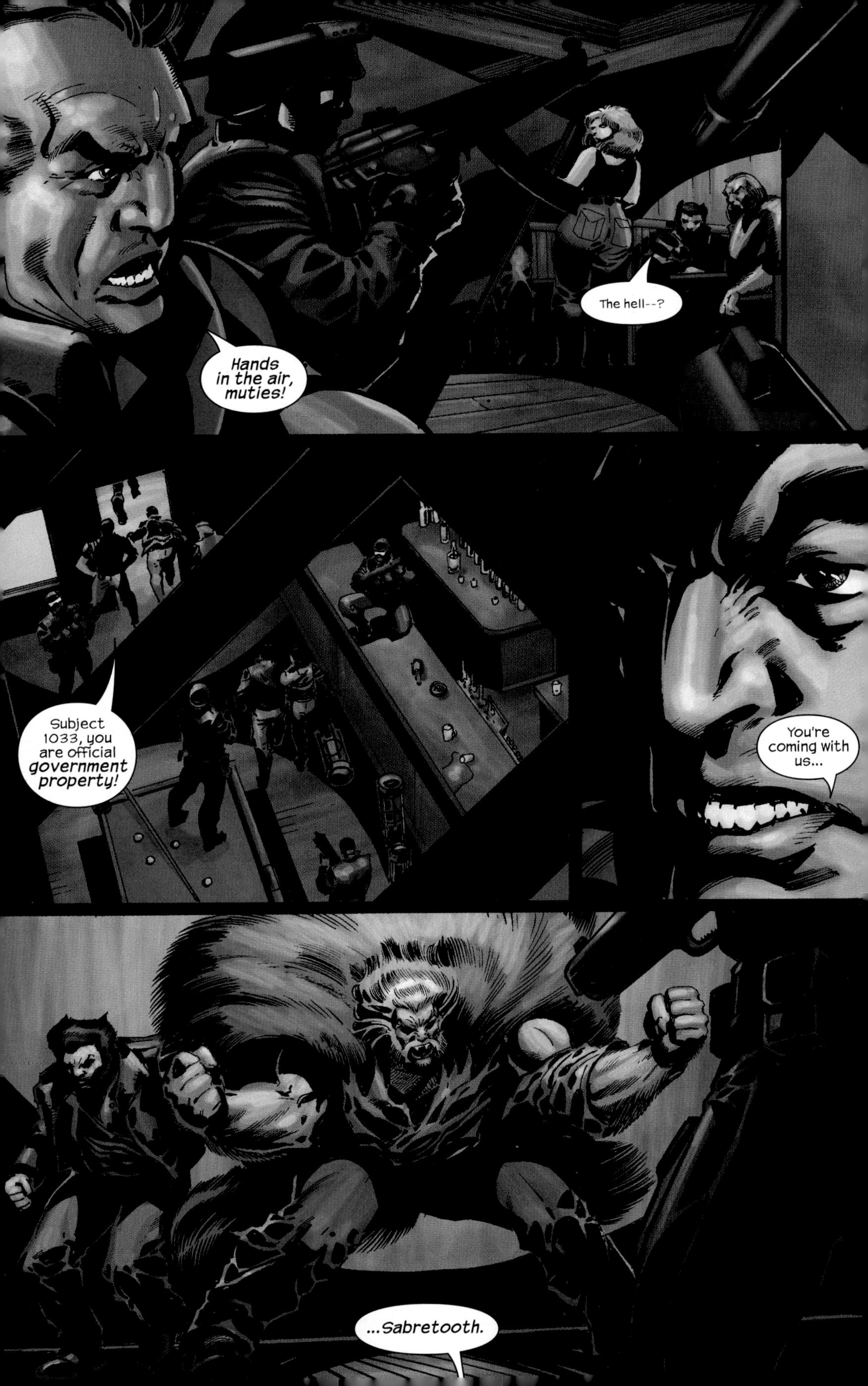
Hands in the air, muties!
The hell--?
Subject 1033, you are official *government property!*
You're coming with us...
...Sabretooth.

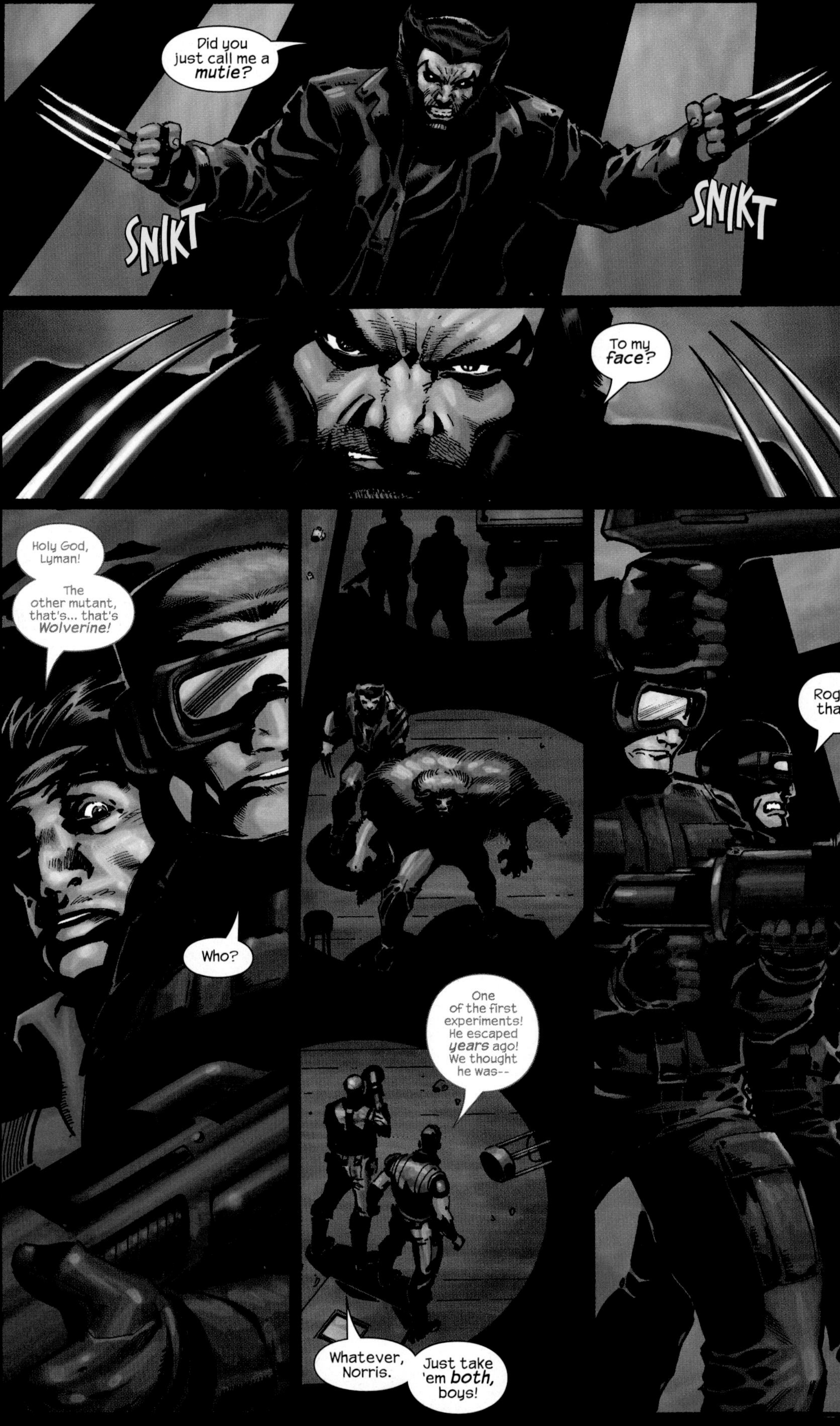
Did you just call me a *mutie?*
SNIKT
SNIKT
To my *face?*
Holy God, Lyman!
The other mutant, that's... that's *Wolverine!*
Who?
One of the first experiments! He escaped *years* ago! We thought he was--
Whatever, Norris.
Just take 'em *both,* boys!
Roger that.

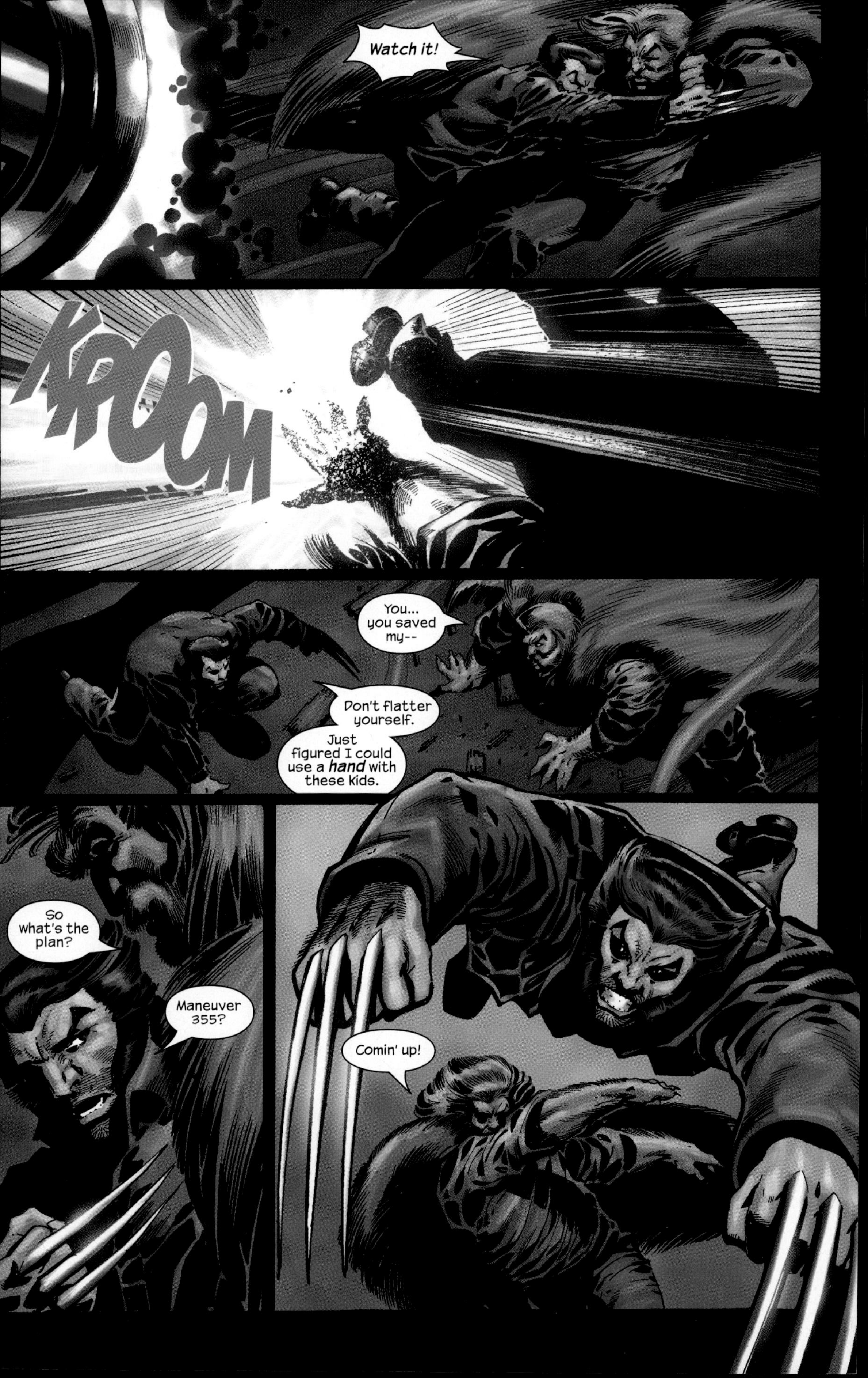
Watch it!
KROOM
You... you saved my--
Don't flatter yourself.
Just figured I could use a *hand* with these kids.
So what's the plan?
Maneuver 355?
Comin' up!

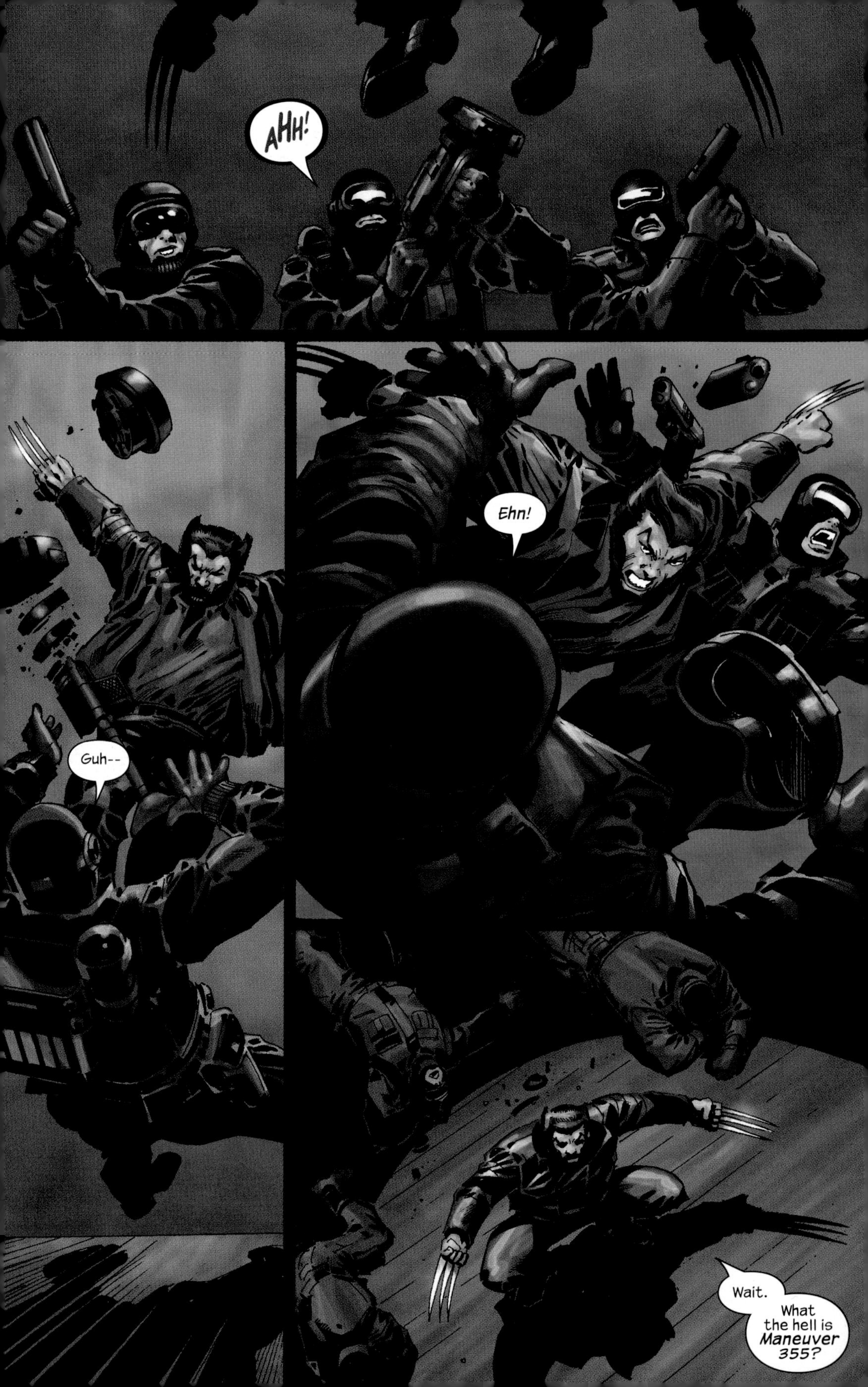
AHH!
Guh--
Ehn!
Wait.
What the hell is Maneuver 355?

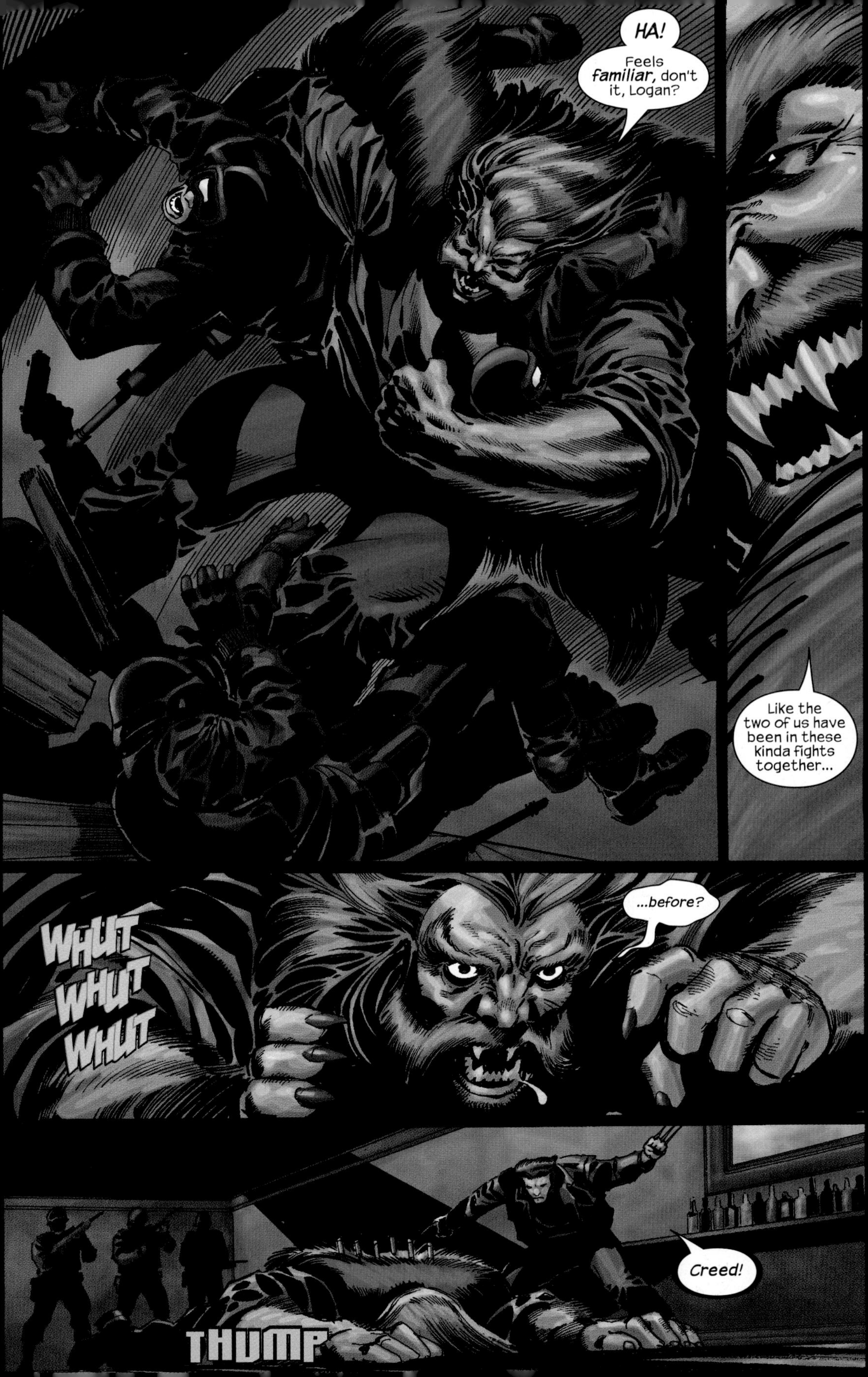
HA!
Feels *familiar,* don't it, Logan?
Like the two of us have been in these kinda fights together...
...before?
WHUT WHUT WHUT
Creed!
THUMP

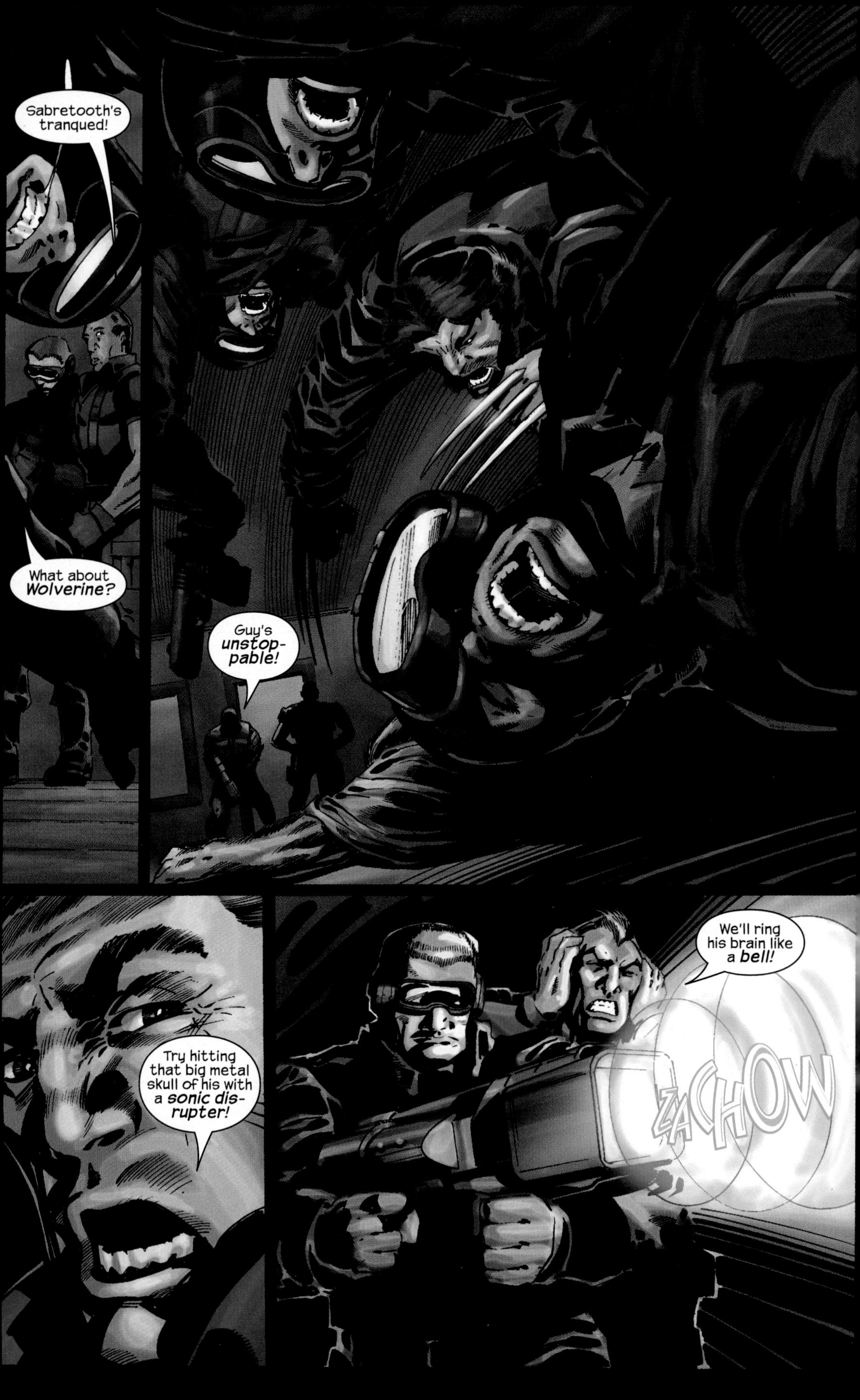
Sabretooth's tranqued!
What about Wolverine?
Guy's unstoppable!
Try hitting that big metal skull of his with a sonic disrupter!
We'll ring his brain like a bell!
ZACHOW

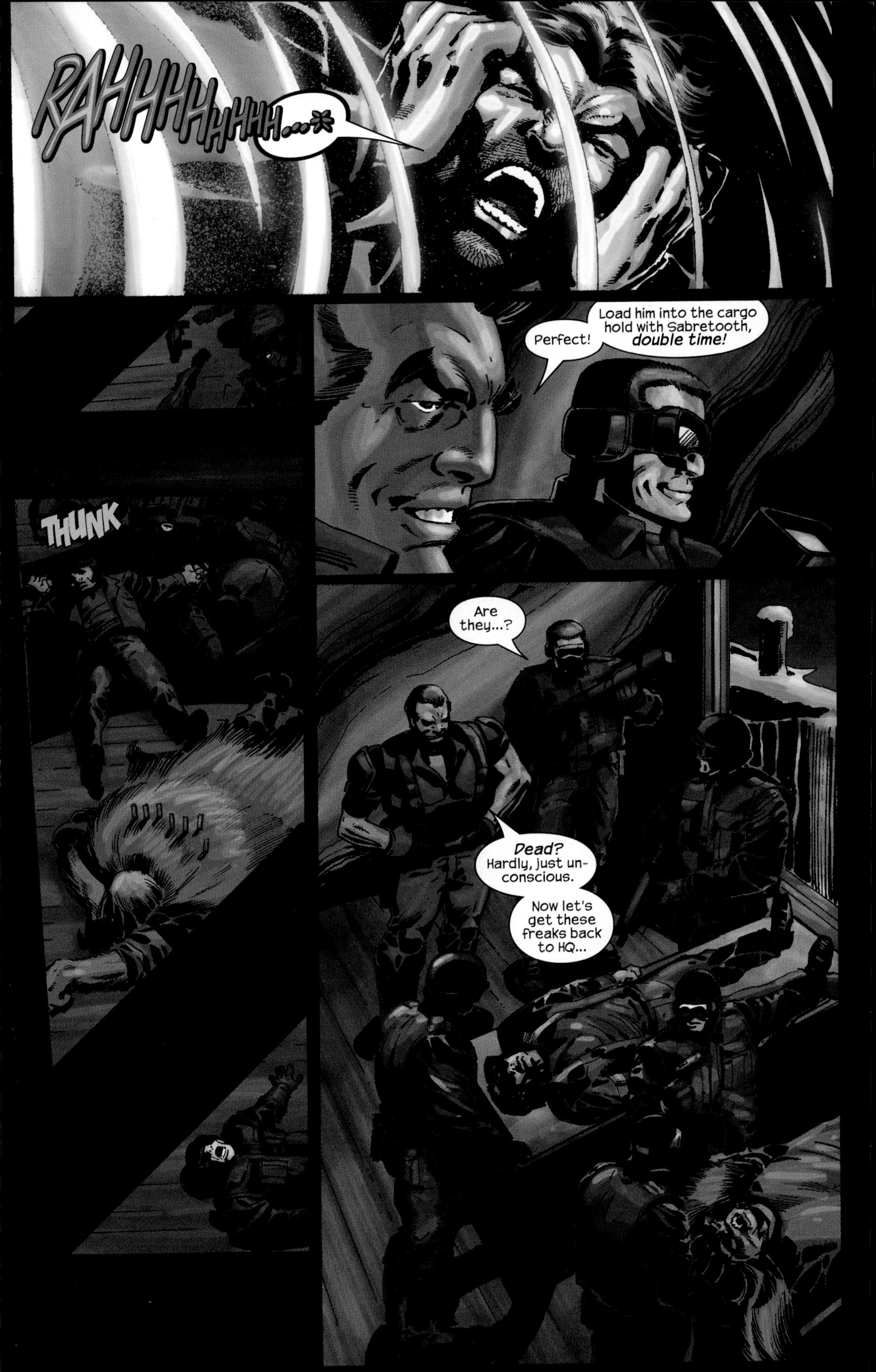
RAHHHHHHHH...*
Perfect!
Load him into the cargo hold with Sabretooth, *double time!*
THUNK
Are they...?
Dead? Hardly, just unconscious.
Now let's get these freaks back to HQ...

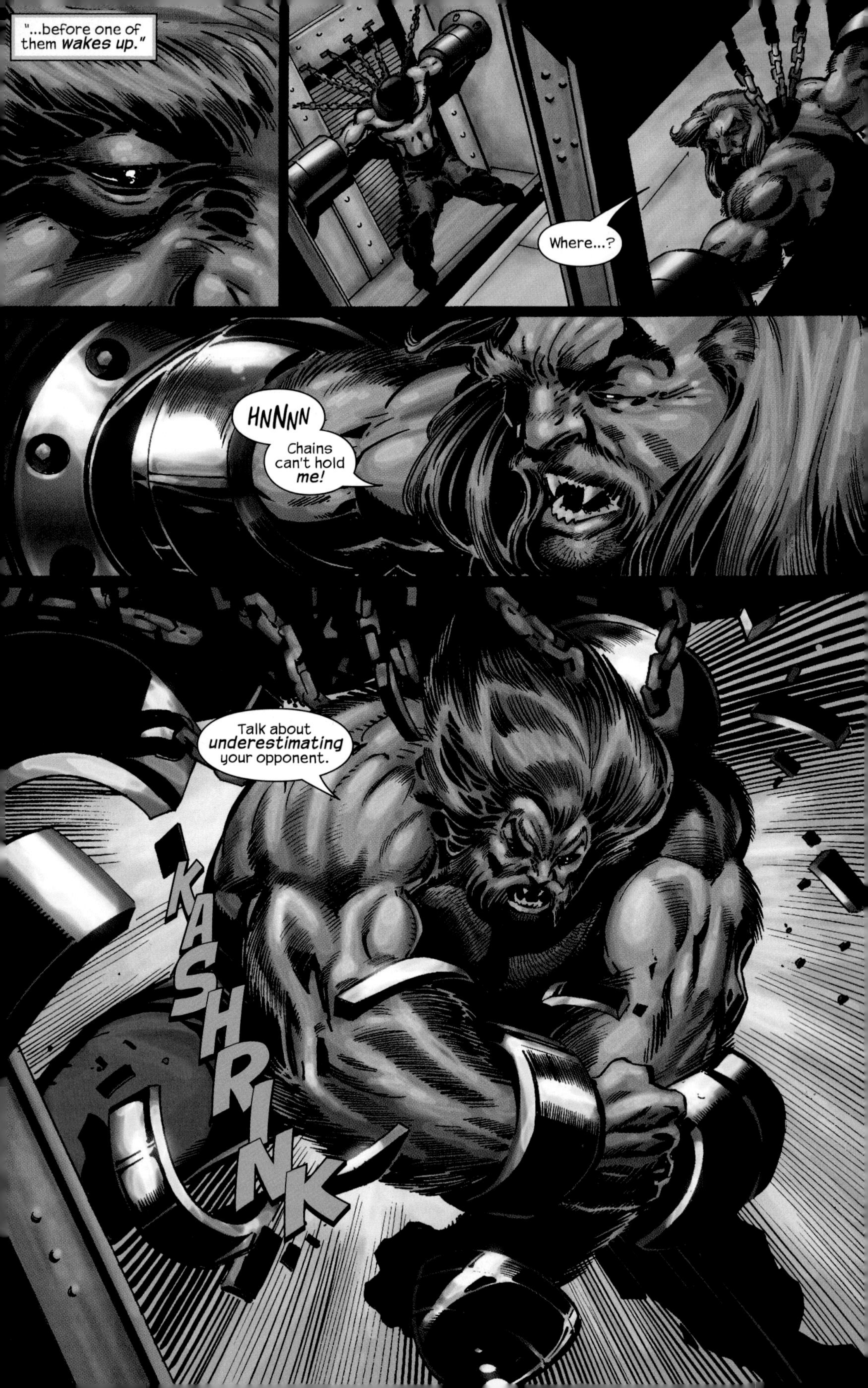
"...before one of them *wakes up.*"
Where...?
HNNNN
Chains can't hold *me!*
Talk about *underestimating* your opponent.
KASHRINK

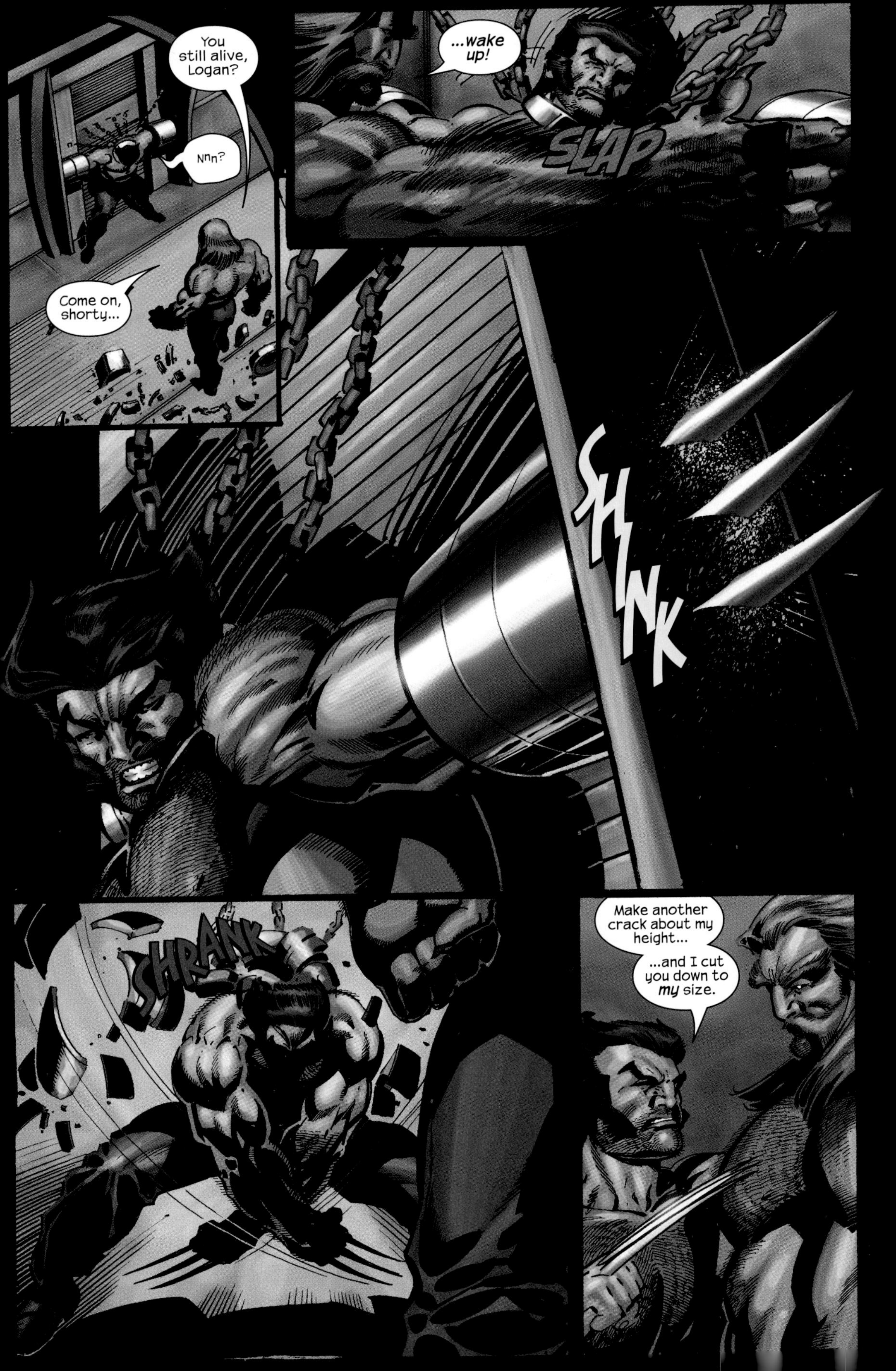
You still alive, Logan?
Nnn?
Come on, shorty...
...wake up!
SLAP
SHINK
SHRANK
Make another crack about my height...
...and I cut you down to *my* size.

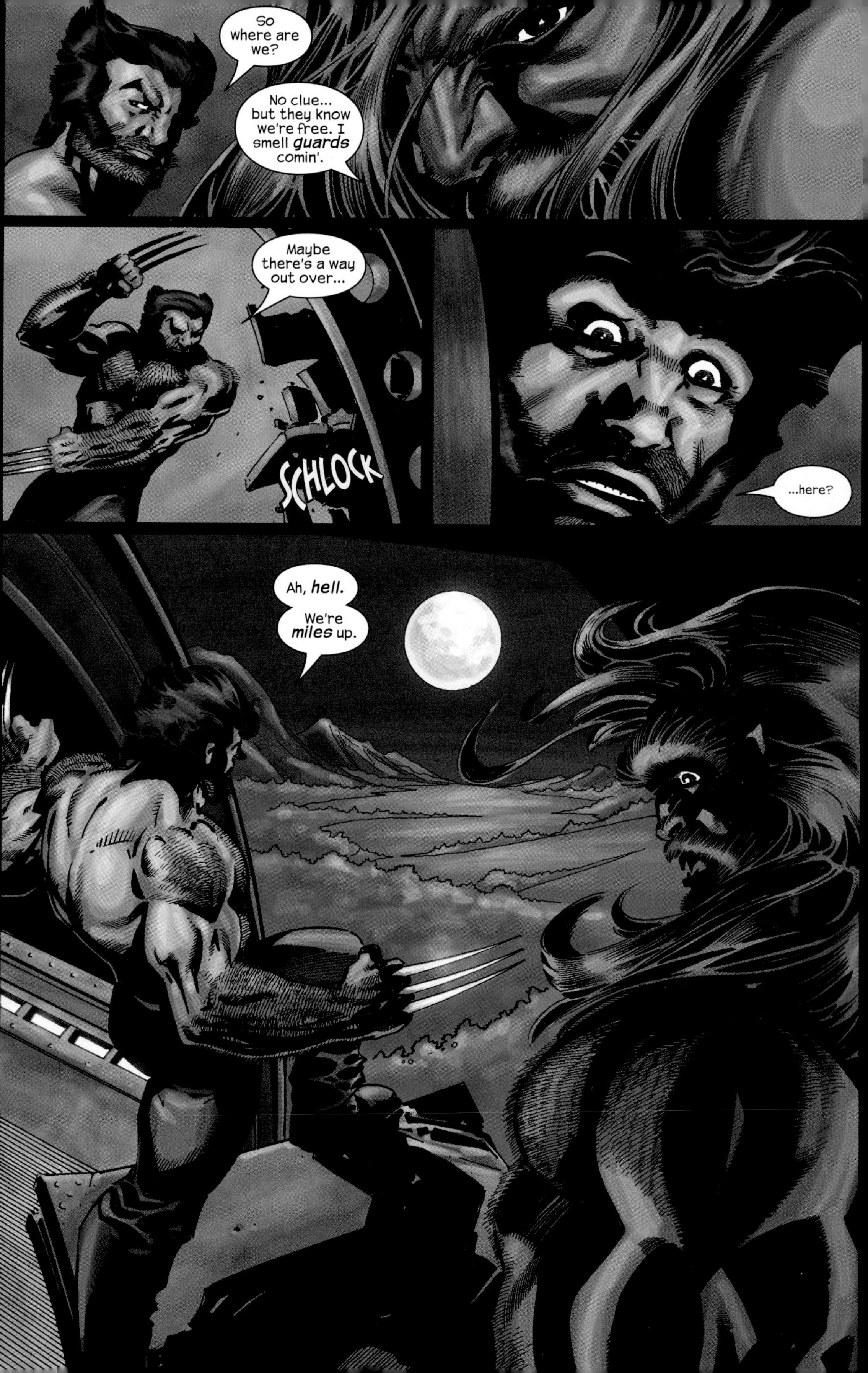
So where are we?
No clue... but they know we're free. I smell guards comin'.
Maybe there's a way out over...
SCHLOCK
...here?
Ah, hell.
We're miles up.

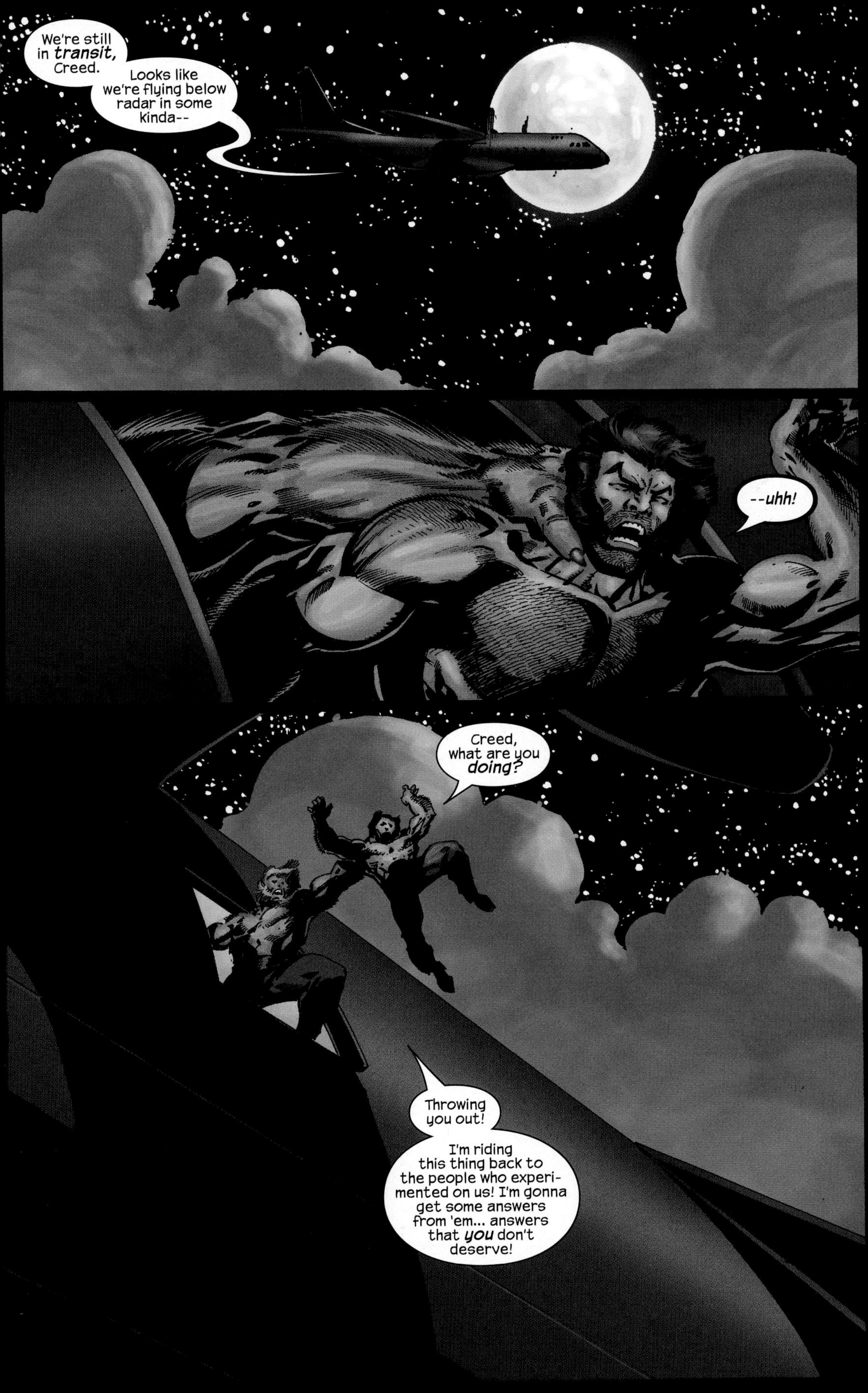

We're still in *transit,* Creed.
Looks like we're flying below radar in some kinda--
--uhh!
Creed, what are you *doing?*
Throwing you out!
I'm riding this thing back to the people who experimented on us! I'm gonna get some answers from 'em... answers that *you* don't deserve!

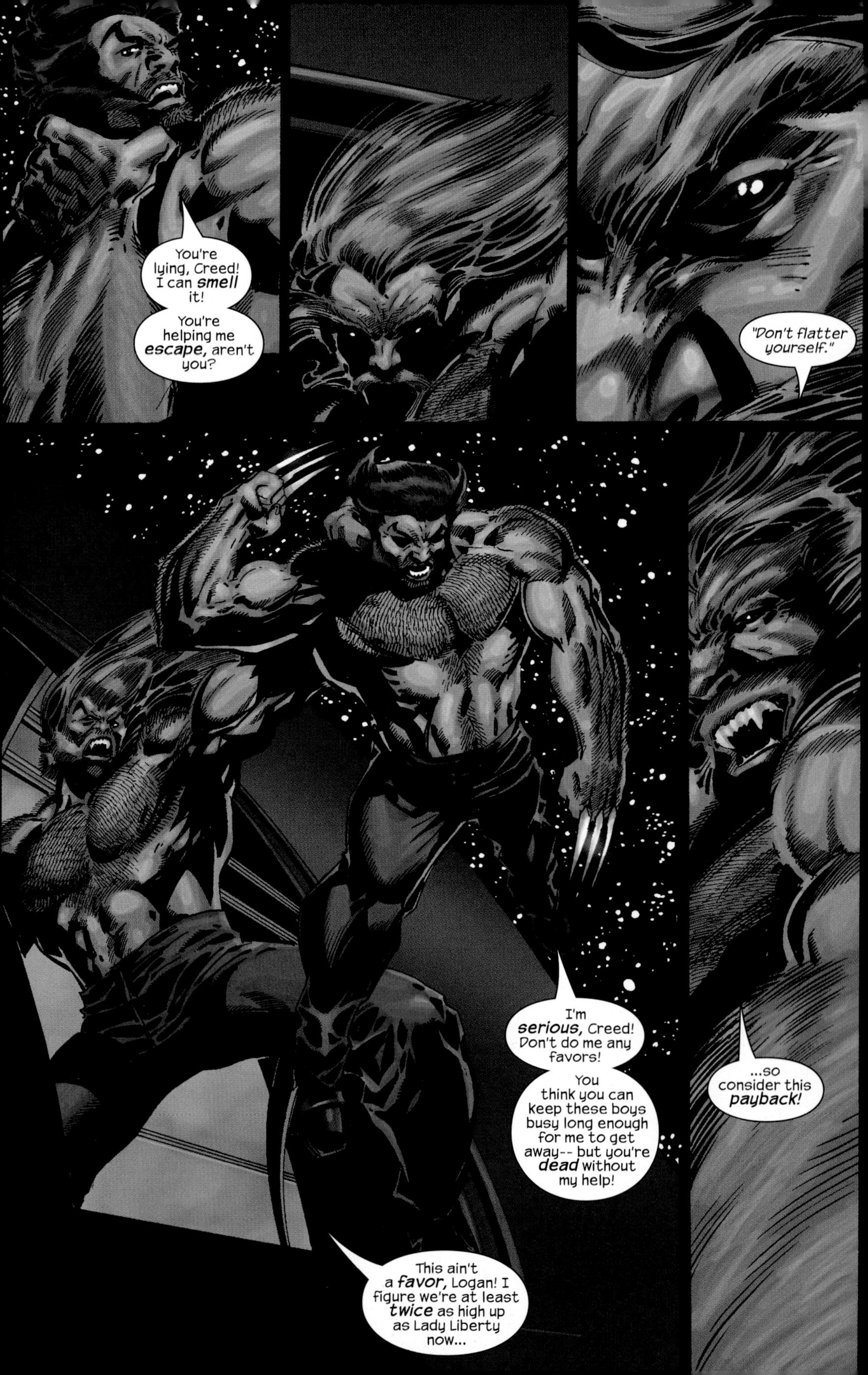
You're lying, Creed! I can smell it!
You're helping me escape, aren't you?
"Don't flatter yourself."
I'm serious, Creed! Don't do me any favors!
You think you can keep these boys busy long enough for me to get away-- but you're dead without my help!
This ain't a favor, Logan! I figure we're at least twice as high up as Lady Liberty now...
...so consider this payback!

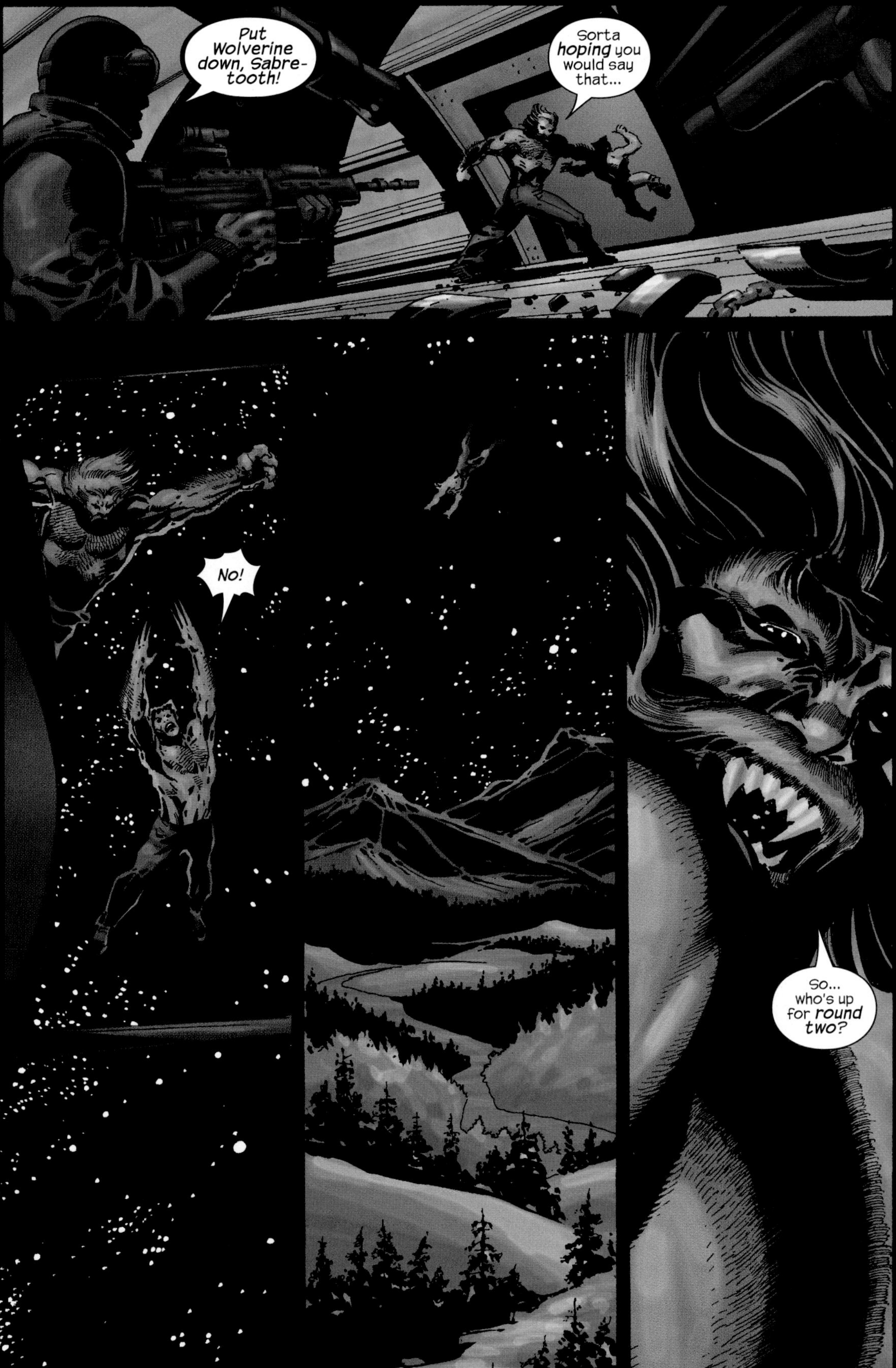

Put Wolverine down, Sabre-tooth!
Sorta hoping you would say that...
No!
So... who's up for round two?

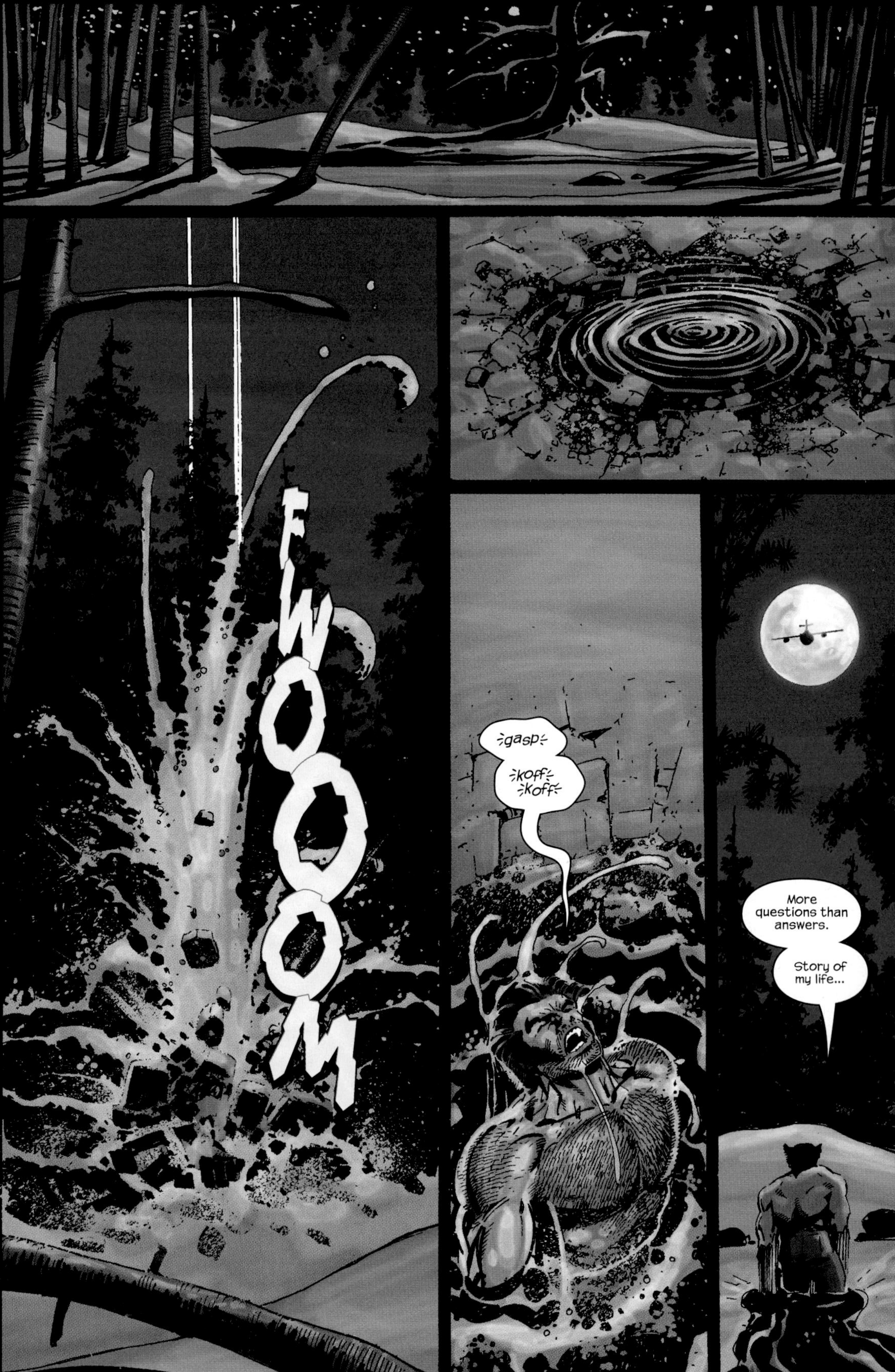
FWOOOOM
gasp
koff koff
More questions than answers.
Story of my life...

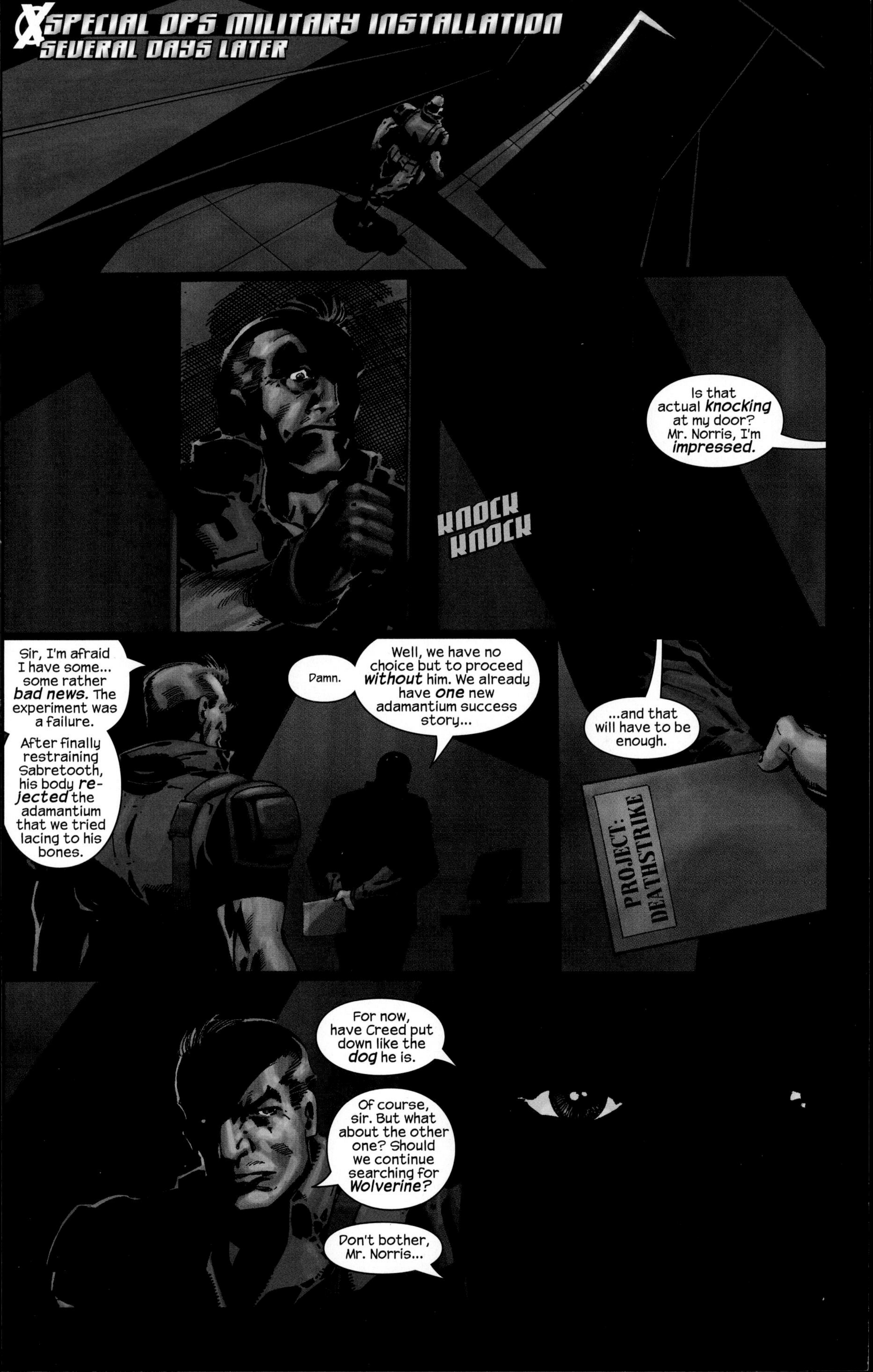
SPECIAL OPS MILITARY INSTALLATION
SEVERAL DAYS LATER
Is that actual knocking at my door? Mr. Norris, I'm impressed.
KNOCK KNOCK
Sir, I'm afraid I have some... some rather bad news. The experiment was a failure.
After finally restraining Sabretooth, his body rejected the adamantium that we tried lacing to his bones.
Damn.
Well, we have no choice but to proceed without him. We already have one new adamantium success story...
...and that will have to be enough.
PROJECT: DEATHSTRIKE
For now, have Creed put down like the dog he is.
Of course, sir. But what about the other one? Should we continue searching for Wolverine?
Don't bother, Mr. Norris...

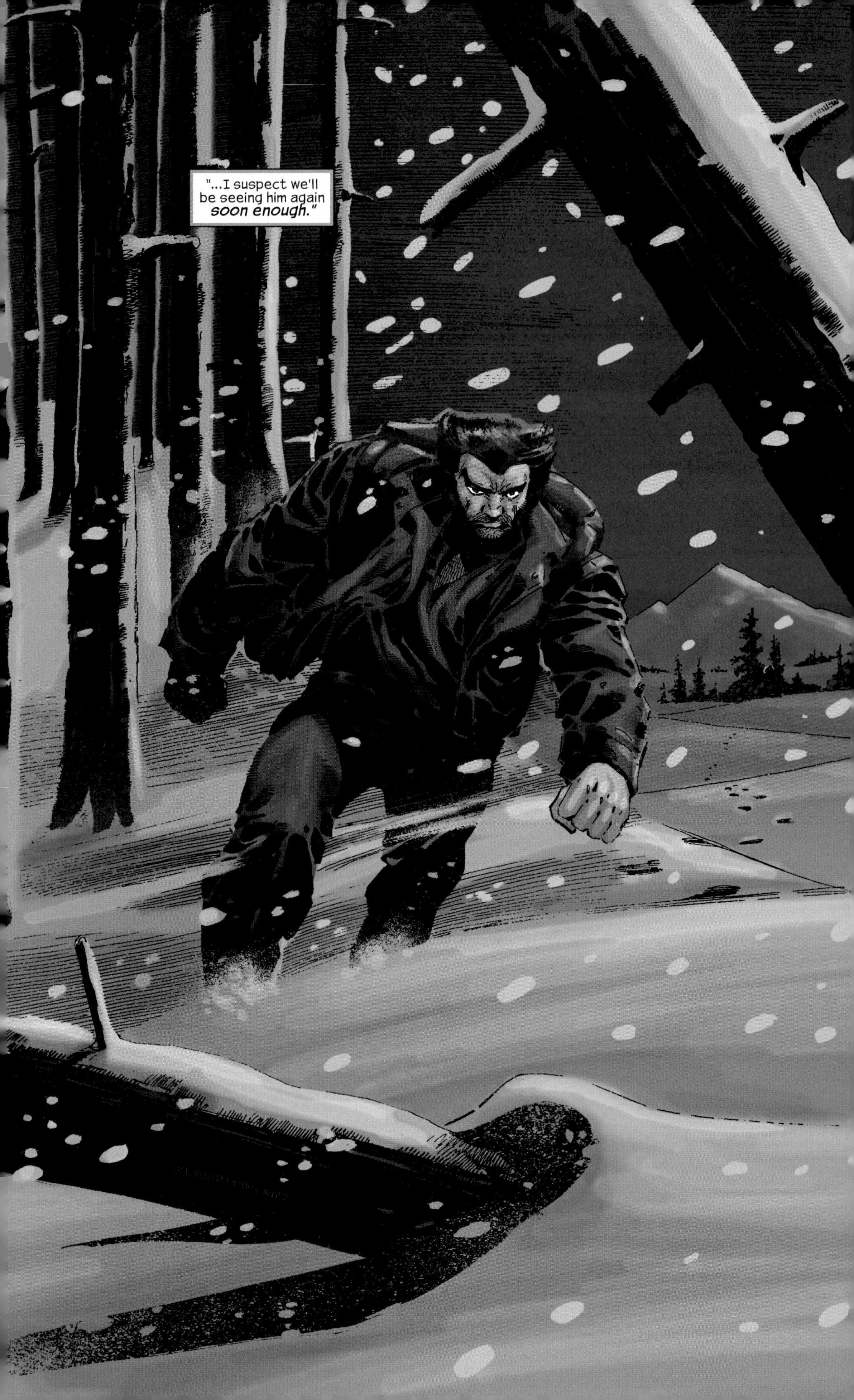
"...I suspect we'll be seeing him again soon enough."

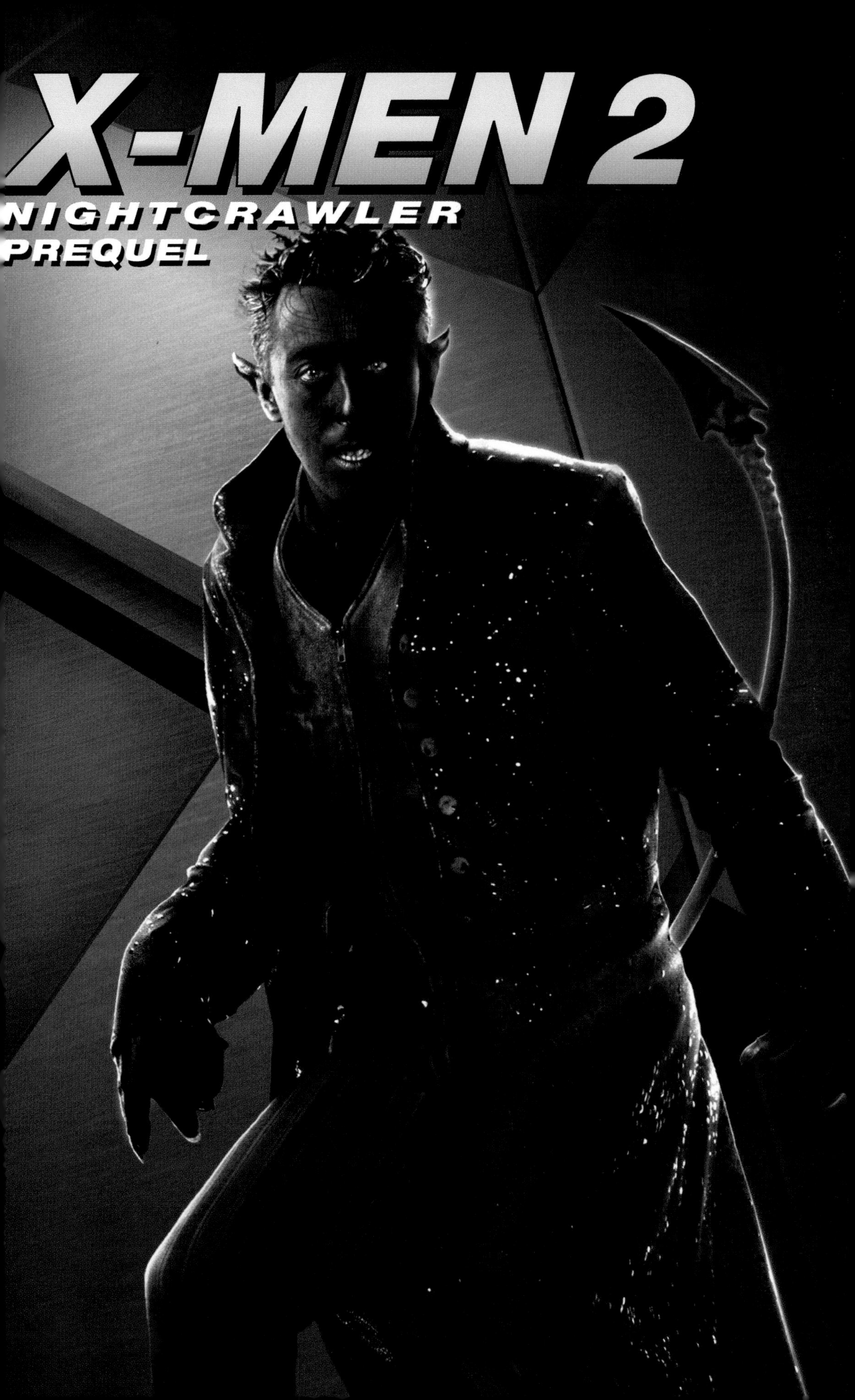
X-MEN 2
NIGHTCRAWLER
PREQUEL

PREVIOUSLY IN X-MEN: THE MOVIE

Mutation.

The result of a natural change in the genetic material -- the DNA -- of the human cell. Though beyond the basic knowledge and theories of evolution, mutation is a common occurrence -- an everyday phenomenon -- and one that is generally unnoticed and largely harmless.

Or rather, it was.

Not long ago, mutations of a more unique power and variety began to appear in certain individuals... individuals branded with the catch-all label of "MUTANTS." Since the discovery of their existence, mutants have been regarded with fear, suspicion, and often hatred. So across the planet, the debate rages -- are mutants the next link in the evolutionary chain... or simply a new species of humanity fighting for their share of the world?

Either way, one fact has been historically proven, time and time again-- sharing the world has never been the shining attribute of humankind.

To make certain that mutants are allowed their rightful chance at survival, Professor Charles Xavier -- a powerful telepathic mutant himself -- has formed the X-MEN, a group of mutants who have sworn to protect a world that both fears and hates them. By offering new mutants the chance to learn about and hone their special powers in the protected environment of his mansion in upstate New York, Professor X has granted new hope to the next generation of young mutants...

...young mutants like Kurt Wagner, a German-born orphan with blue skin and a tail who finds himself quite at home with the traveling circus that adopted him at an early age. But when his strange teleportational powers attract the attention of a mysterious organization, the warmth and safety of Kurt's life may come to an abrupt end...

NIGHTCRAWLER

CHUCK AUSTEN   KARL KERSCHL   JUNG CHOI'S TRANSPARENCY DIGITAL   PAUL TUTRONE
    writer   artist   colorist   letterer

MIKE RAICHT & NOVA REN SUMA   MIKE MARTS   JOE QUESADA   BILL JEMAS
        assistant editors   editor   editor in chief   president

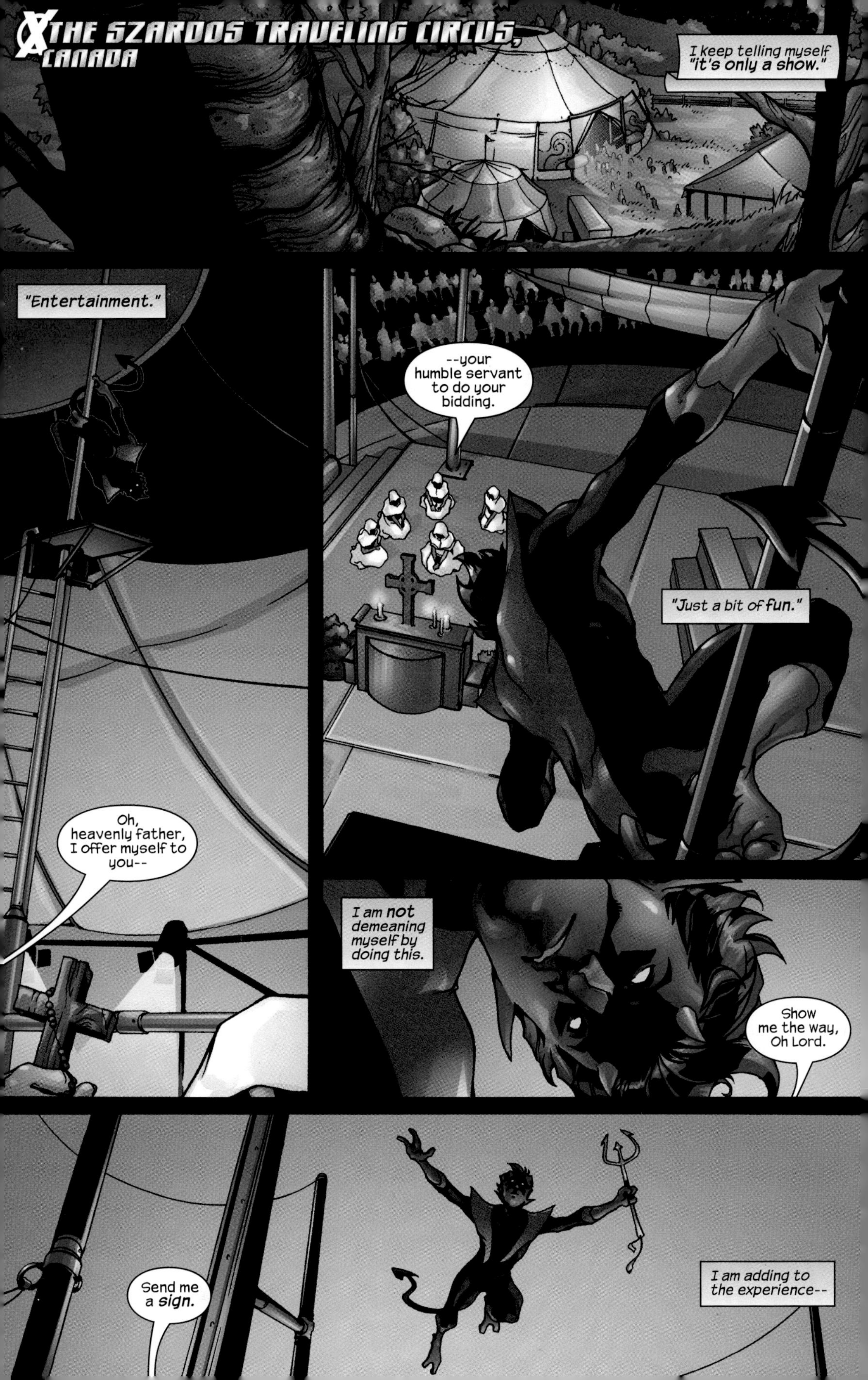
THE SZARDOS TRAVELING CIRCUS, CANADA
I keep telling myself "it's only a show."
"Entertainment."
Oh, heavenly father, I offer myself to you--
--your humble servant to do your bidding.
"Just a bit of fun."
I am not demeaning myself by doing this.
Show me the way, Oh Lord.
Send me a sign.
I am adding to the experience--

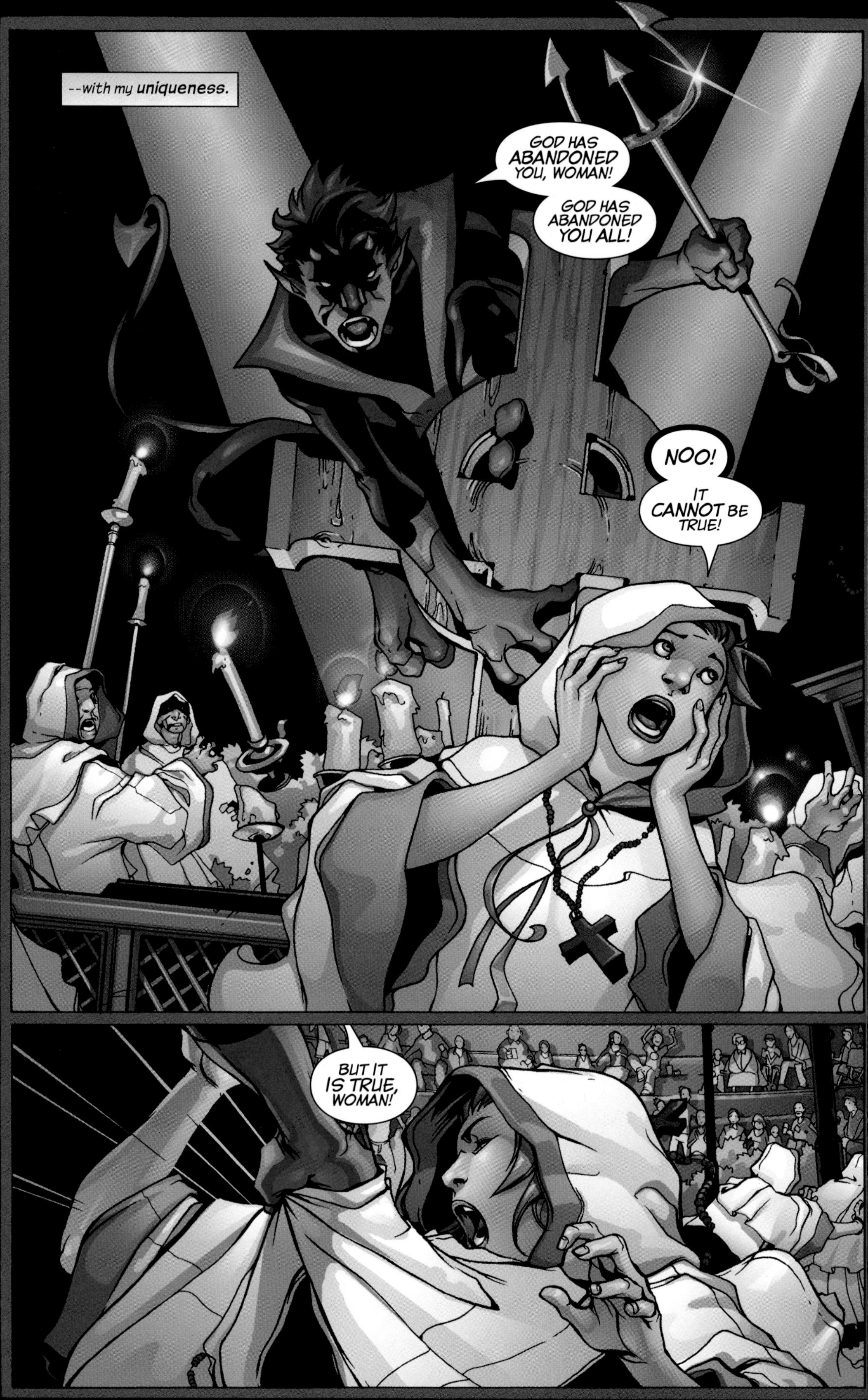
--with my uniqueness.
GOD HAS ABANDONED YOU, WOMAN!
GOD HAS ABANDONED YOU ALL!
NOO!
IT CANNOT BE TRUE!
BUT IT IS TRUE, WOMAN!

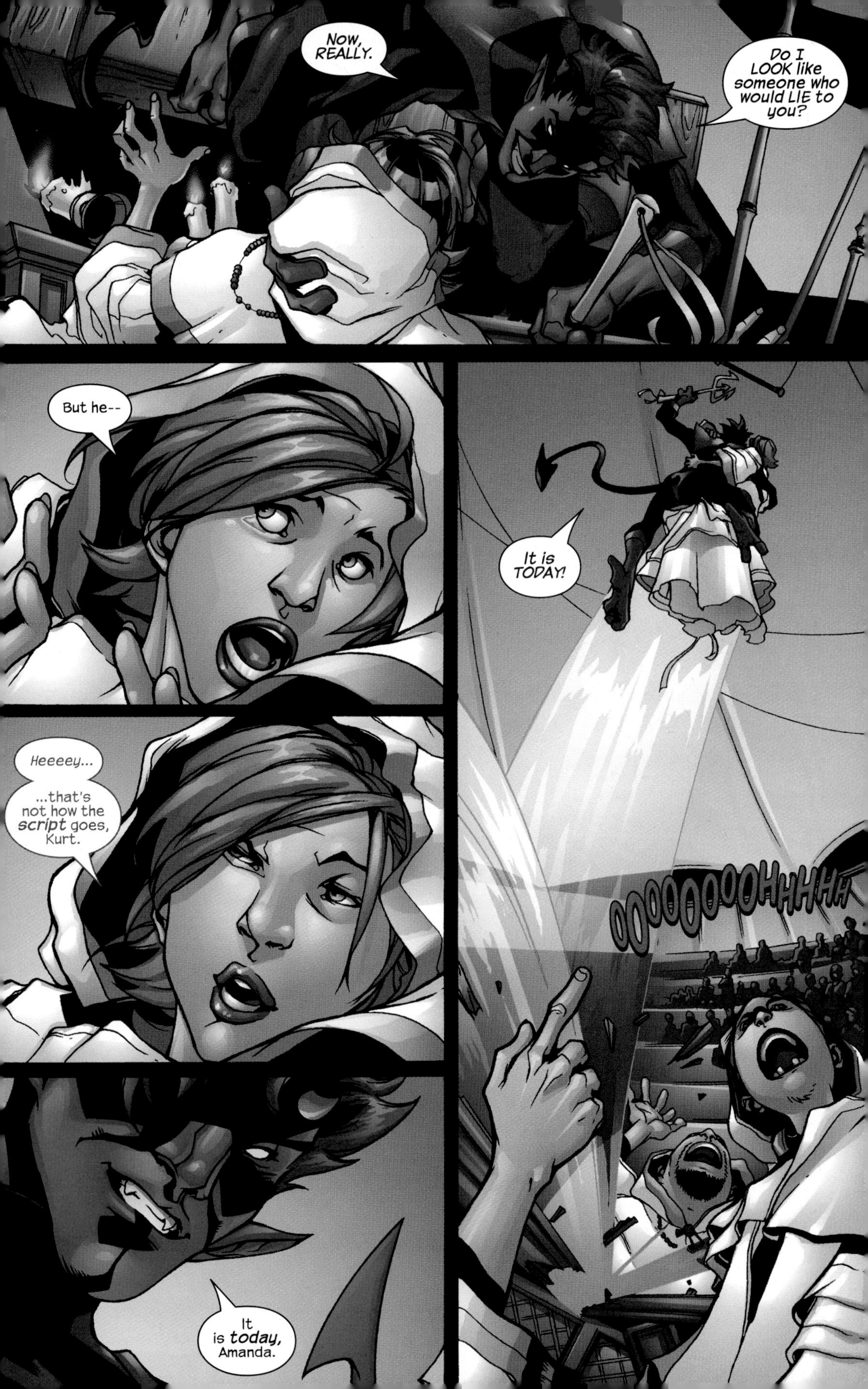

NOW, REALLY.
Do I LOOK like someone who would LIE to you?
But he--
Heeeey...
...that's not how the script goes, Kurt.
It is today, Amanda.
It is TODAY!
OOOOOOOOHHHHH

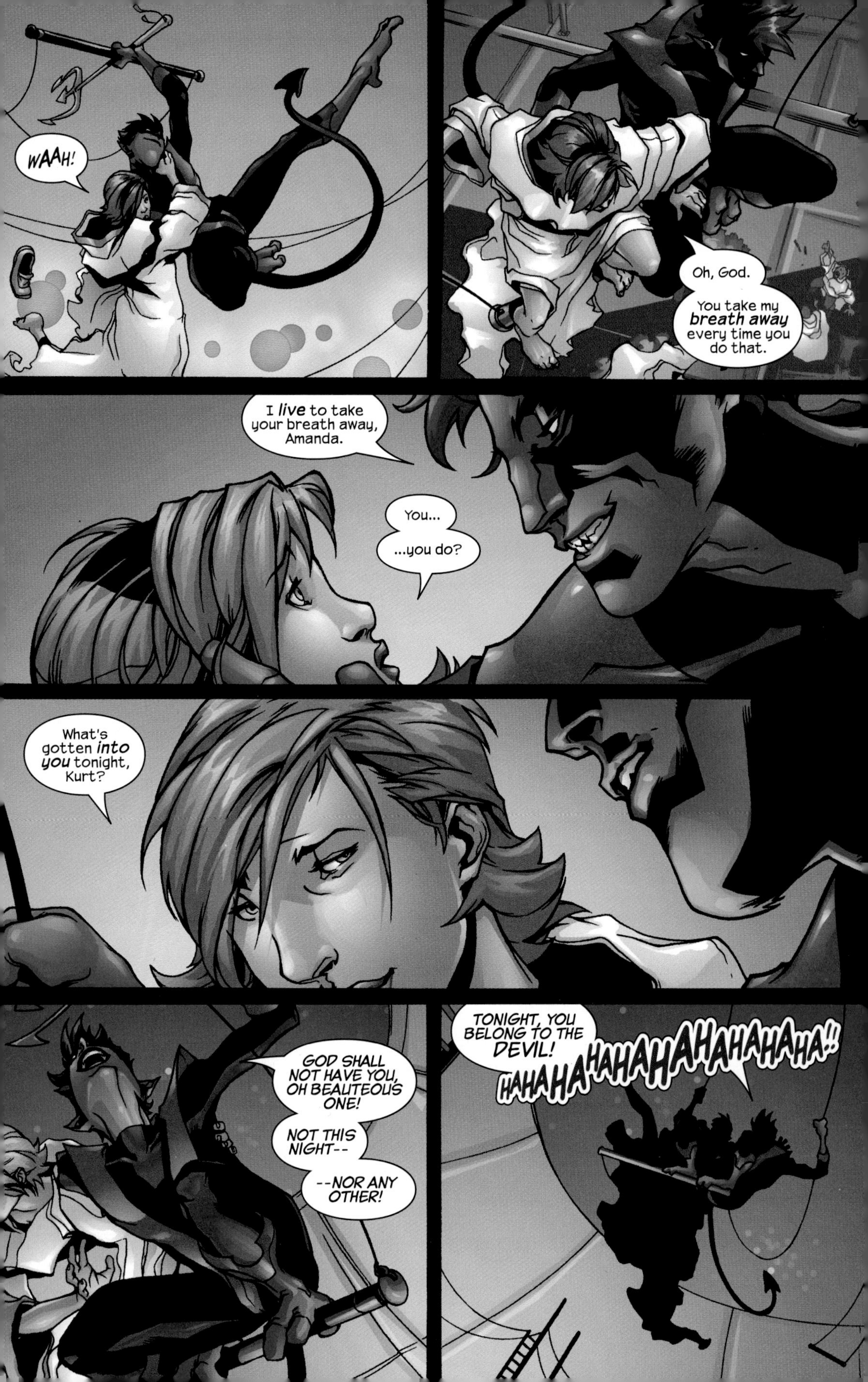
WAAH!
Oh, God.
You take my **breath away** every time you do that.
I *live* to take your breath away, Amanda.
You...
...you do?
What's gotten ***into you*** tonight, Kurt?
GOD SHALL NOT HAVE YOU, OH BEAUTEOUS ONE!
NOT THIS NIGHT--
--NOR ANY OTHER!
TONIGHT, YOU BELONG TO THE DEVIL!
HAHAHAHAHAHAHAHAHA!!

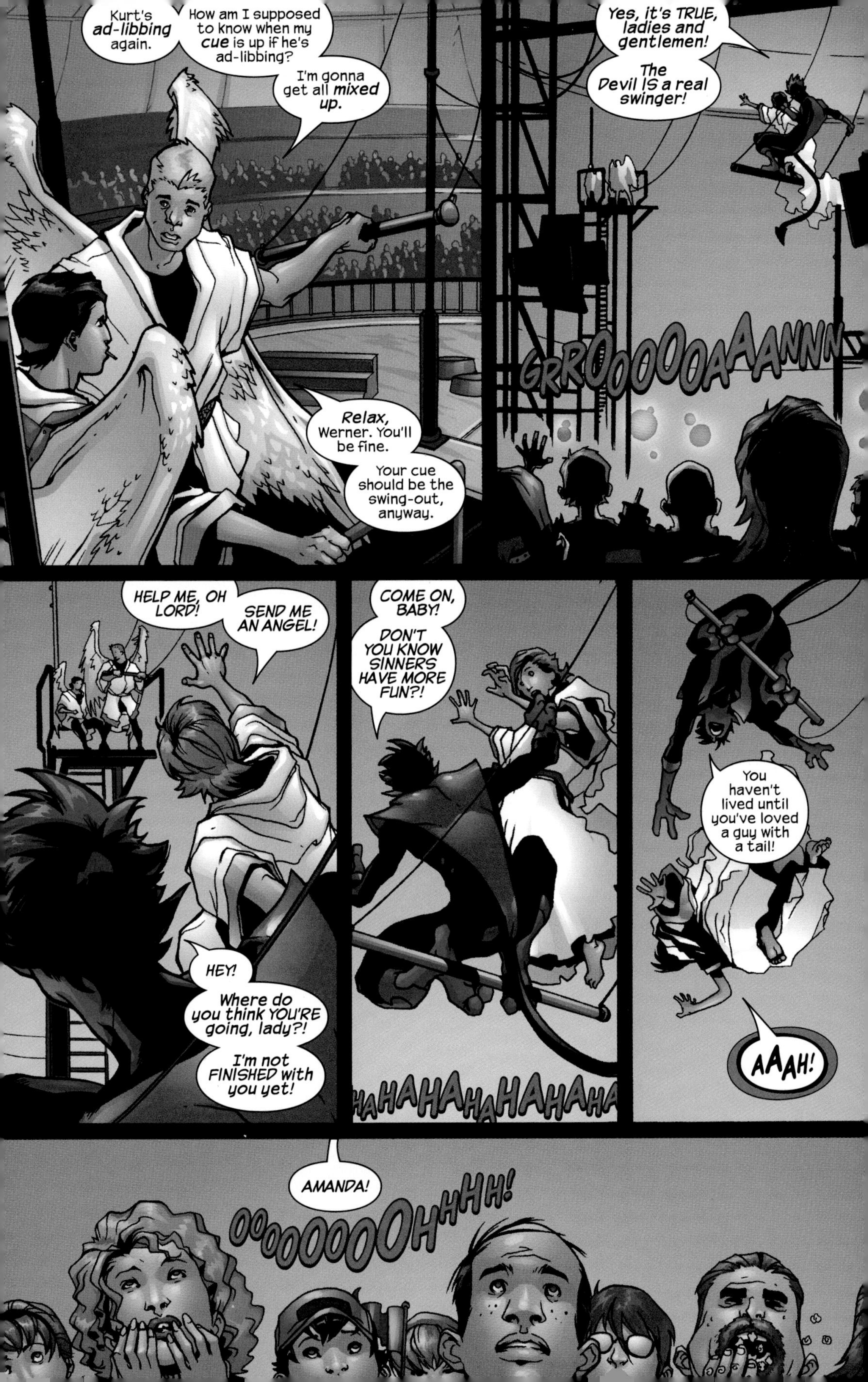

Kurt's *ad-libbing* again.
How am I supposed to know when my *cue* is up if he's ad-libbing?
I'm gonna get all *mixed up.*
Relax, Werner. You'll be fine.
Your cue should be the swing-out, anyway.
Yes, it's TRUE, ladies and gentlemen!
The Devil IS a real swinger!
GRROOOOOOAAANNN
HELP ME, OH LORD!
SEND ME AN ANGEL!
HEY!
Where do you think YOU'RE going, lady?!
I'm not FINISHED with you yet!
COME ON, BABY!
DON'T YOU KNOW SINNERS HAVE MORE FUN?!
HAHAHAHAHAHAHAHA
You haven't lived until you've loved a guy with a tail!
AAAH!
AMANDA!
OOOOOOOOOHHHHH!

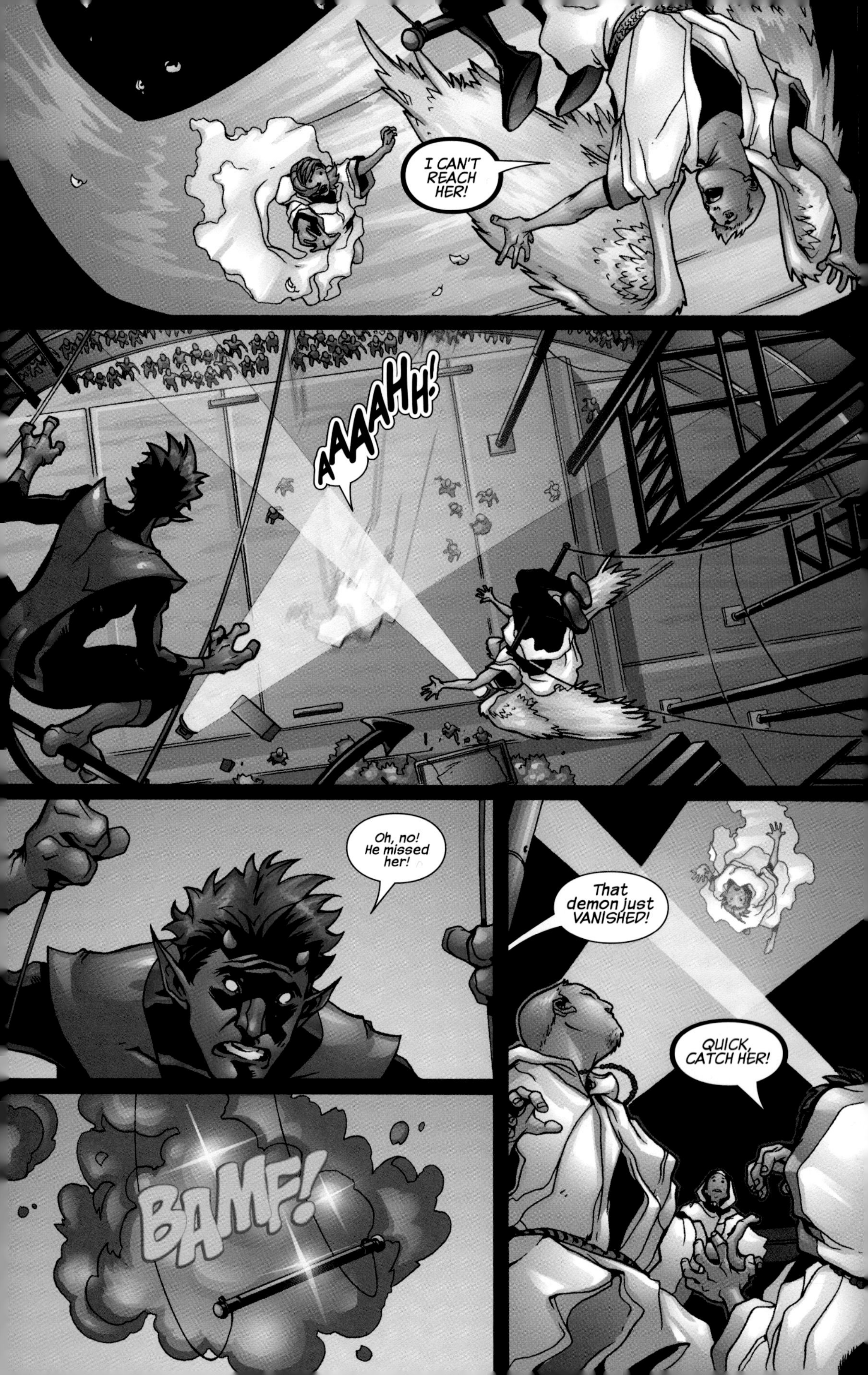
I CAN'T REACH HER!
AAAAHH!
Oh, no! He missed her!
BAMF!
That demon just VANISHED!
QUICK, CATCH HER!

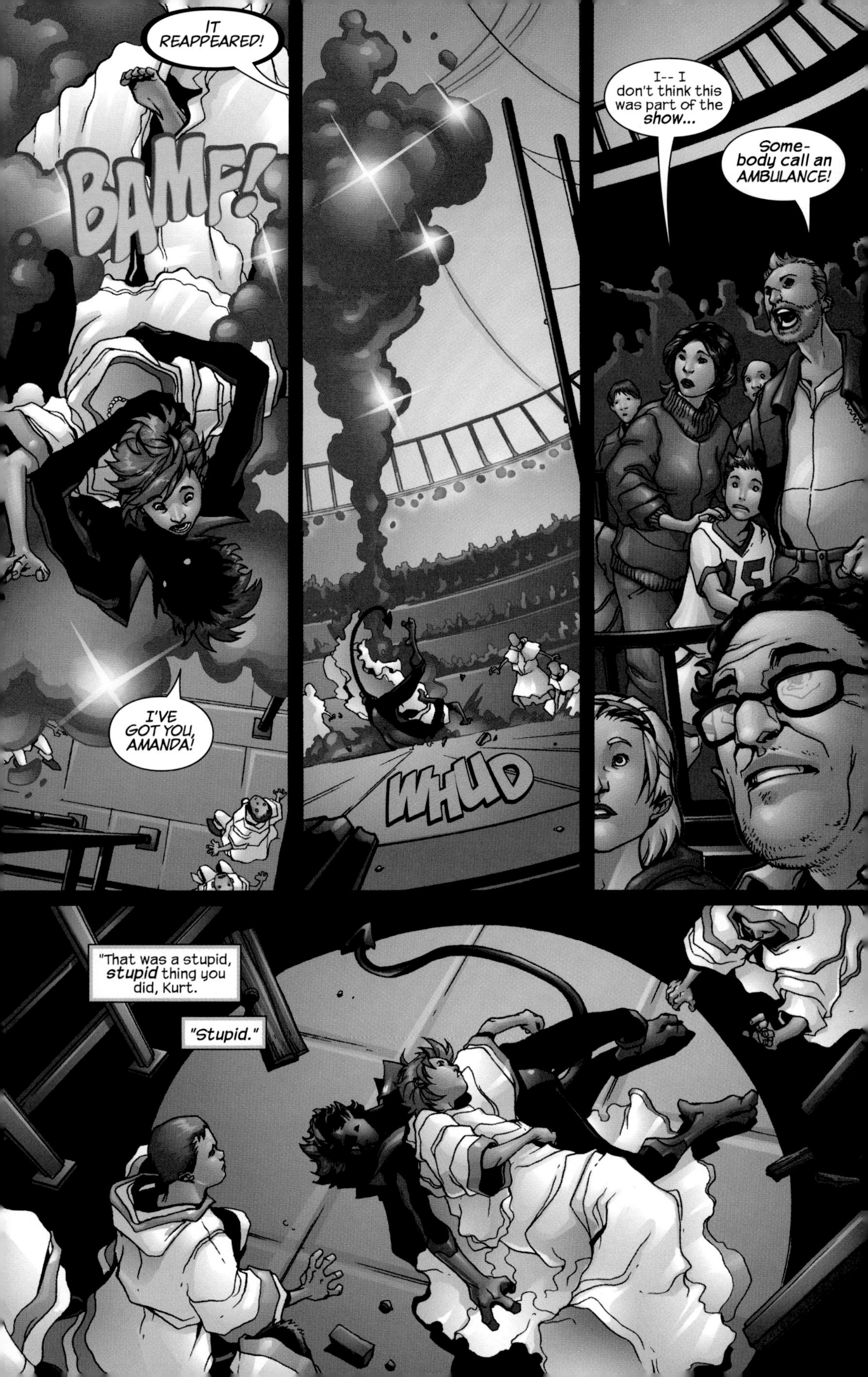
IT REAPPEARED!
BAMF!
I'VE GOT YOU, AMANDA!
WHUD
I-- I don't think this was part of the show...
Some-body call an AMBULANCE!
"That was a stupid, stupid thing you did, Kurt.
"Stupid."

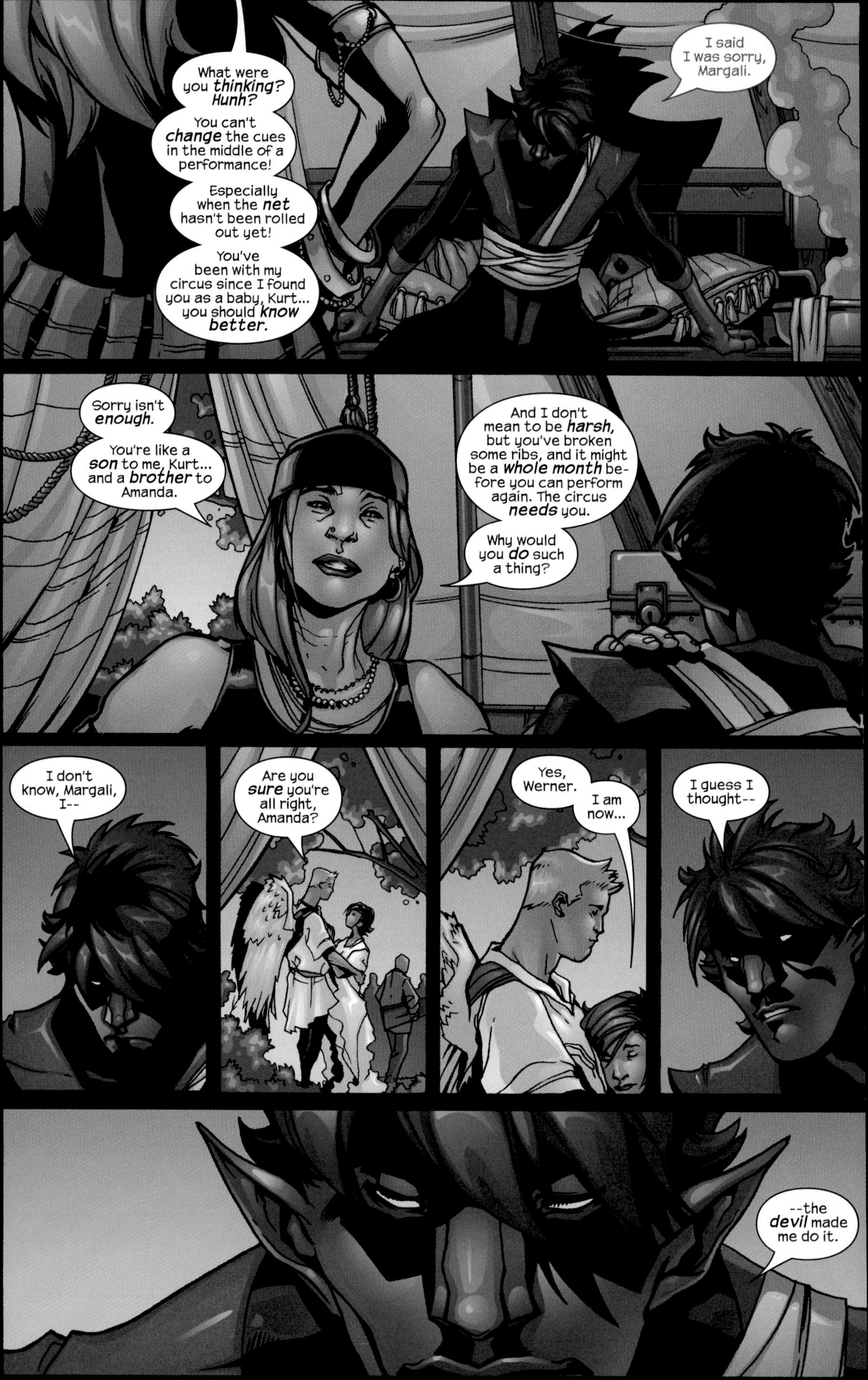
What were you *thinking*? *Hunh*?
You can't *change* the cues in the middle of a performance!
Especially when the *net* hasn't been rolled out yet!
You've been with my circus since I found you as a baby, Kurt... you should *know better*.
I said I was sorry, Margali.
Sorry isn't *enough*.
You're like a *son* to me, Kurt... and a *brother* to Amanda.
And I don't mean to be *harsh*, but you've broken some ribs, and it might be a *whole month* before you can perform again. The circus *needs* you.
Why would you *do* such a thing?
I don't know, Margali, I--
Are you *sure* you're all right, Amanda?
Yes, Werner.
I am now...
I guess I thought--
--the *devil* made me do it.

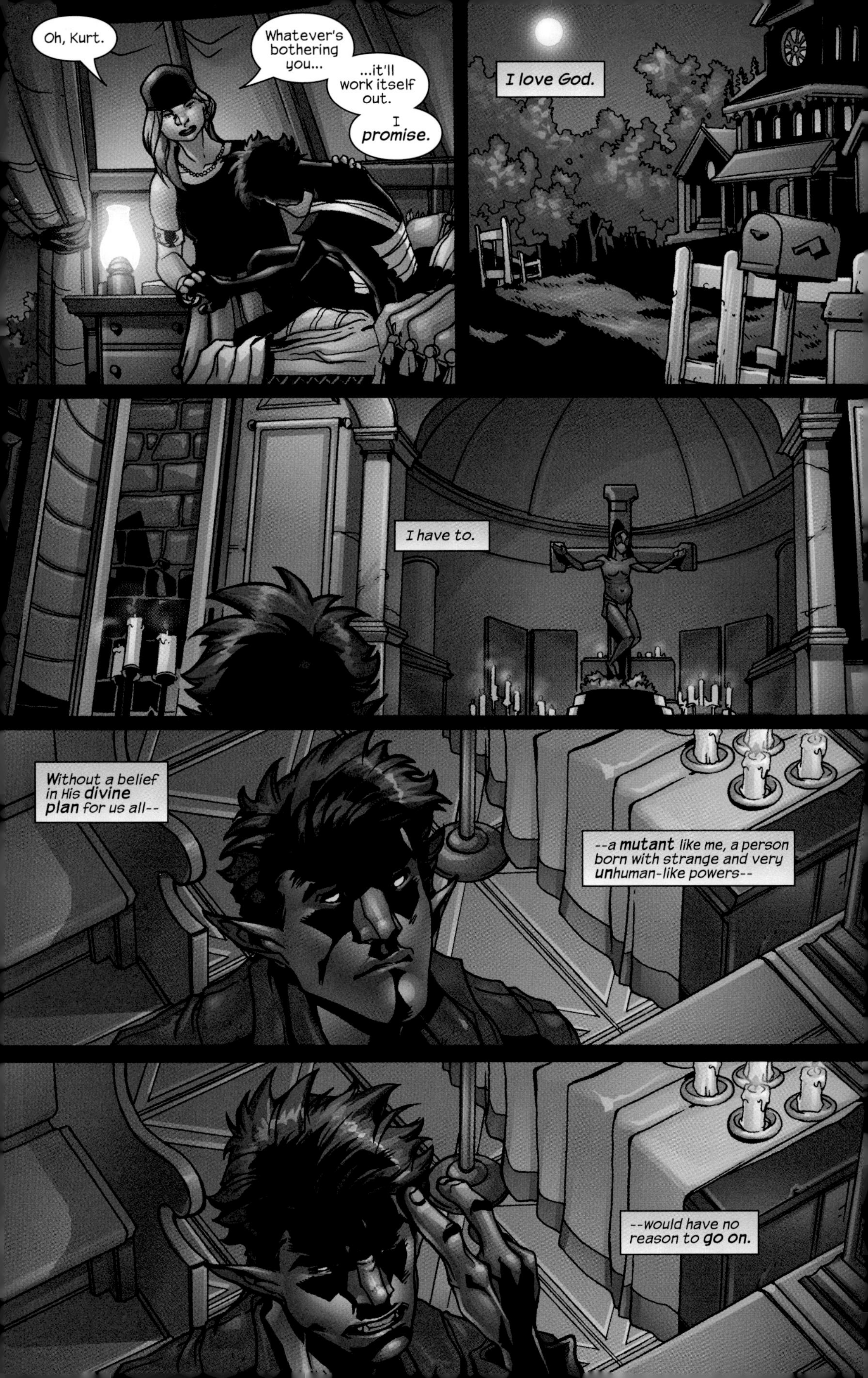

Oh, Kurt.
Whatever's bothering you...
...it'll work itself out.
I promise.
I love God.
I have to.
Without a belief in His divine plan for us all--
--a mutant like me, a person born with strange and very unhuman-like powers--
--would have no reason to go on.

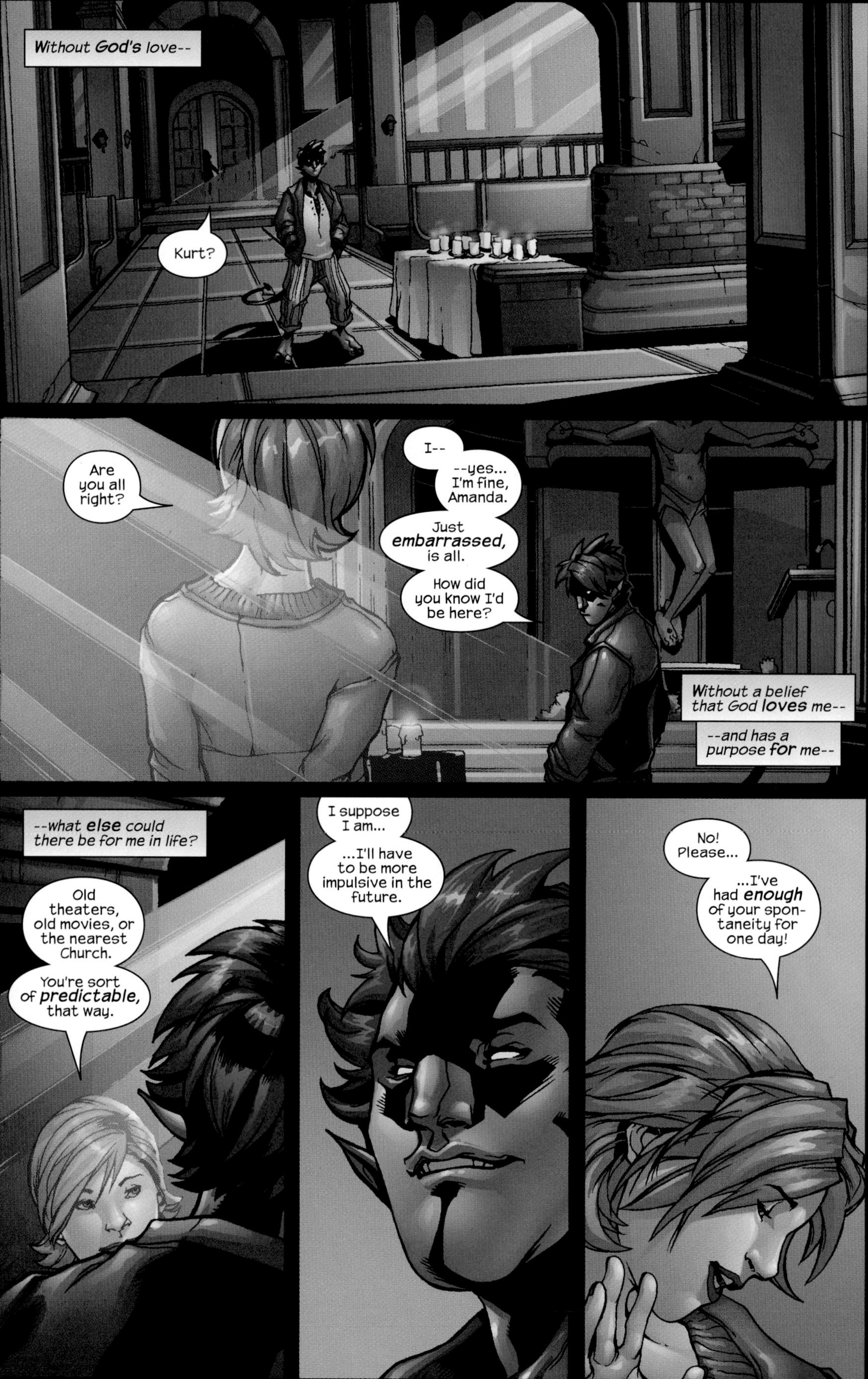
Without God's love--
Kurt?
Are you all right?
I--
--yes... I'm fine, Amanda.
Just embarrassed, is all.
How did you know I'd be here?
Without a belief that God loves me--
--and has a purpose for me--
--what else could there be for me in life?
Old theaters, old movies, or the nearest Church.
You're sort of predictable, that way.
I suppose I am...
...I'll have to be more impulsive in the future.
No! Please...
...I've had enough of your spontaneity for one day!

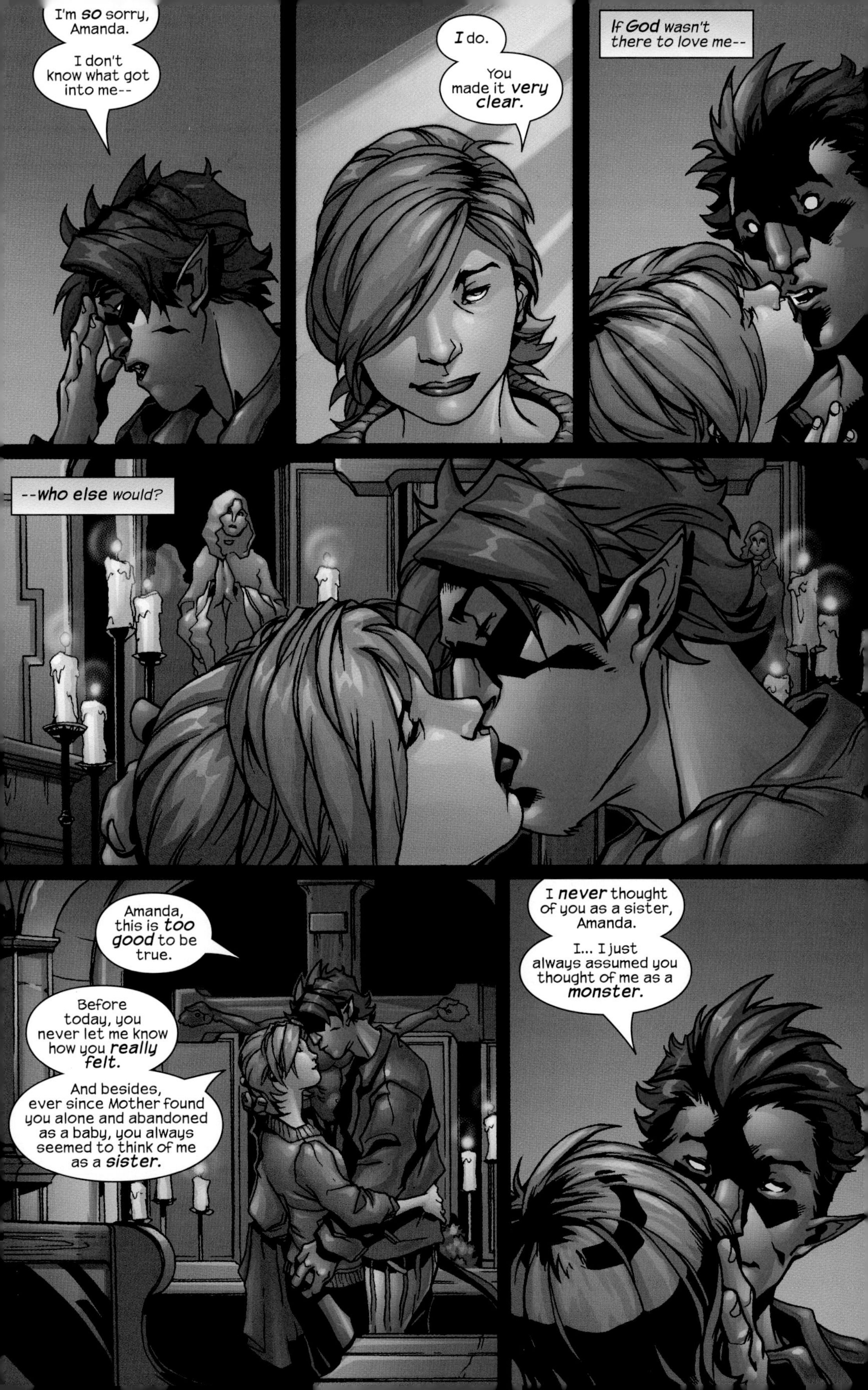
I'm SO sorry, Amanda.
I don't know what got into me--
I do.
You made it very clear.
If God wasn't there to love me--
--who else would?
Amanda, this is too good to be true.
Before today, you never let me know how you really felt.
And besides, ever since Mother found you alone and abandoned as a baby, you always seemed to think of me as a sister.
I never thought of you as a sister, Amanda.
I... I just always assumed you thought of me as a monster.

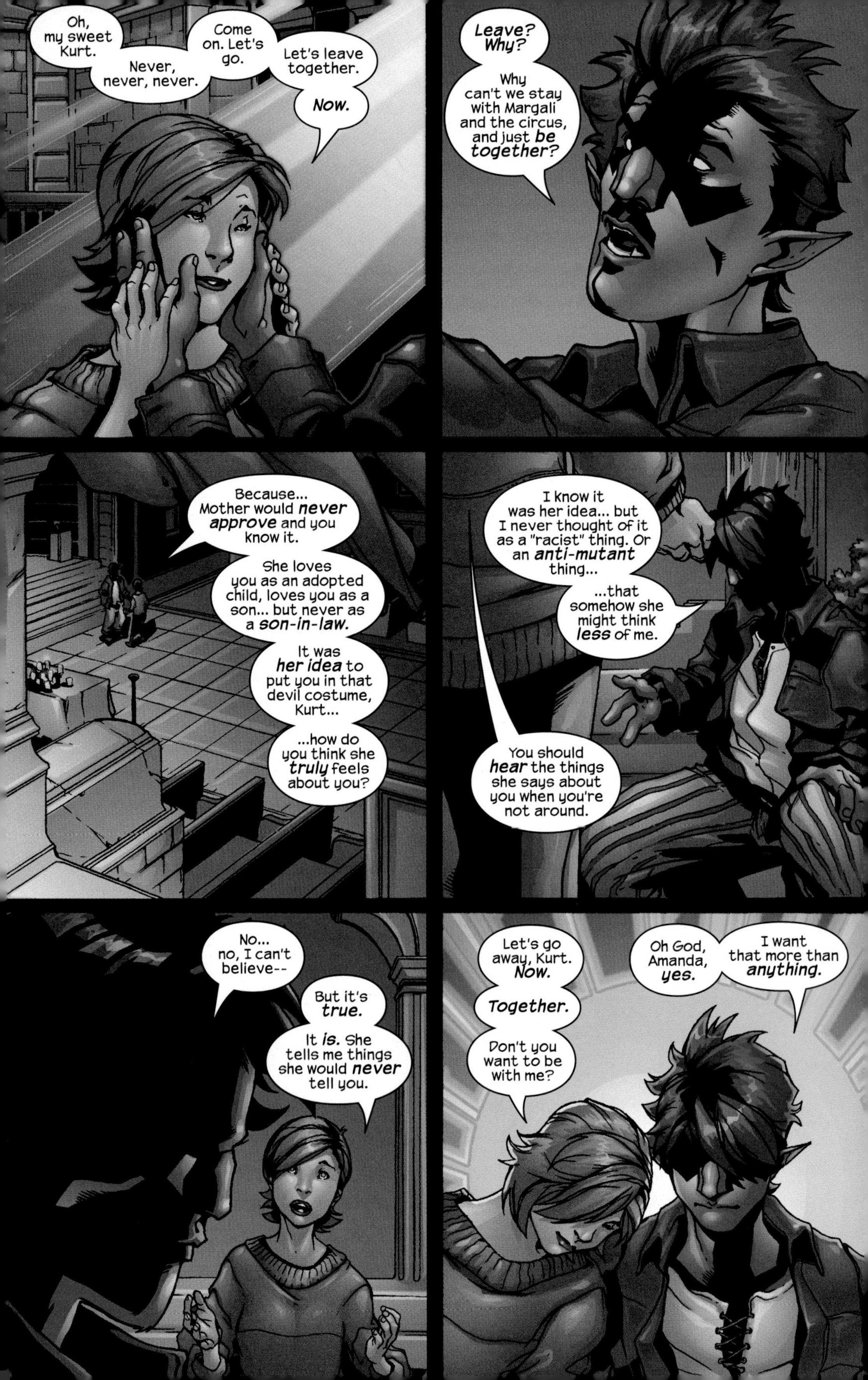
Oh, my sweet Kurt.
Never, never, never.
Come on. Let's go.
Let's leave together.
Now.
Leave? Why?
Why can't we stay with Margali and the circus, and just be together?
Because... Mother would never approve and you know it.
She loves you as an adopted child, loves you as a son... but never as a son-in-law.
It was her idea to put you in that devil costume, Kurt...
...how do you think she truly feels about you?
I know it was her idea... but I never thought of it as a "racist" thing. Or an anti-mutant thing...
...that somehow she might think less of me.
You should hear the things she says about you when you're not around.
No... no, I can't believe--
But it's true.
It is. She tells me things she would never tell you.
Let's go away, Kurt. Now.
Together.
Don't you want to be with me?
Oh God, Amanda, yes.
I want that more than anything.

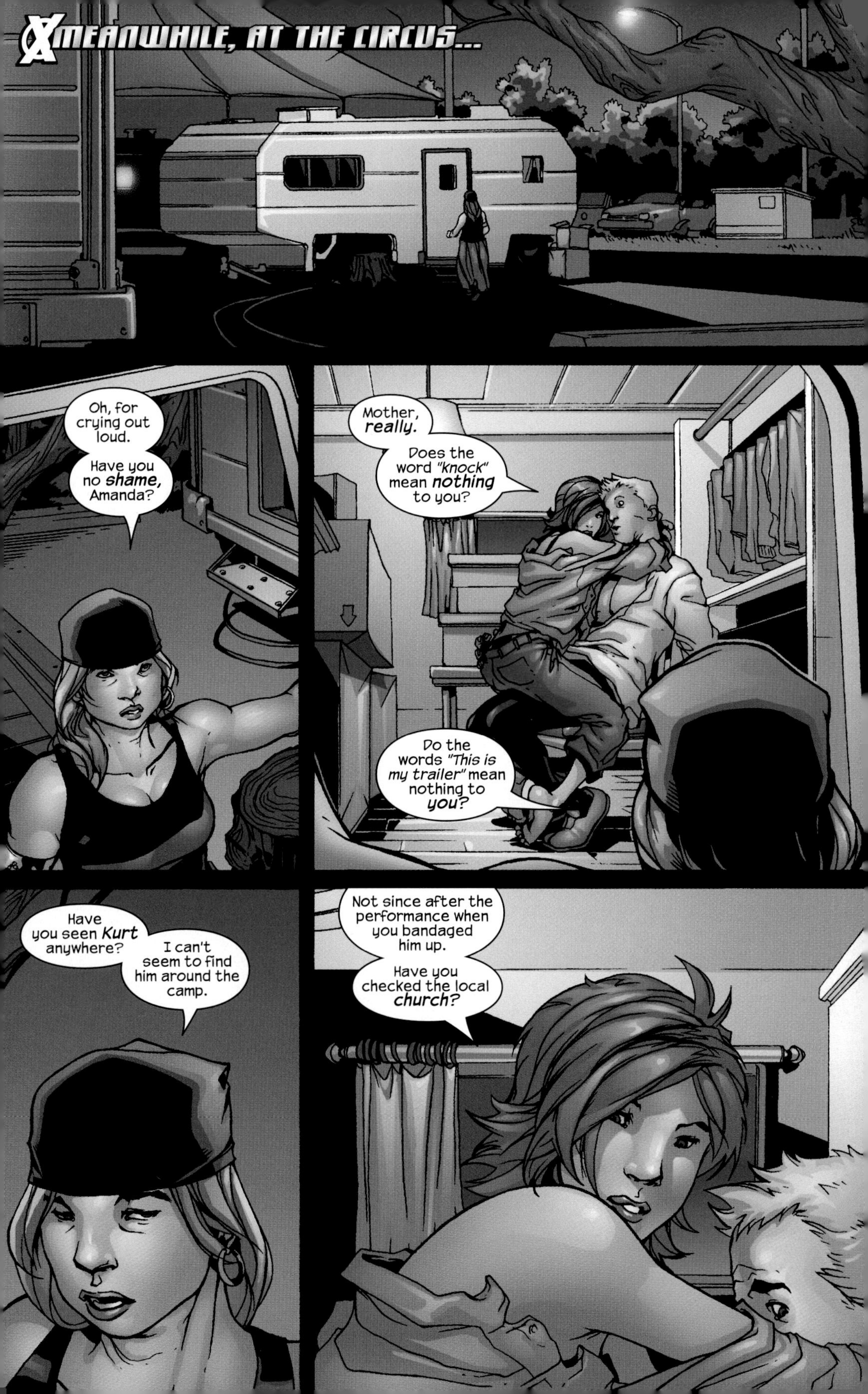
MEANWHILE, AT THE CIRCUS...
Oh, for crying out loud.
Have you no *shame,* Amanda?
Mother, *really.*
Does the word *"knock"* mean *nothing* to you?
Do the words *"This is my trailer"* mean nothing to *you?*
Have you seen *Kurt* anywhere?
I can't seem to find him around the camp.
Not since after the performance when you bandaged him up.
Have you checked the local *church?*

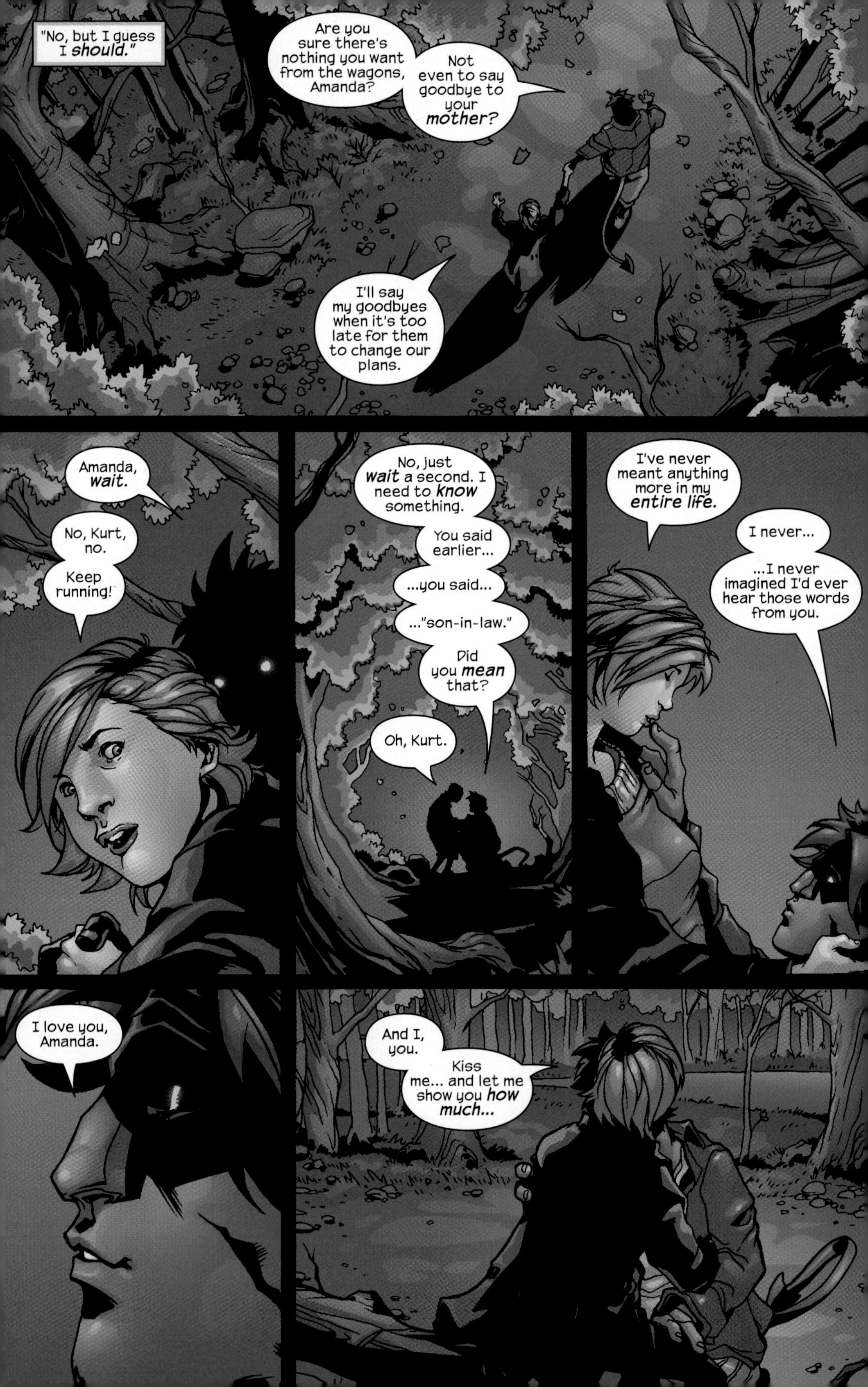

"No, but I guess I *should.*"
Are you sure there's nothing you want from the wagons, Amanda?
Not even to say goodbye to your *mother?*
I'll say my goodbyes when it's too late for them to change our plans.
Amanda, *wait.*
No, Kurt, no.
Keep running!
No, just *wait* a second. I need to *know* something.
You said earlier...
...you said...
..."son-in-law."
Did you *mean* that?
Oh, Kurt.
I've never meant anything more in my *entire life.*
I never...
...I never imagined I'd ever hear those words from you.
I love you, Amanda.
And I, you.
Kiss me... and let me show you *how much...*

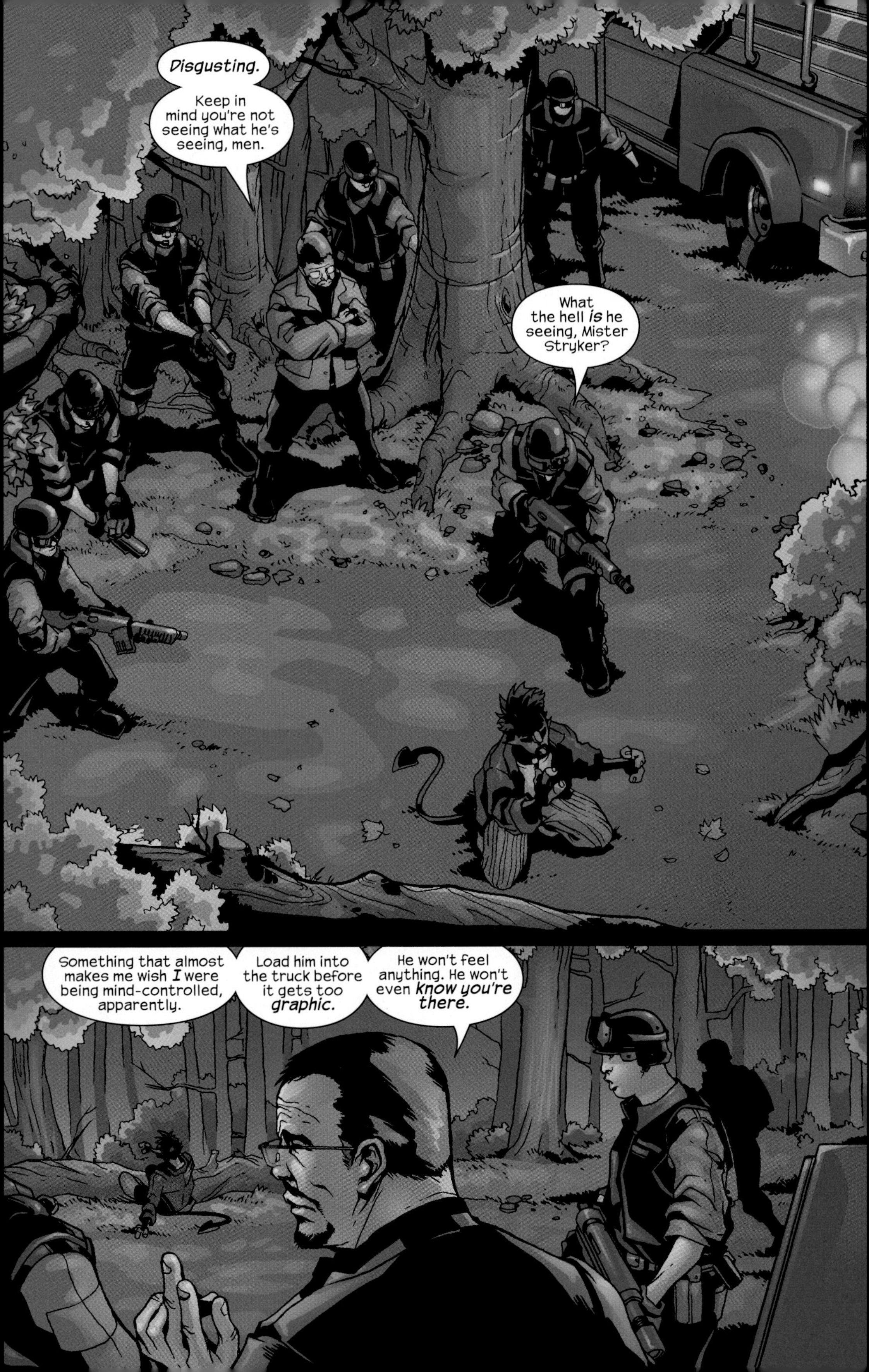
Disgusting.
Keep in mind you're not seeing what he's seeing, men.
What the hell *is* he seeing, Mister Stryker?
Something that almost makes me wish *I* were being mind-controlled, apparently.
Load him into the truck before it gets too *graphic.*
He won't feel anything. He won't even *know you're there.*

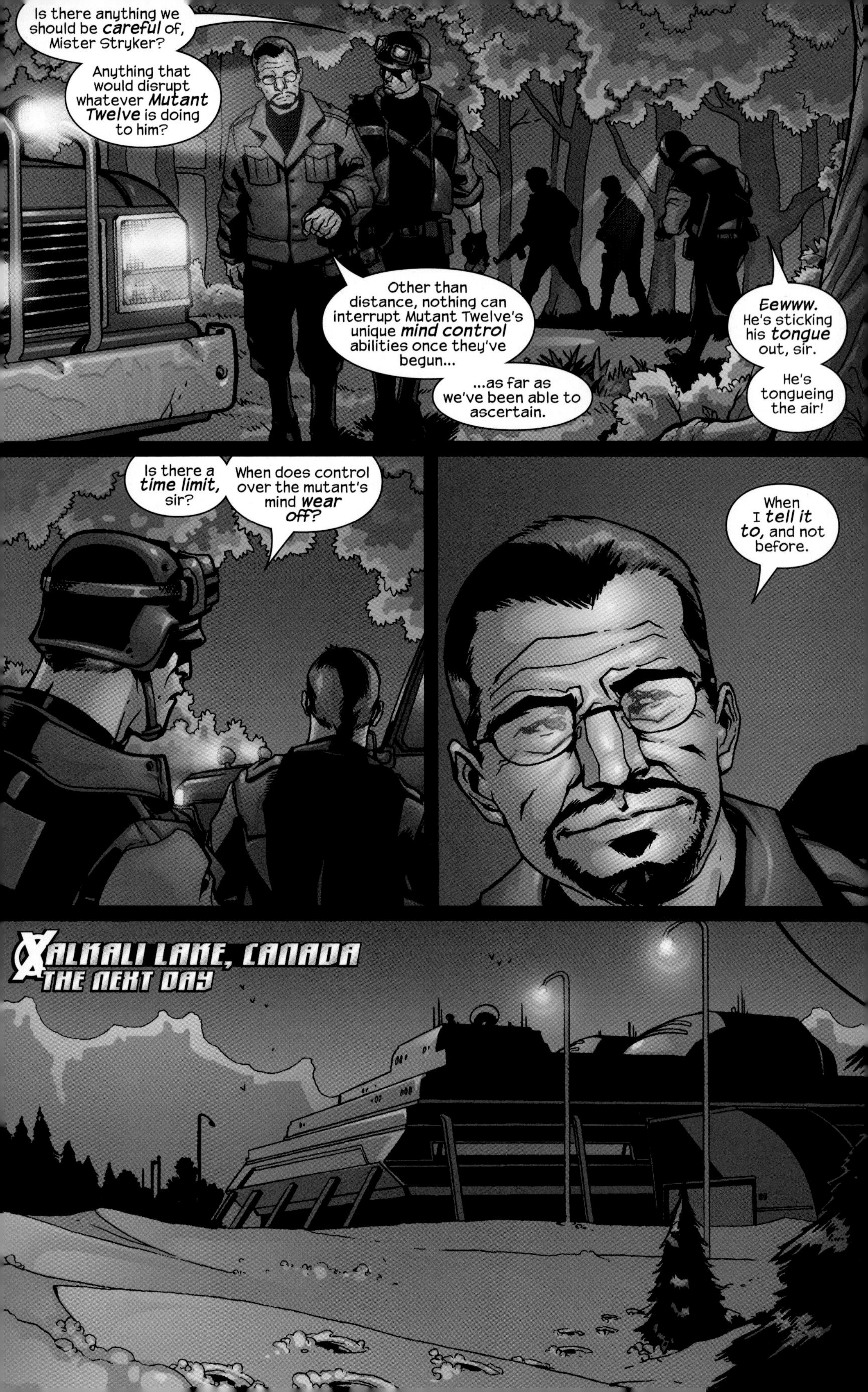
Is there anything we should be careful of, Mister Stryker?
Anything that would disrupt whatever Mutant Twelve is doing to him?
Other than distance, nothing can interrupt Mutant Twelve's unique mind control abilities once they've begun...
...as far as we've been able to ascertain.
Eewww. He's sticking his tongue out, sir.
He's tongueing the air!
Is there a time limit, sir?
When does control over the mutant's mind wear off?
When I tell it to, and not before.
ALKALI LAKE, CANADA
THE NEXT DAY

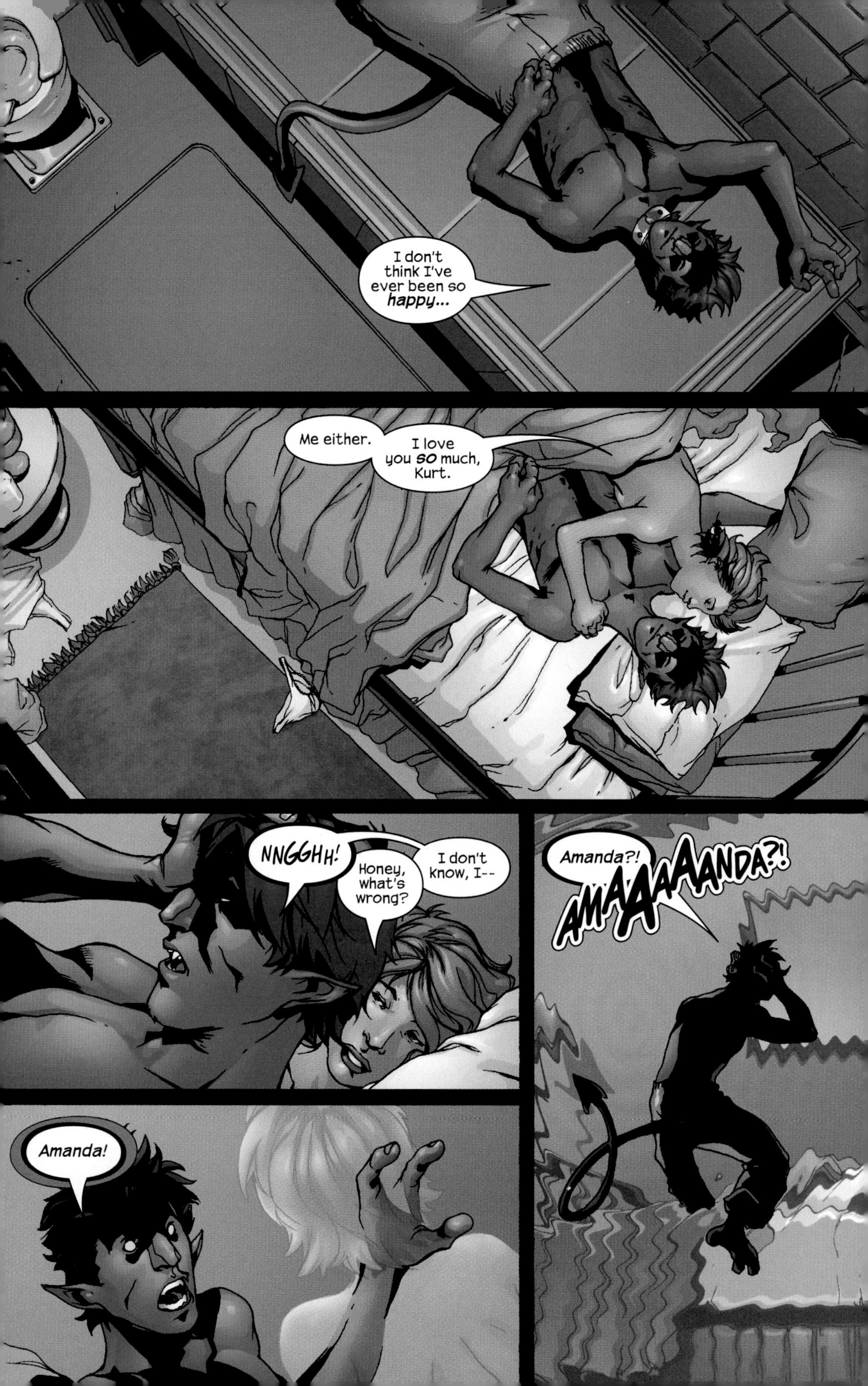
I don't think I've ever been so *happy...*
Me either.
I love you *SO* much, Kurt.
NNGGHH!
Honey, what's wrong?
I don't know, I--
Amanda?!
AMAAAAAANDA?!
Amanda!

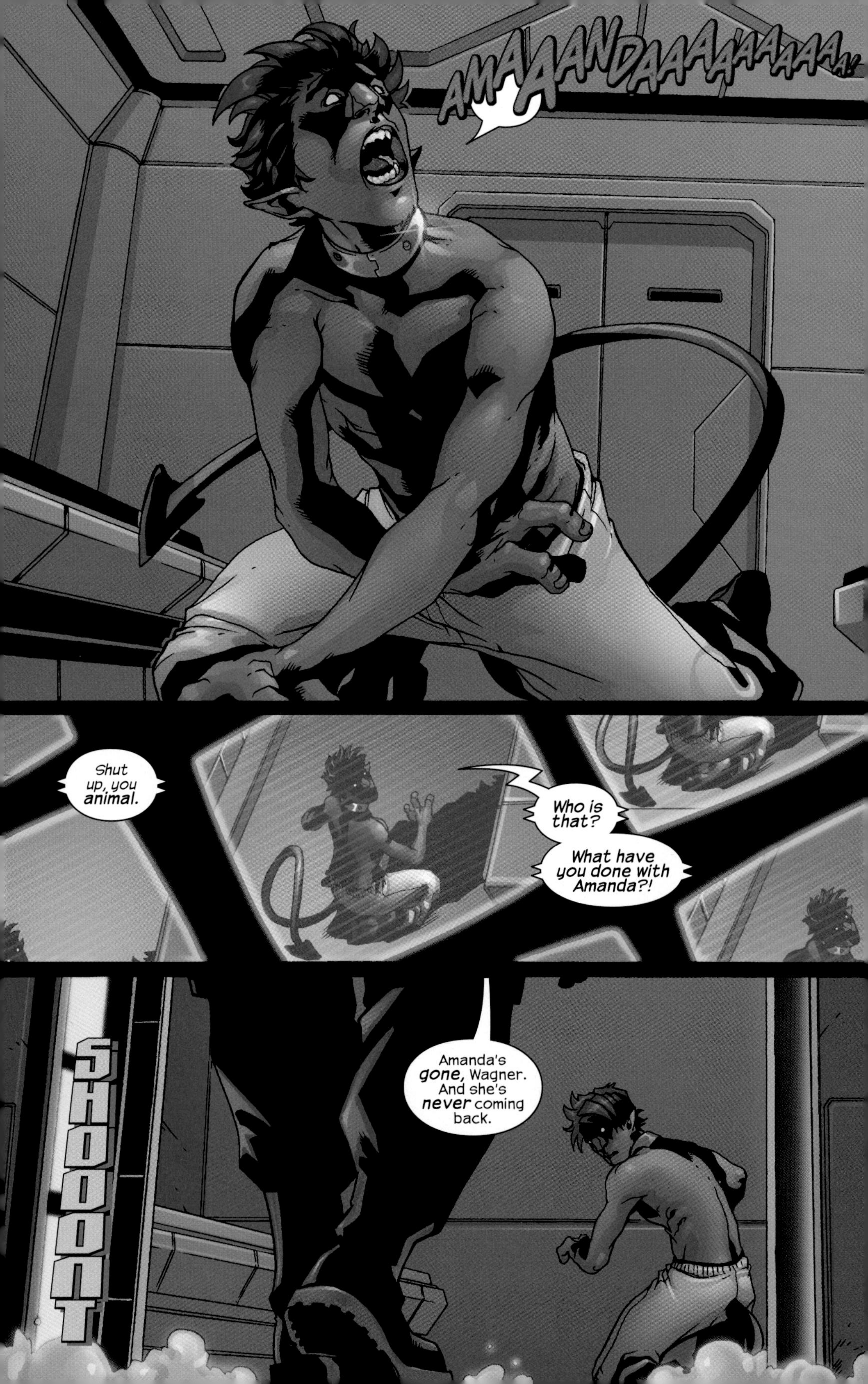
AMAAANDAAAAAAAAA!
Shut up, you animal.
Who is that?
What have you done with Amanda?!
SHOOOOT
Amanda's gone, Wagner. And she's never coming back.

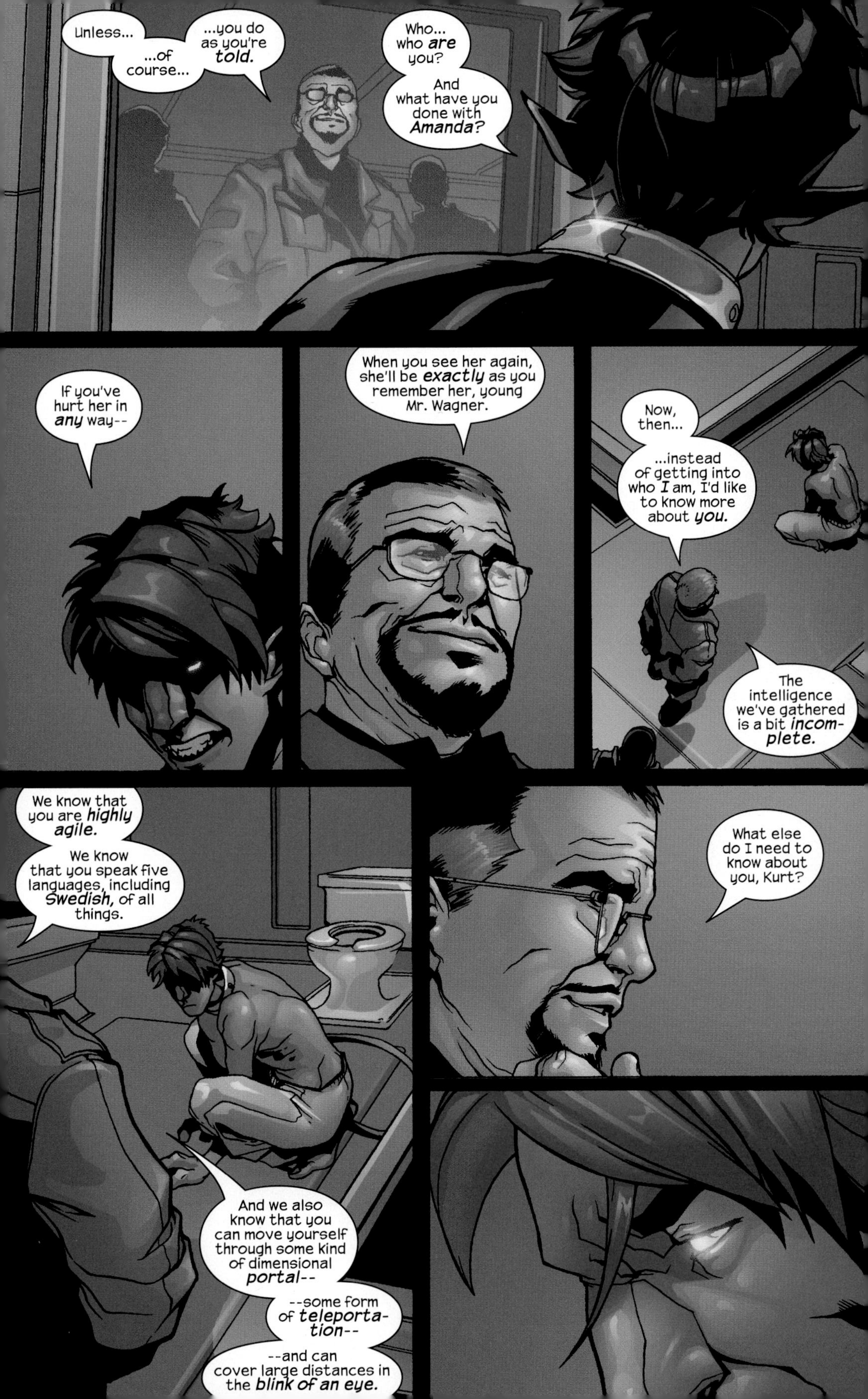

Unless...
...of course...
...you do as you're *told.*
Who... who *are* you?
And what have you done with *Amanda?*
If you've hurt her in *any* way--
When you see her again, she'll be *exactly* as you remember her, young Mr. Wagner.
Now, then...
...instead of getting into who *I* am, I'd like to know more about *you.*
The intelligence we've gathered is a bit *incomplete.*
We know that you are *highly agile.*
We know that you speak five languages, including *Swedish,* of all things.
And we also know that you can move yourself through some kind of dimensional *portal*--
--some form of *teleportation*--
--and can cover large distances in the *blink of an eye.*
What else do I need to know about you, Kurt?

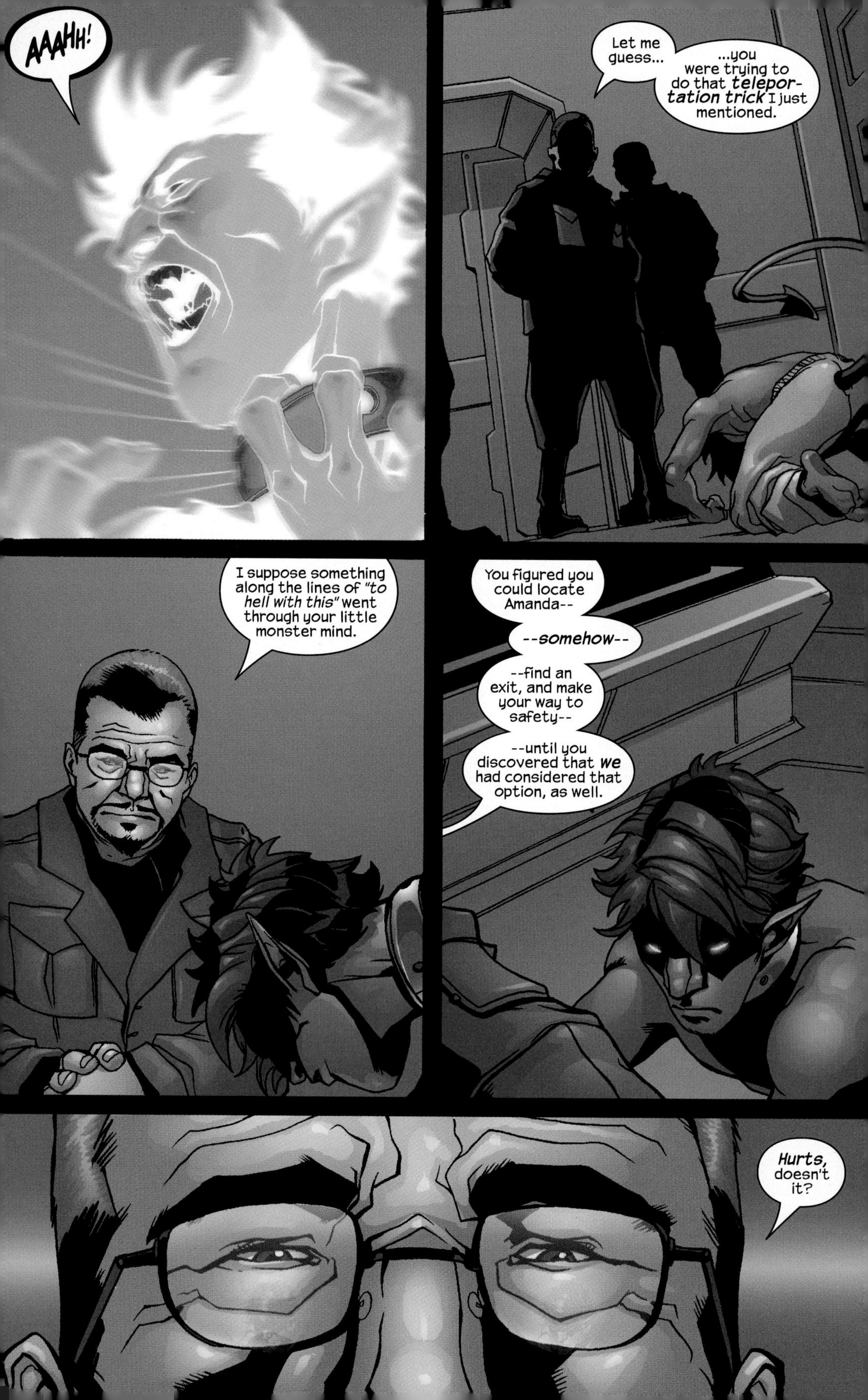
AAAHH!
Let me guess...
...you were trying to do that teleportation trick I just mentioned.
I suppose something along the lines of "to hell with this" went through your little monster mind.
You figured you could locate Amanda--
--somehow--
--find an exit, and make your way to safety--
--until you discovered that we had considered that option, as well.
Hurts, doesn't it?

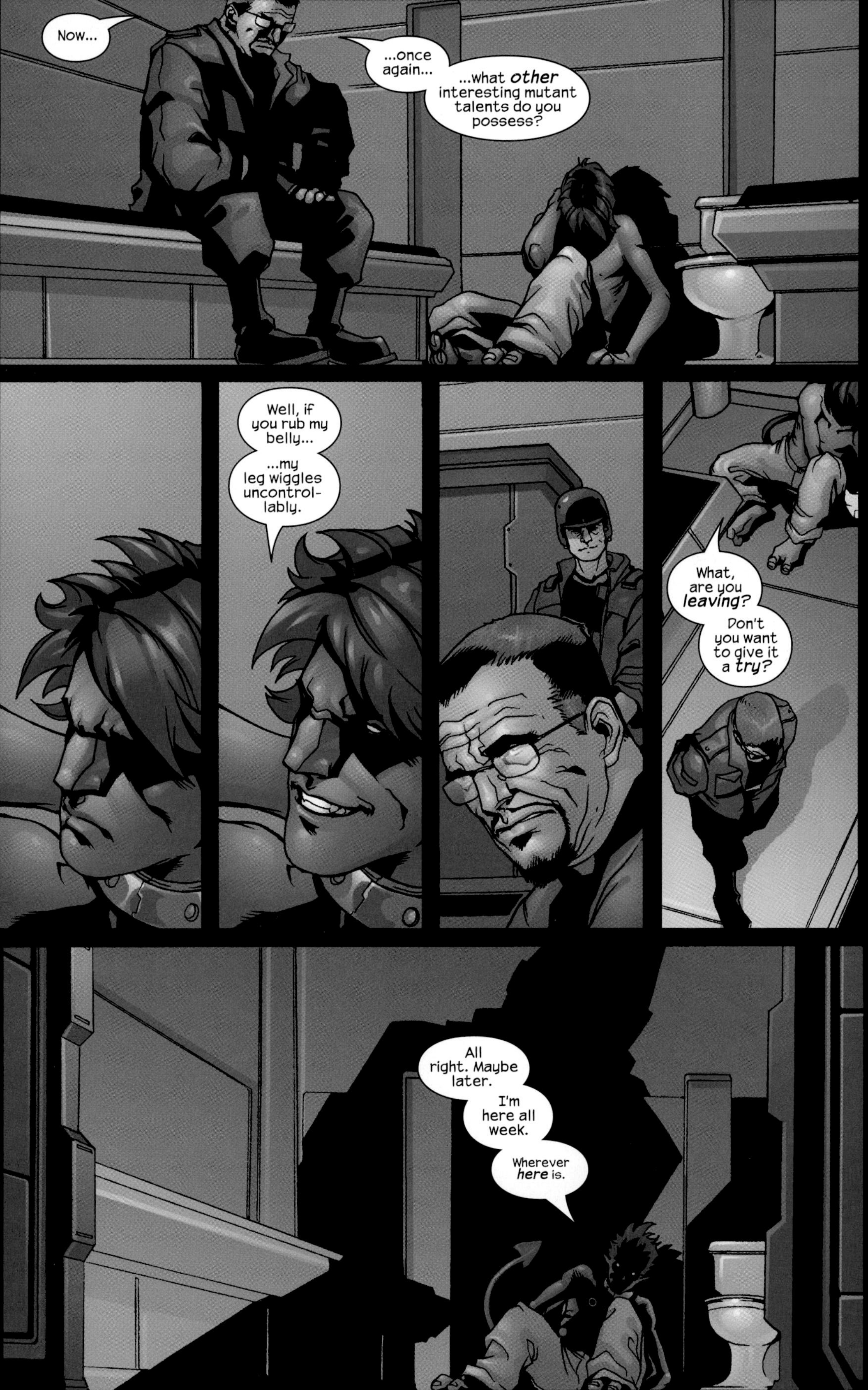

Now...
...once again...
...what other interesting mutant talents do you possess?
Well, if you rub my belly...
...my leg wiggles uncontrol-lably.
What, are you leaving?
Don't you want to give it a try?
All right. Maybe later.
I'm here all week.
Wherever here is.

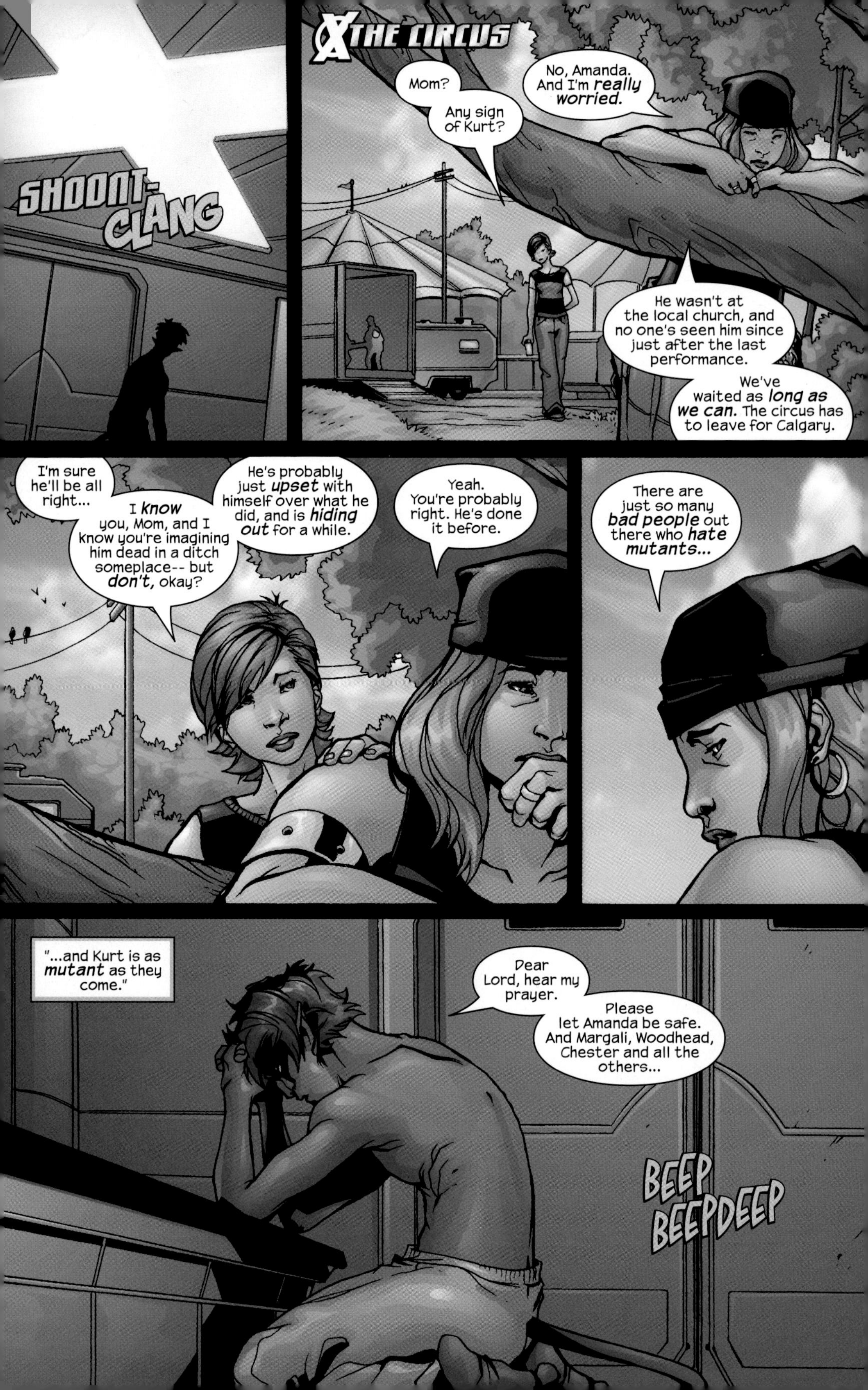
SHOONT-CLANG
THE CIRCUS
Mom?
Any sign of Kurt?
No, Amanda. And I'm *really worried.*
He wasn't at the local church, and no one's seen him since just after the last performance.
We've waited as *long as we can.* The circus has to leave for Calgary.
I'm sure he'll be all right...
I *know* you, Mom, and I know you're imagining him dead in a ditch someplace-- but *don't,* okay?
He's probably just *upset* with himself over what he did, and is *hiding out* for a while.
Yeah. You're probably right. He's done it before.
There are just so many *bad people* out there who *hate mutants...*
"...and Kurt is as *mutant* as they come."
Dear Lord, hear my prayer.
Please let Amanda be safe. And Margali, Woodhead, Chester and all the others...
BEEP BEEPDEEP

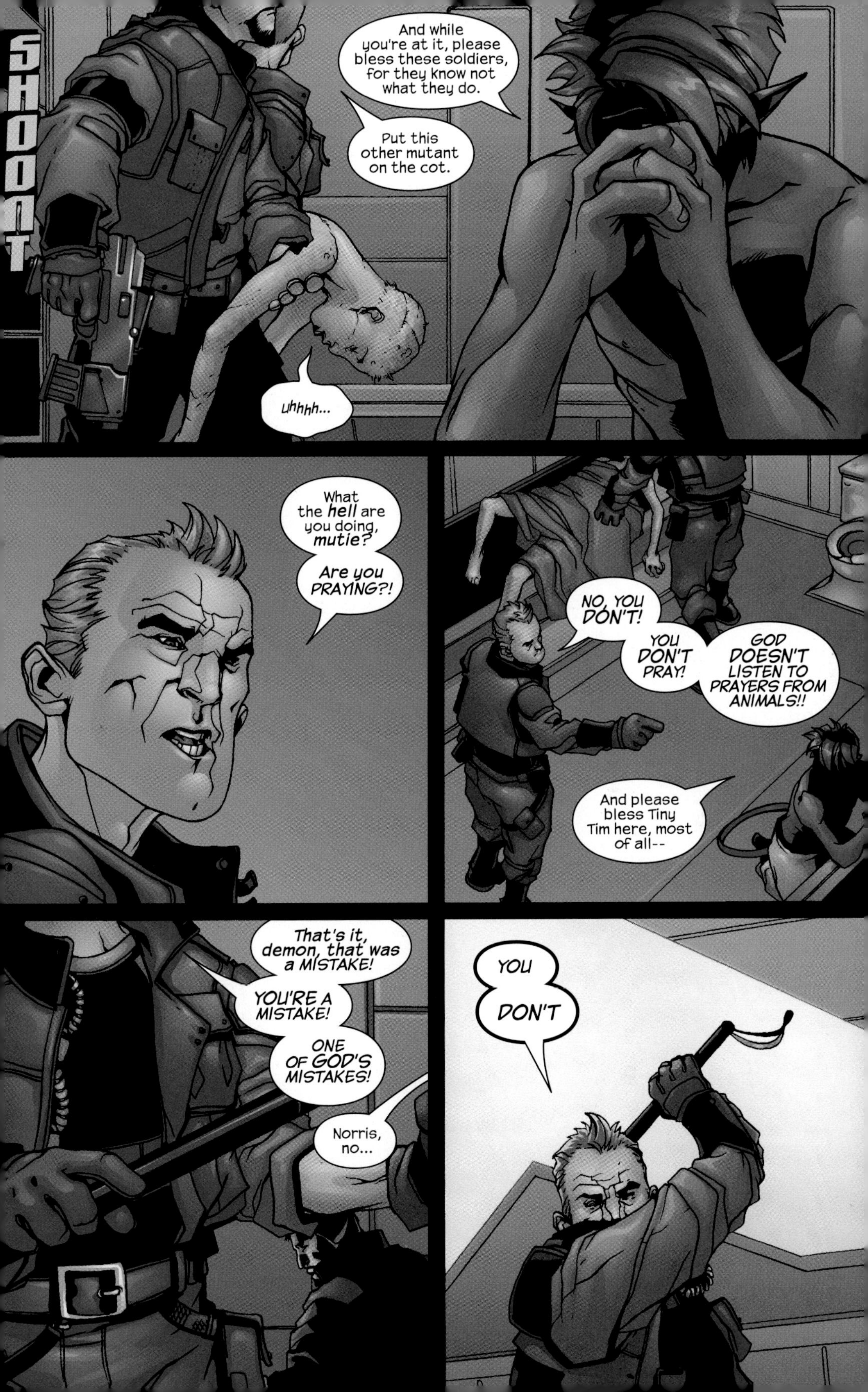

And while you're at it, please bless these soldiers, for they know not what they do.
Put this other mutant on the cot.
uhhhh...
What the hell are you doing, mutie?
Are you PRAYING?!
NO, YOU DON'T!
YOU DON'T PRAY!
GOD DOESN'T LISTEN TO PRAYERS FROM ANIMALS!!
And please bless Tiny Tim here, most of all--
That's it, demon, that was a MISTAKE!
YOU'RE A MISTAKE!
ONE OF GOD'S MISTAKES!
Norris, no...
YOU
DON'T

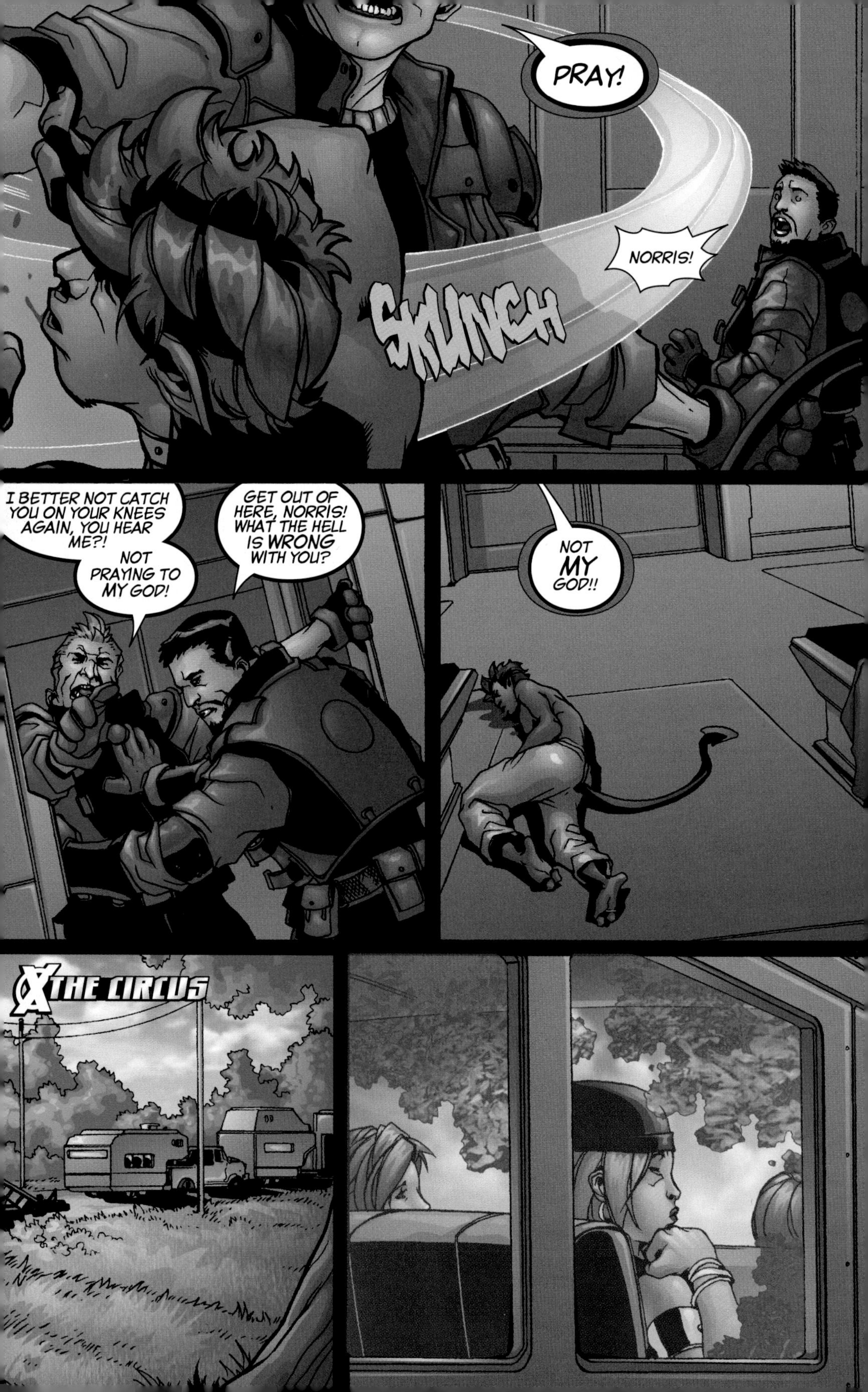
PRAY!
NORRIS!
SKUNCH
I BETTER NOT CATCH YOU ON YOUR KNEES AGAIN, YOU HEAR ME?!
NOT PRAYING TO MY GOD!
GET OUT OF HERE, NORRIS! WHAT THE HELL IS WRONG WITH YOU?
NOT MY GOD!!
THE CIRCUS

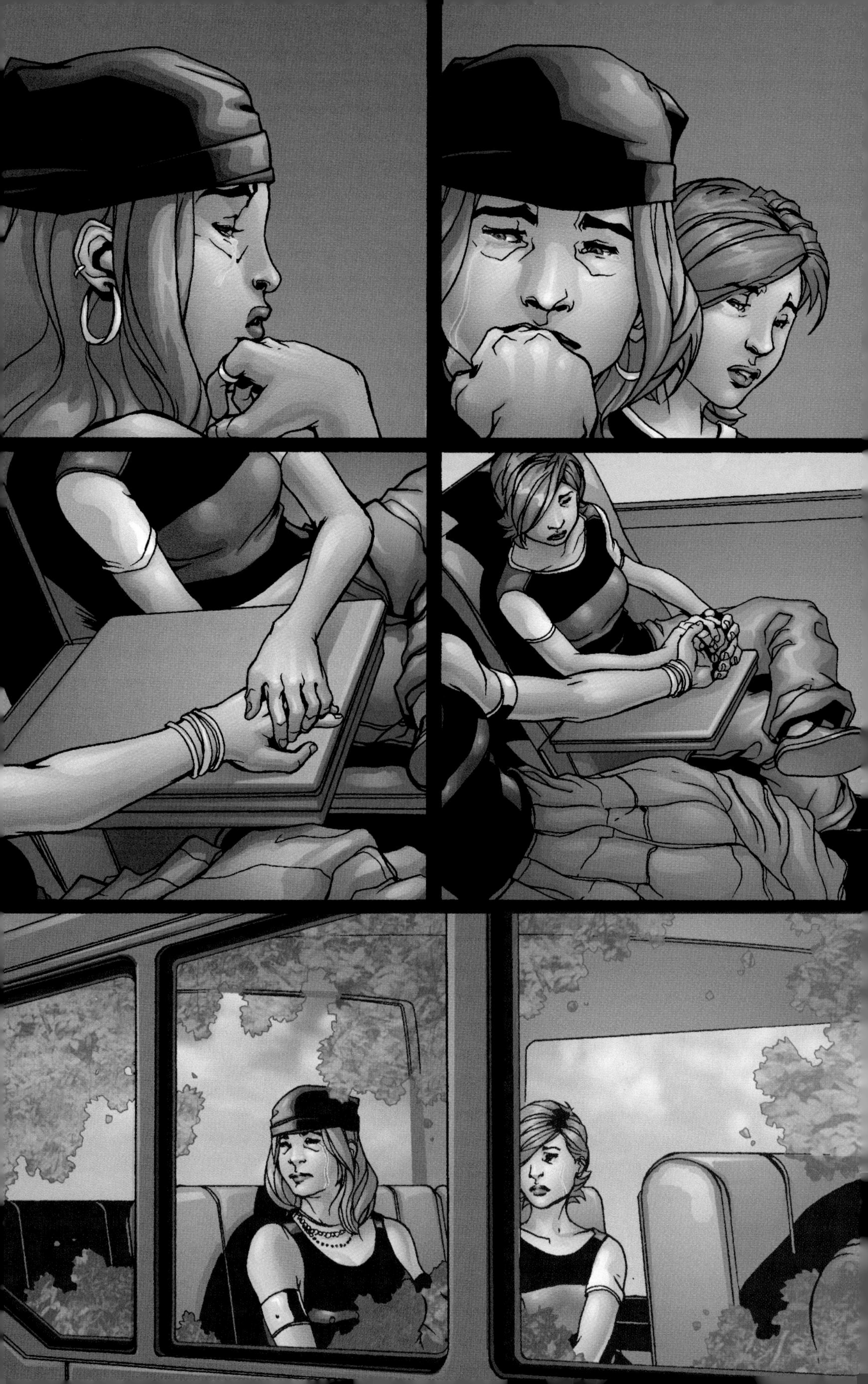

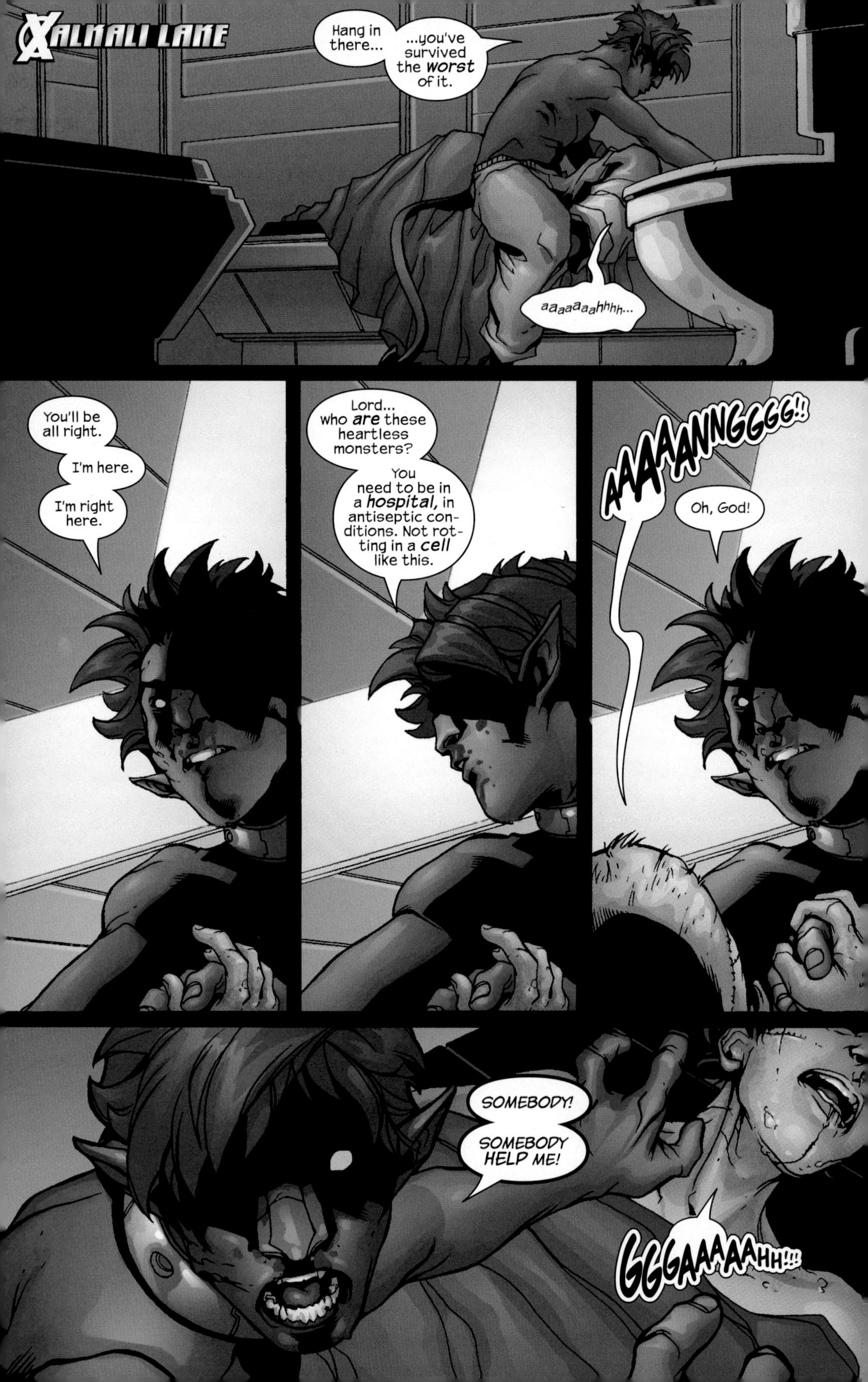
ALKALI LAKE
Hang in there...
...you've survived the worst of it.
aaaaaaahhhh...
You'll be all right.
I'm here.
I'm right here.
Lord... who are these heartless monsters?
You need to be in a hospital, in antiseptic conditions. Not rotting in a cell like this.
AAAAANNGGGG!!
Oh, God!
SOMEBODY!
SOMEBODY HELP ME!
GGGAAAAAHH!!!

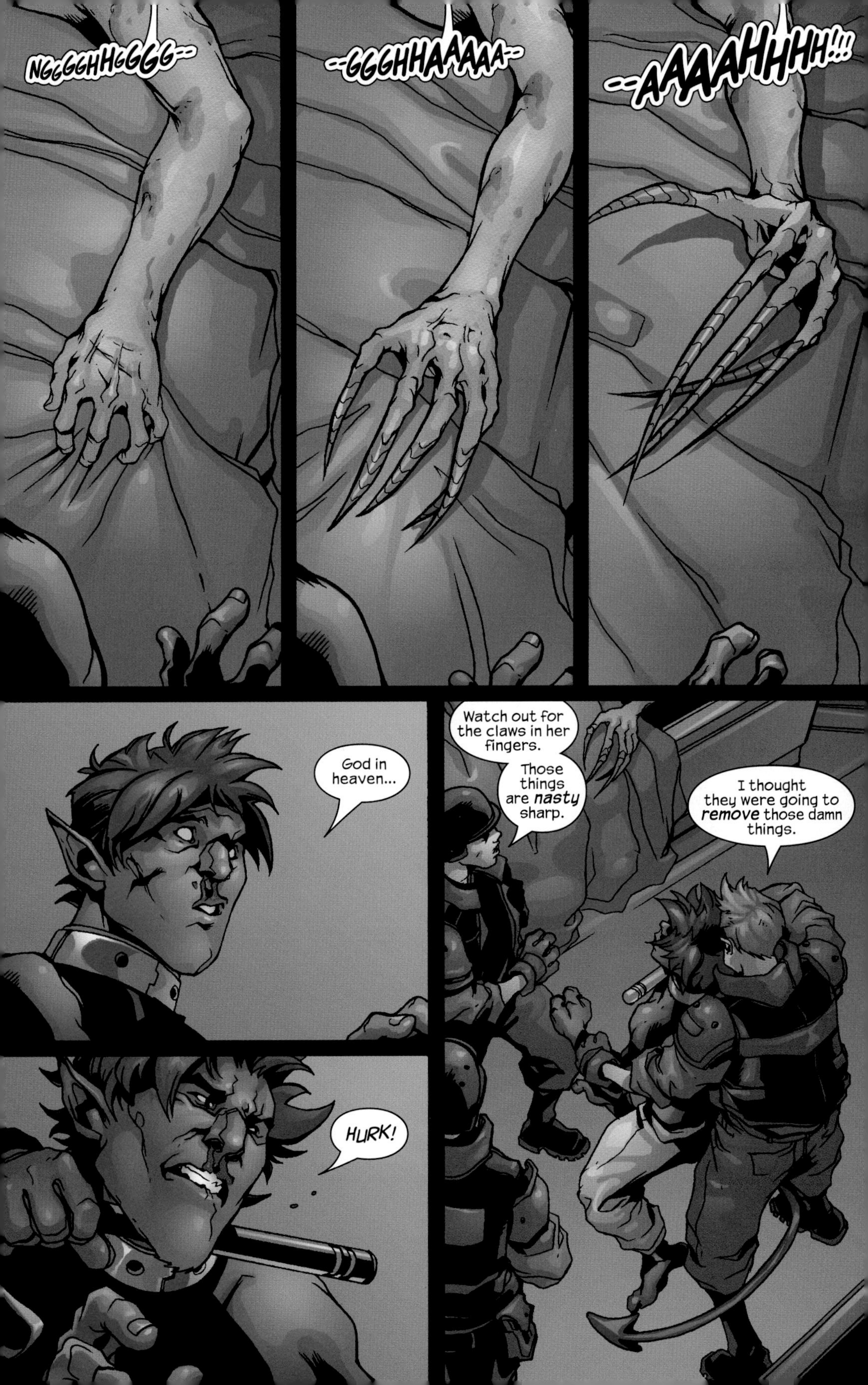
NGGGGHHGGGG--
--GGGHHAAAAA--
--AAAAHHHH!!!
God in heaven...
Watch out for the claws in her fingers.
Those things are nasty sharp.
I thought they were going to remove those damn things.
HURK!

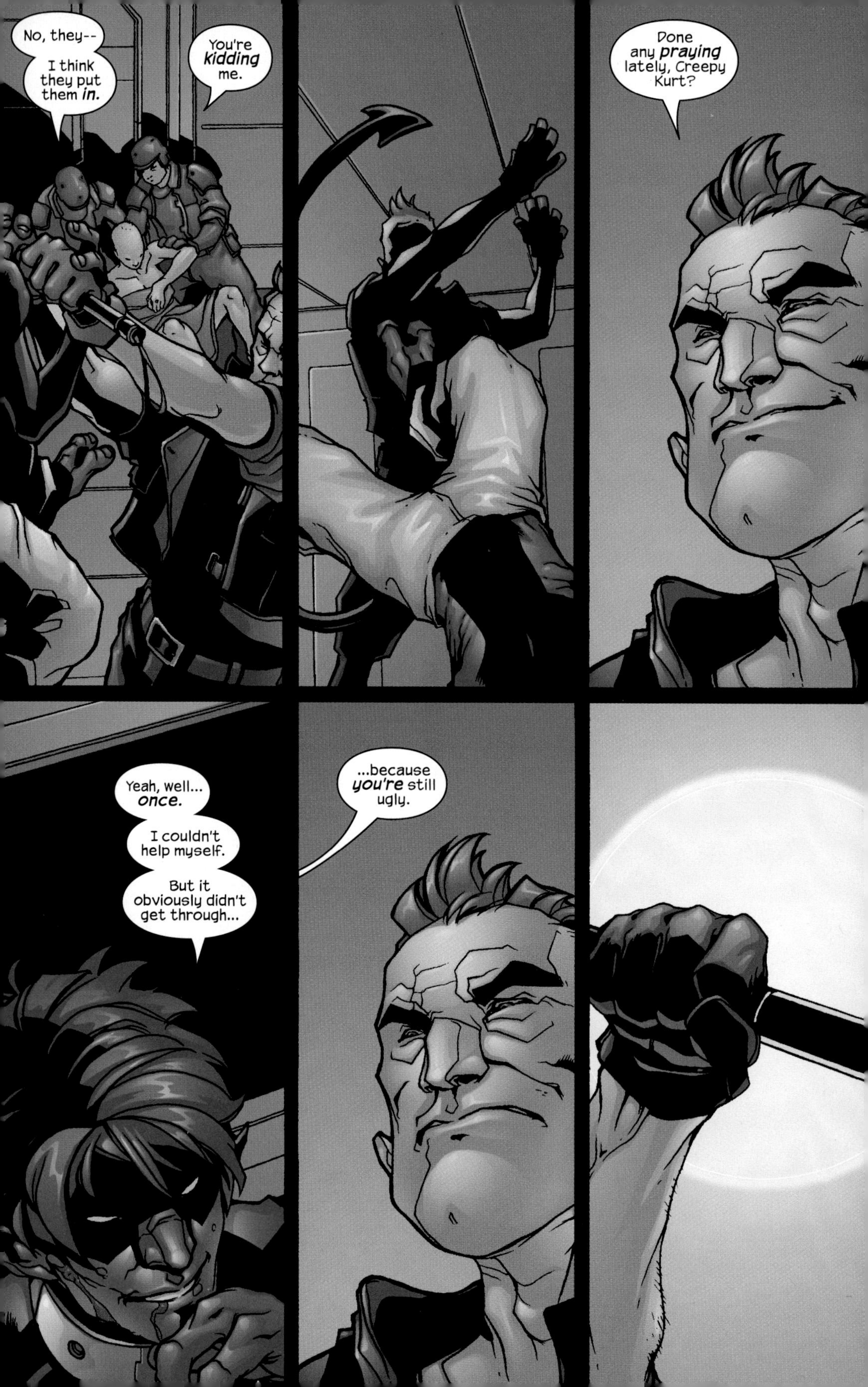
No, they--
I think they put them *in.*
You're *kidding* me.
Done any *praying* lately, Creepy Kurt?
Yeah, well... *once.*
I couldn't help myself.
But it obviously didn't get through...
...because *you're* still ugly.

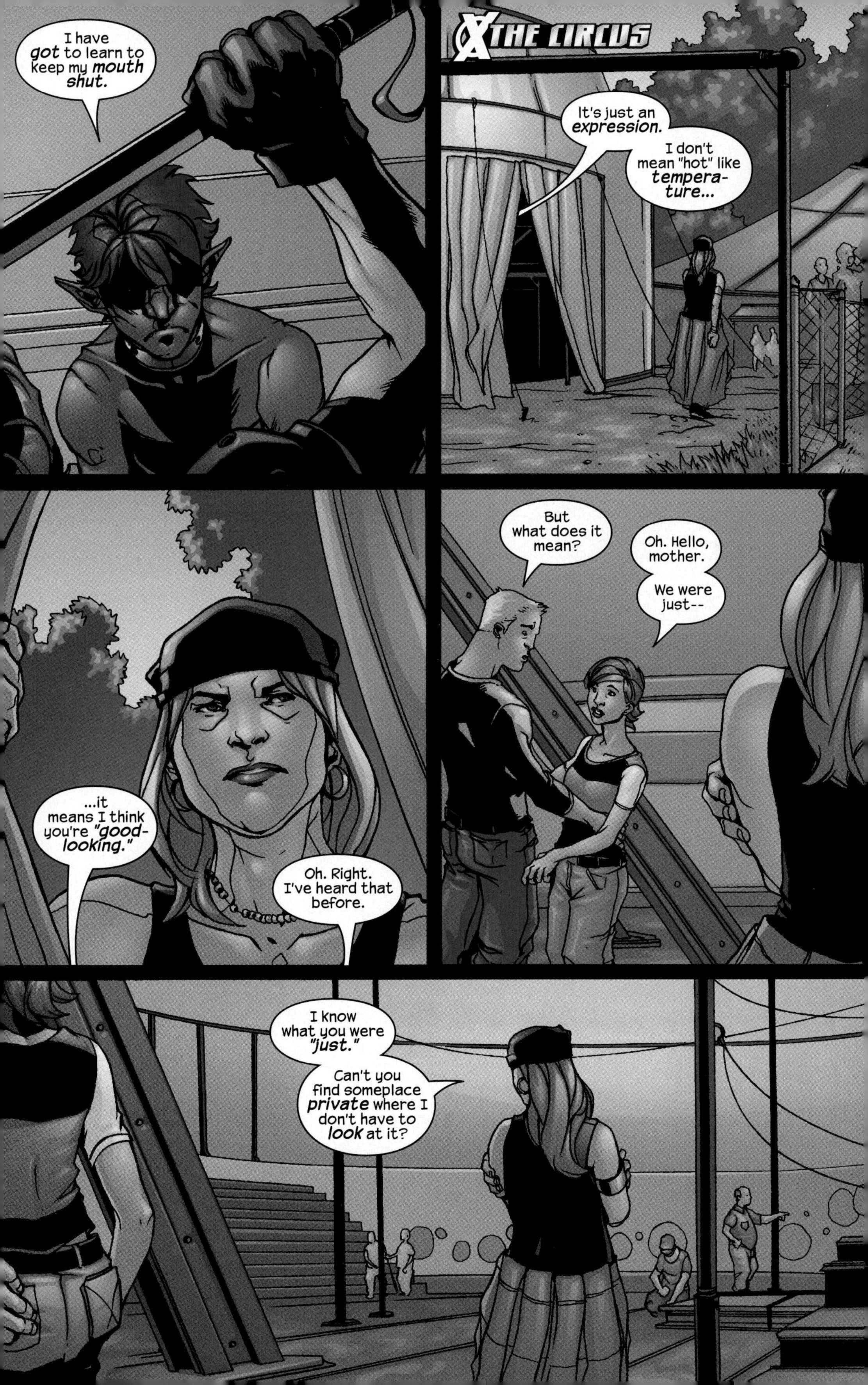
I have got to learn to keep my mouth shut.
THE CIRCUS
It's just an expression.
I don't mean "hot" like tempera-ture...
...it means I think you're "good-looking."
Oh. Right. I've heard that before.
But what does it mean?
Oh. Hello, mother.
We were just--
I know what you were "just."
Can't you find someplace private where I don't have to look at it?

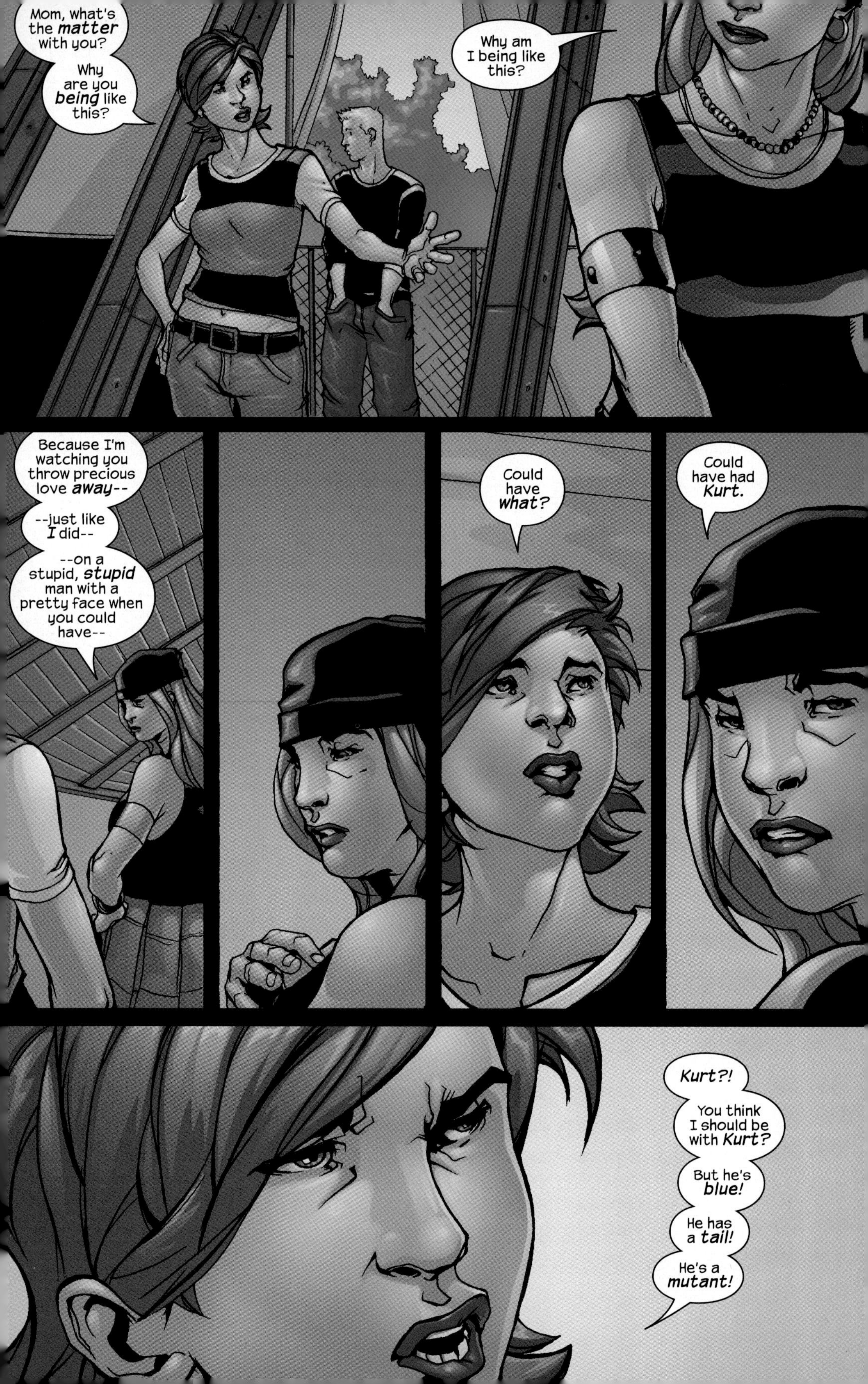
Mom, what's the matter with you?
Why are you being like this?
Why am I being like this?
Because I'm watching you throw precious love away--
--just like I did--
--on a stupid, stupid man with a pretty face when you could have--
Could have what?
Could have had Kurt.
Kurt?!
You think I should be with Kurt?
But he's blue!
He has a tail!
He's a mutant!

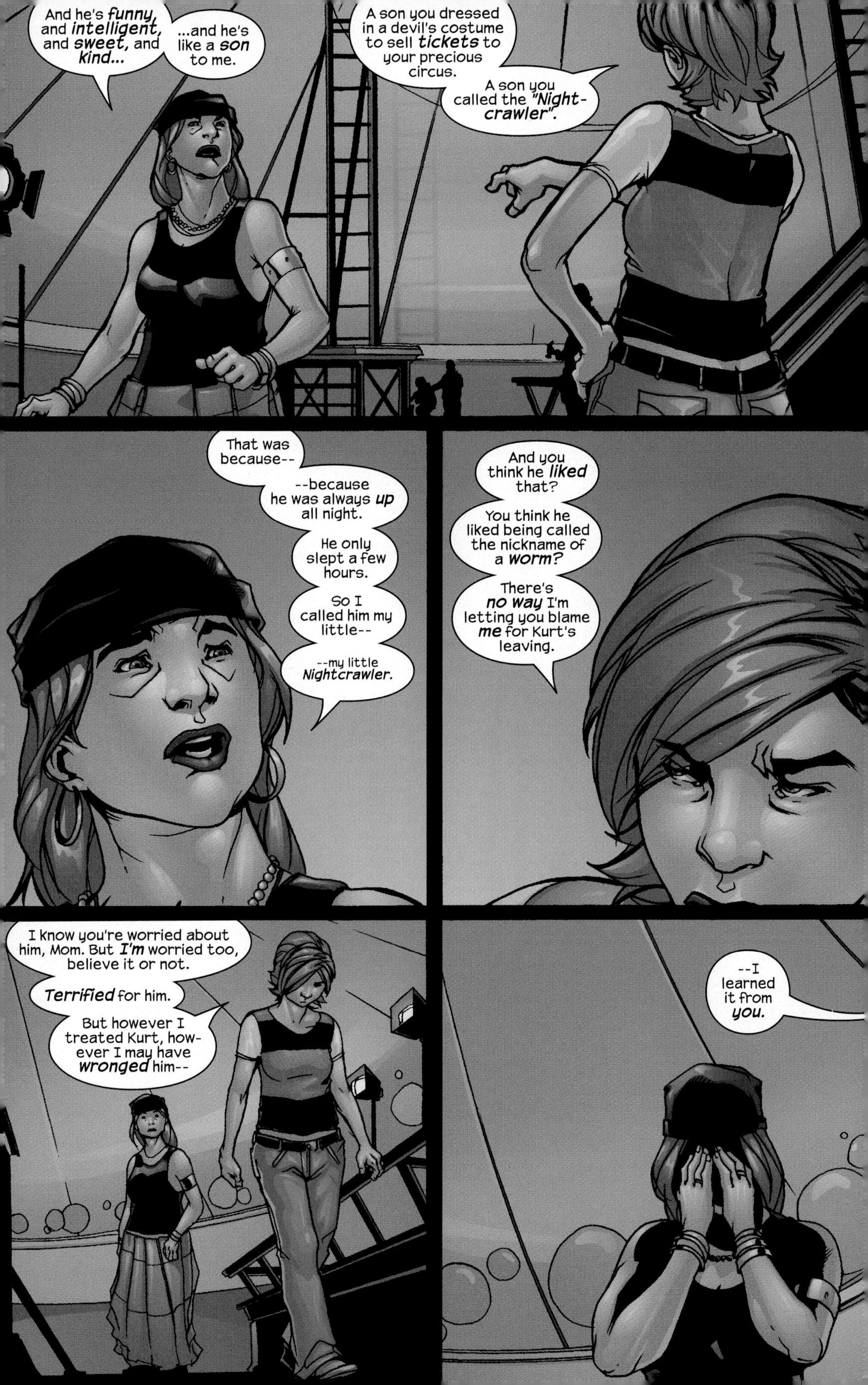
And he's funny, and intelligent, and sweet, and kind...
...and he's like a son to me.
A son you dressed in a devil's costume to sell tickets to your precious circus.
A son you called the "Night-crawler".
That was because--
--because he was always up all night.
He only slept a few hours.
So I called him my little--
--my little Nightcrawler.
And you think he liked that?
You think he liked being called the nickname of a worm?
There's no way I'm letting you blame me for Kurt's leaving.
I know you're worried about him, Mom. But I'm worried too, believe it or not.
Terrified for him.
But however I treated Kurt, how-ever I may have wronged him--
--I learned it from you.

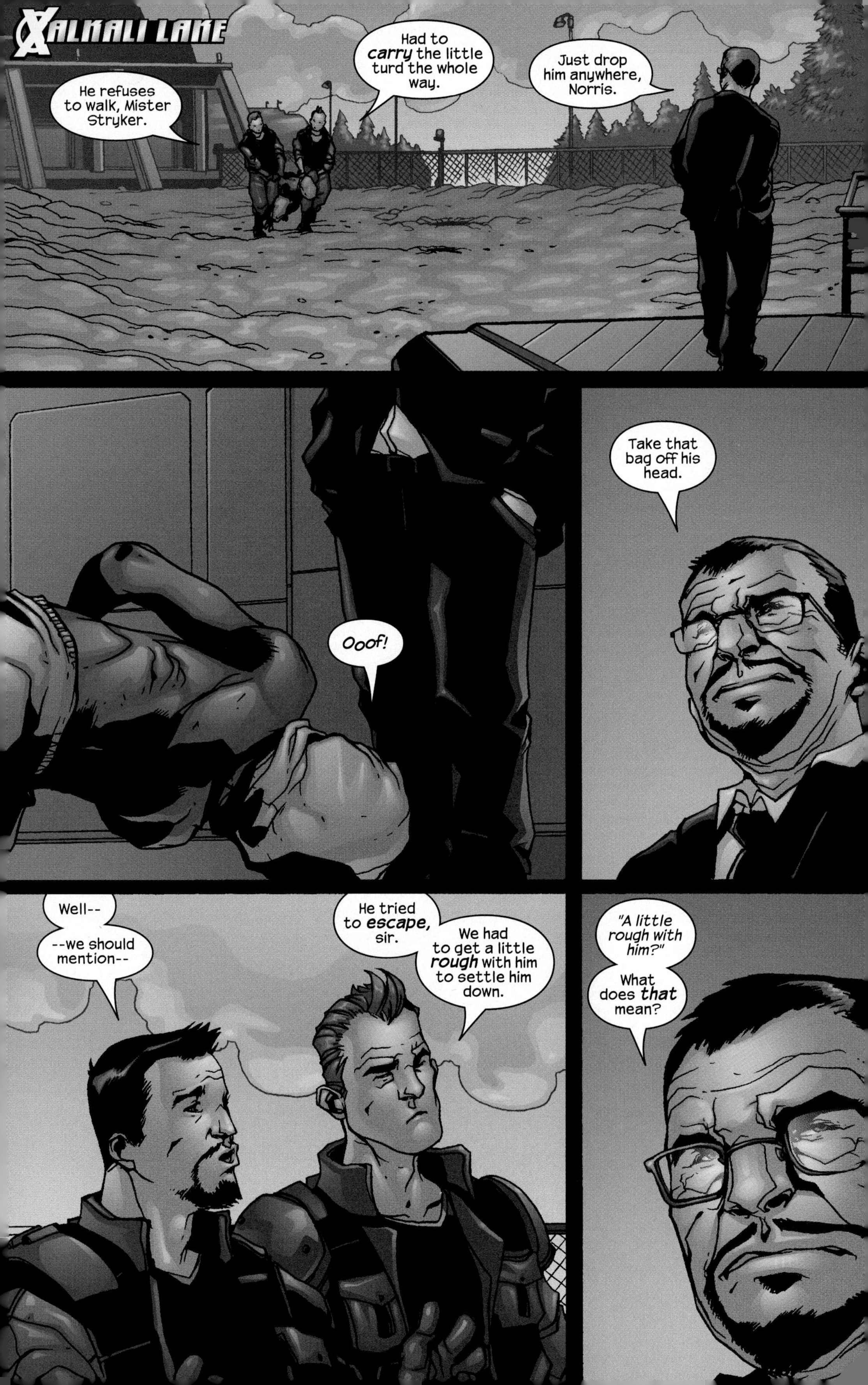
ALKALI LAKE
He refuses to walk, Mister Stryker.
Had to *carry* the little turd the whole way.
Just drop him anywhere, Norris.
Ooof!
Take that bag off his head.
Well--
--we should mention--
He tried to *escape,* sir.
We had to get a little *rough* with him to settle him down.
"A little rough with him?"
What does *that* mean?

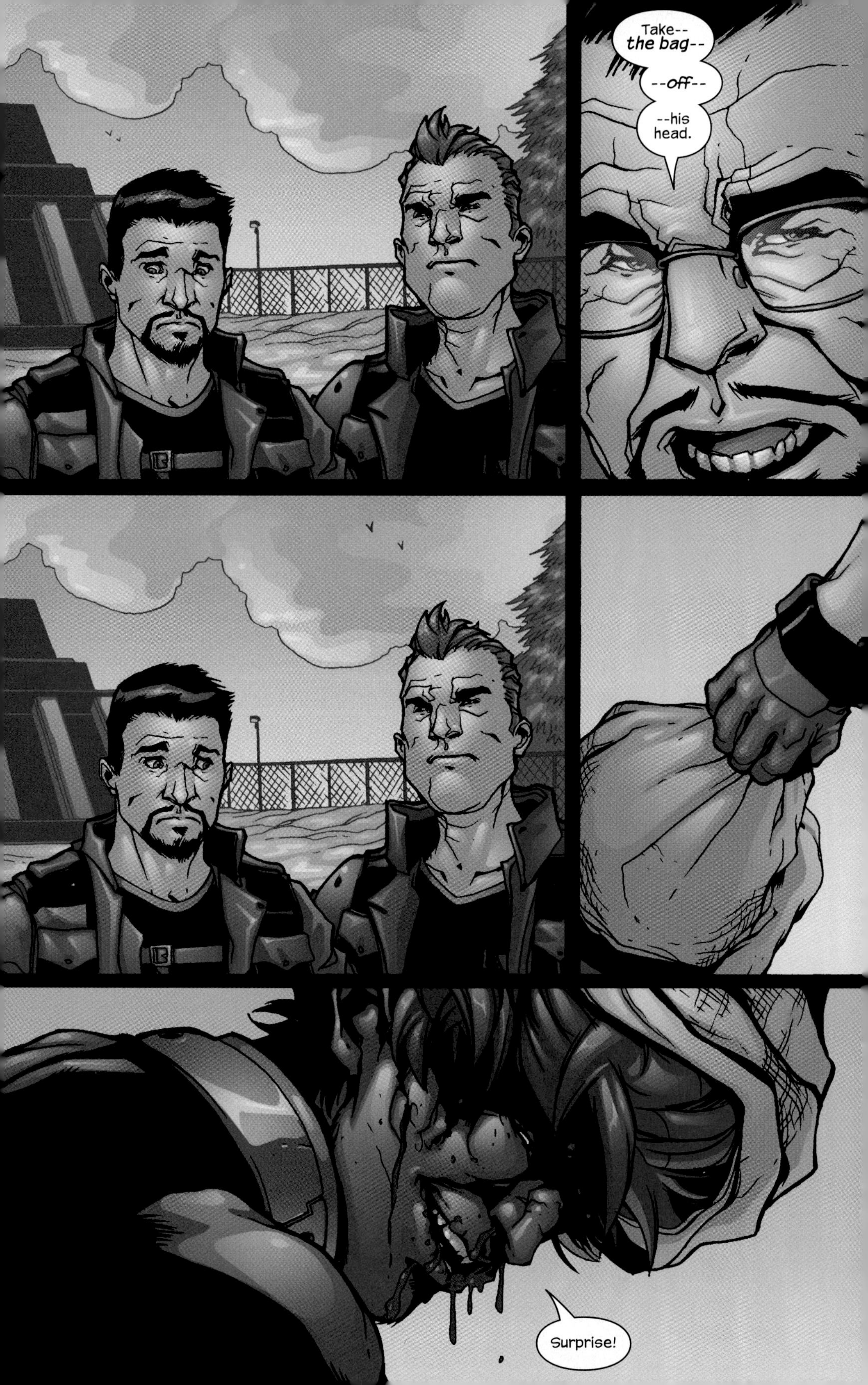
Take-- *the bag*--
--*off*--
--his head.
Surprise!

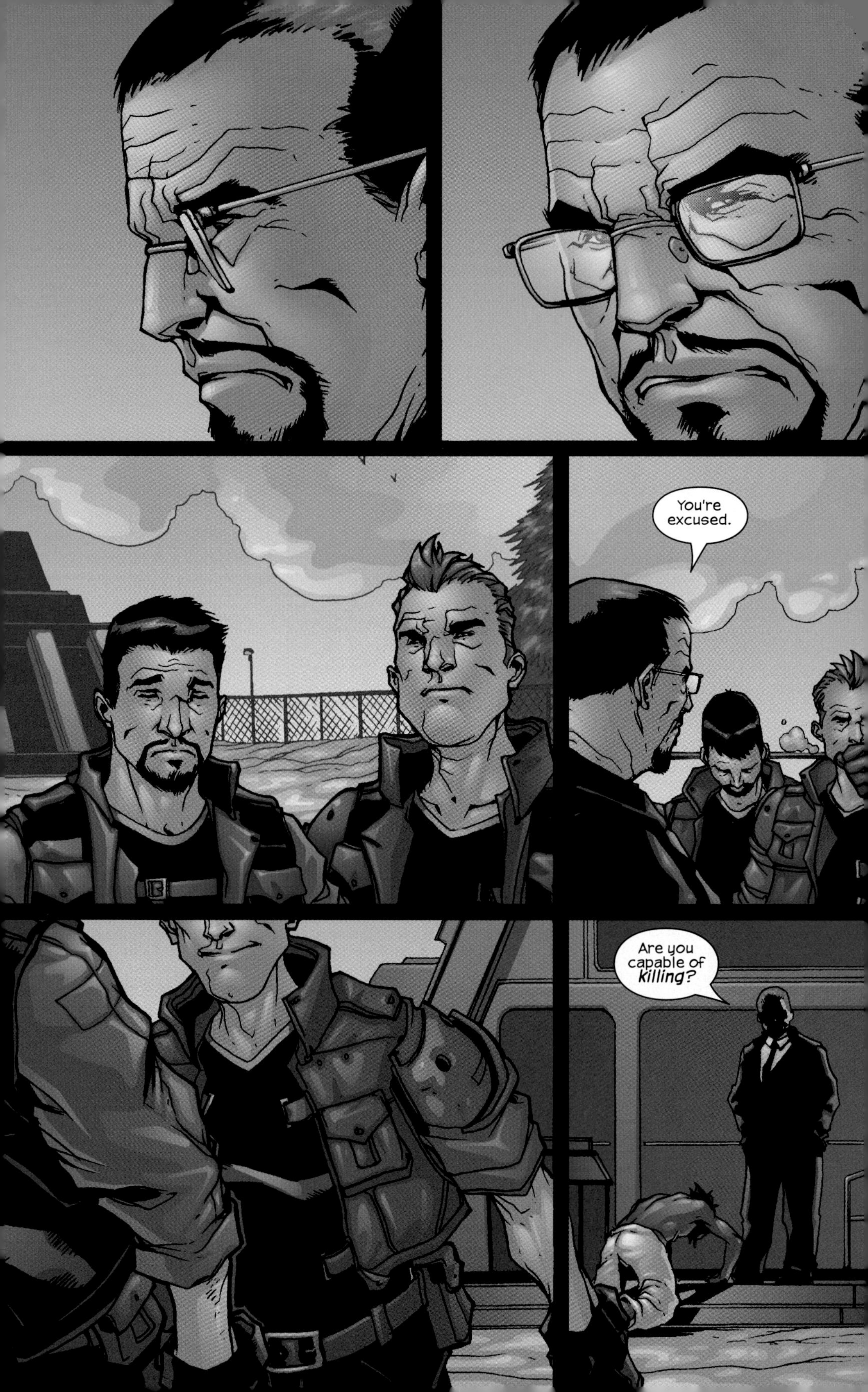
You're excused.
Are you capable of *killing?*

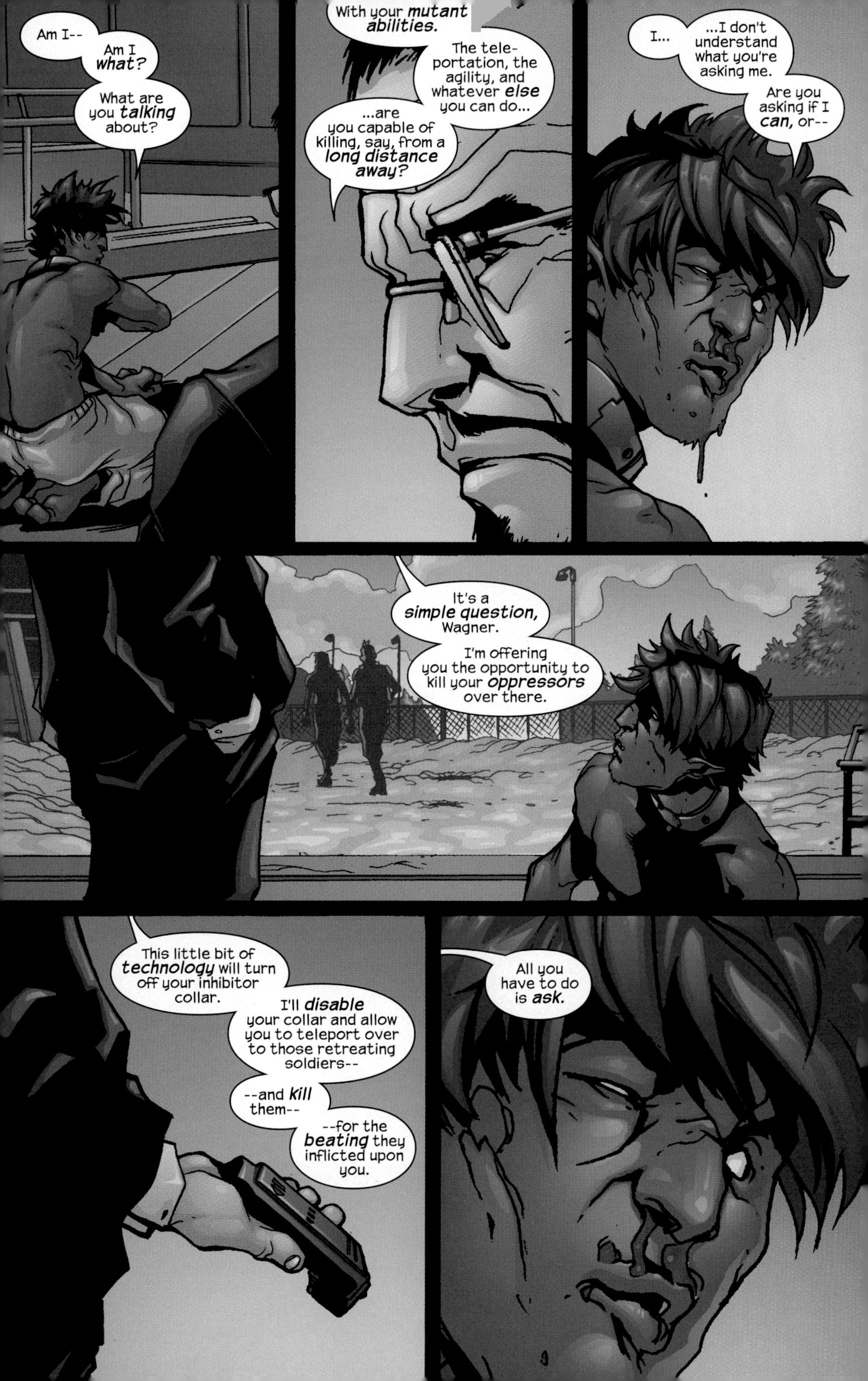

Am I--
Am I what?
What are you talking about?
With your mutant abilities.
The teleportation, the agility, and whatever else you can do...
...are you capable of killing, say, from a long distance away?
I...
...I don't understand what you're asking me.
Are you asking if I can, or--
It's a simple question, Wagner.
I'm offering you the opportunity to kill your oppressors over there.
This little bit of technology will turn off your inhibitor collar.
I'll disable your collar and allow you to teleport over to those retreating soldiers--
--and kill them--
--for the beating they inflicted upon you.
All you have to do is ask.

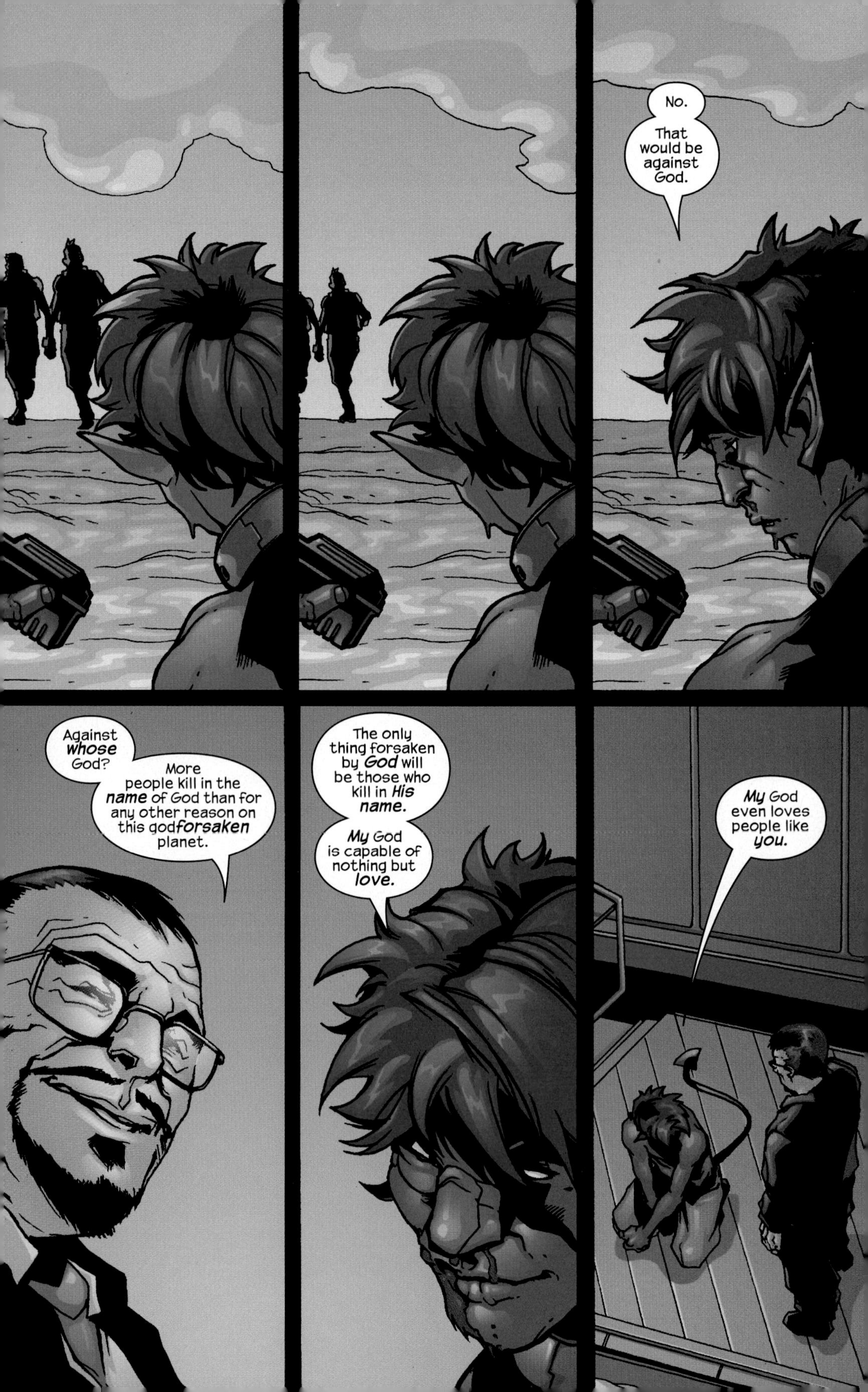
No.
That would be against God.
Against whose God?
More people kill in the name of God than for any other reason on this godforsaken planet.
The only thing forsaken by God will be those who kill in His name.
My God is capable of nothing but love.
My God even loves people like you.

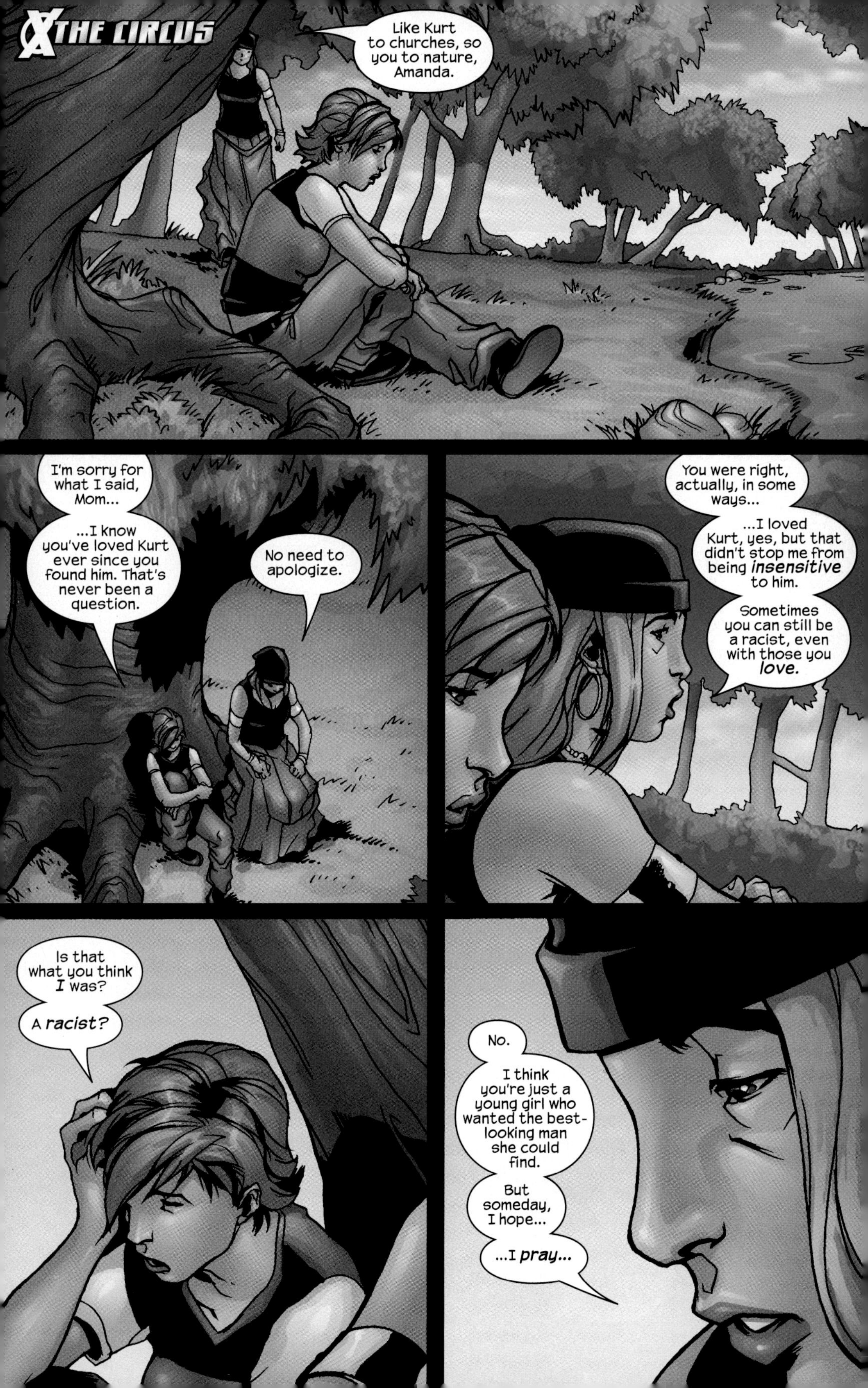
THE CIRCUS
Like Kurt to churches, so you to nature, Amanda.
I'm sorry for what I said, Mom...
...I know you've loved Kurt ever since you found him. That's never been a question.
No need to apologize.
You were right, actually, in some ways...
...I loved Kurt, yes, but that didn't stop me from being *insensitive* to him.
Sometimes you can still be a racist, even with those you *love.*
Is that what you think *I* was?
A *racist?*
No.
I think you're just a young girl who wanted the best-looking man she could find.
But someday, I hope...
...I *pray...*

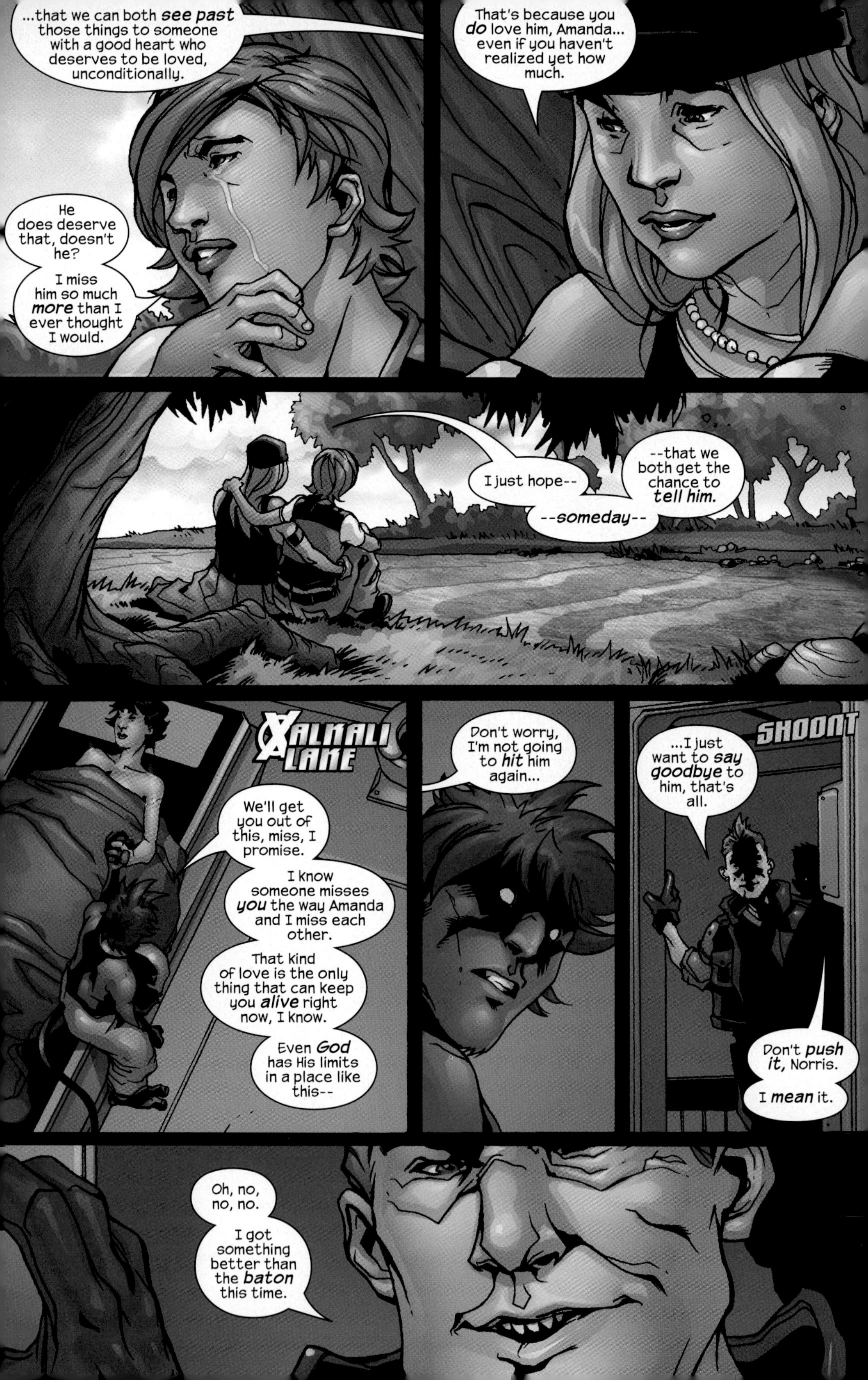
...that we can both see past those things to someone with a good heart who deserves to be loved, unconditionally.
That's because you do love him, Amanda... even if you haven't realized yet how much.
He does deserve that, doesn't he?
I miss him so much more than I ever thought I would.
I just hope--
--someday--
--that we both get the chance to tell him.
ALKALI LAKE
We'll get you out of this, miss, I promise.
I know someone misses you the way Amanda and I miss each other.
That kind of love is the only thing that can keep you alive right now, I know.
Even God has His limits in a place like this--
Don't worry, I'm not going to hit him again...
SHOONT
...I just want to say goodbye to him, that's all.
Don't push it, Norris.
I mean it.
Oh, no, no, no.
I got something better than the baton this time.

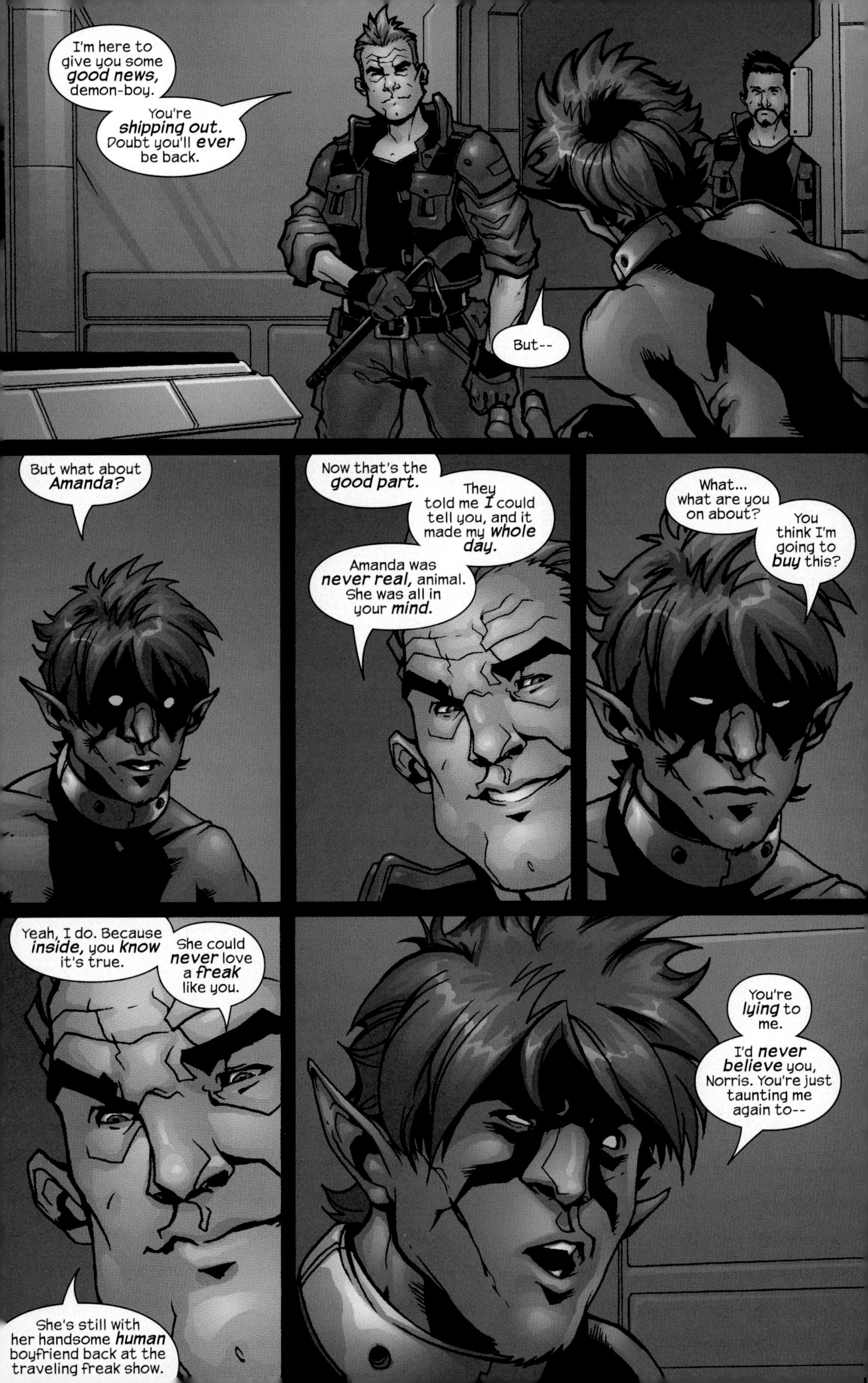

I'm here to give you some *good news,* demon-boy.
You're *shipping out.* Doubt you'll *ever* be back.
But--
But what about *Amanda?*
Now that's the *good part.*
They told me *I* could tell you, and it made my *whole day.*
Amanda was *never real,* animal. She was all in your *mind.*
What... what are you on about?
You think I'm going to *buy* this?
Yeah, I do. Because *inside,* you *know* it's true.
She could *never* love a *freak* like you.
She's still with her handsome *human* boyfriend back at the traveling freak show.
You're *lying* to me.
I'd *never believe* you, Norris. You're just taunting me again to--

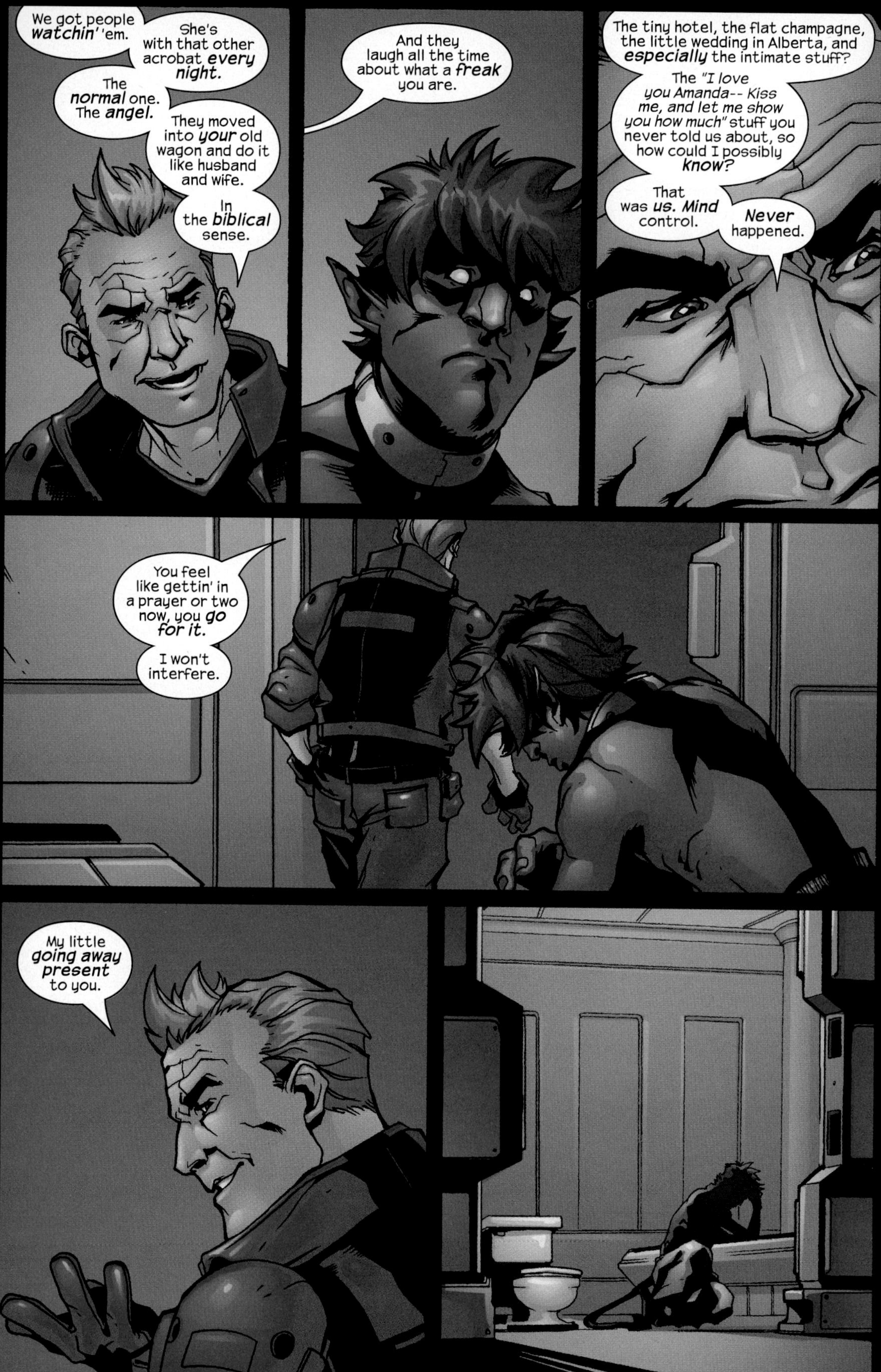
We got people watchin' 'em.
She's with that other acrobat every night.
The normal one. The angel.
They moved into your old wagon and do it like husband and wife.
In the biblical sense.
And they laugh all the time about what a freak you are.
The tiny hotel, the flat champagne, the little wedding in Alberta, and especially the intimate stuff?
The "I love you Amanda-- Kiss me, and let me show you how much" stuff you never told us about, so how could I possibly know?
That was us. Mind control.
Never happened.
You feel like gettin' in a prayer or two now, you go for it.
I won't interfere.
My little going away present to you.

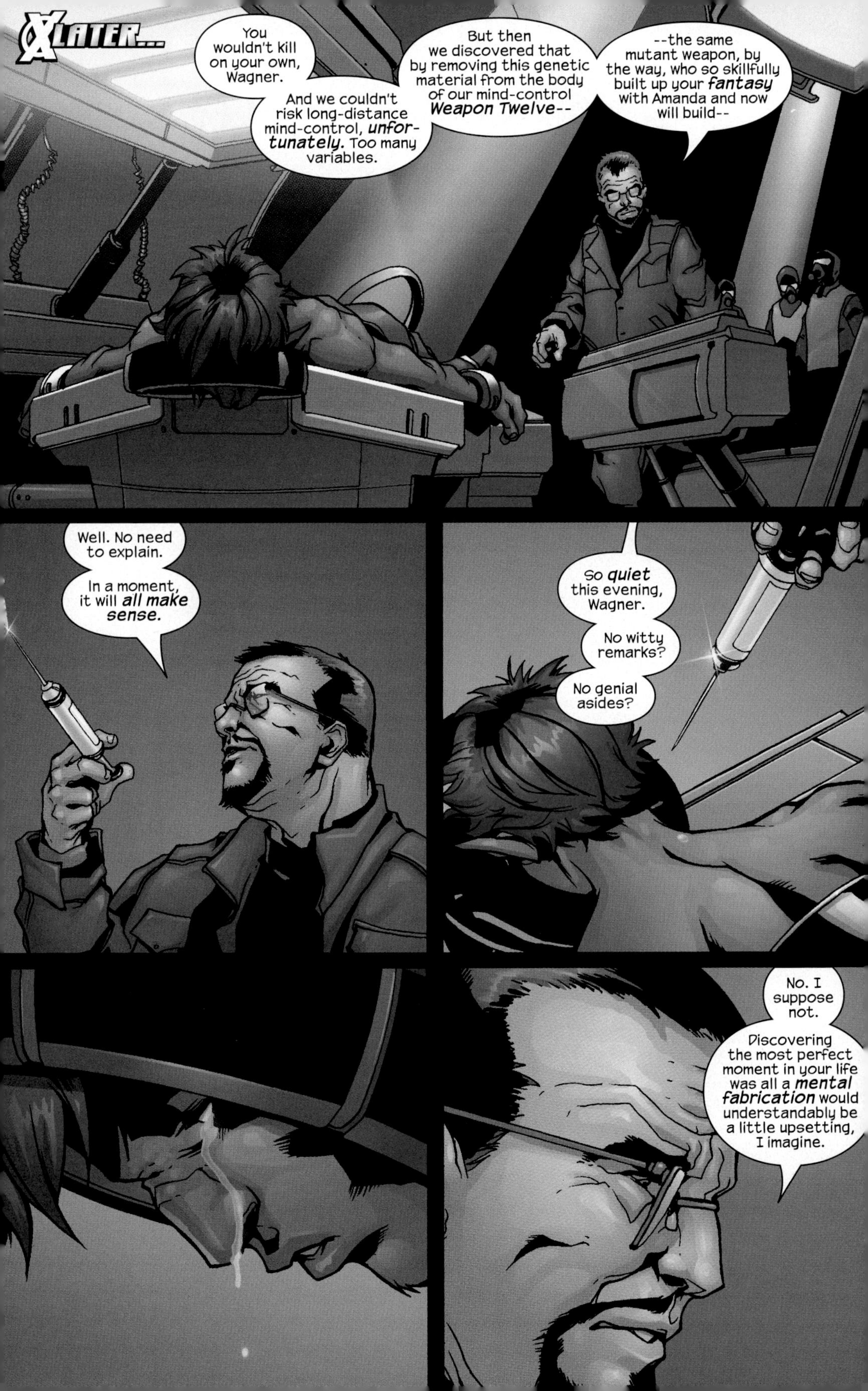
LATER...
You wouldn't kill on your own, Wagner.
And we couldn't risk long-distance mind-control, unfortunately. Too many variables.
But then we discovered that by removing this genetic material from the body of our mind-control Weapon Twelve--
--the same mutant weapon, by the way, who so skillfully built up your fantasy with Amanda and now will build--
Well. No need to explain.
In a moment, it will all make sense.
So quiet this evening, Wagner.
No witty remarks?
No genial asides?
No. I suppose not.
Discovering the most perfect moment in your life was all a mental fabrication would understandably be a little upsetting, I imagine.

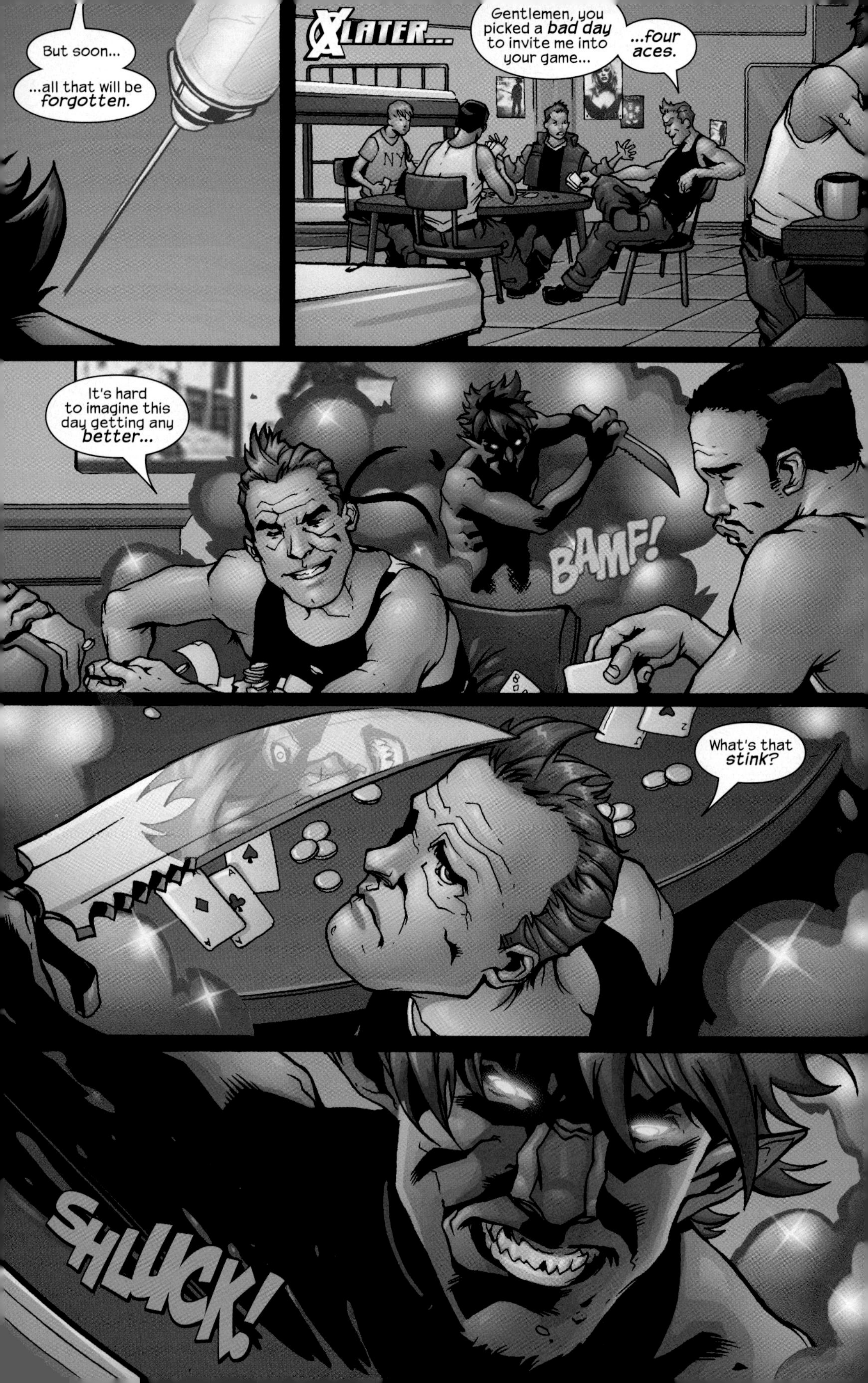
But soon...
...all that will be forgotten.
LATER...
Gentlemen, you picked a bad day to invite me into your game...
...four aces.
It's hard to imagine this day getting any better...
BAMF!
What's that stink?
SHUCK!

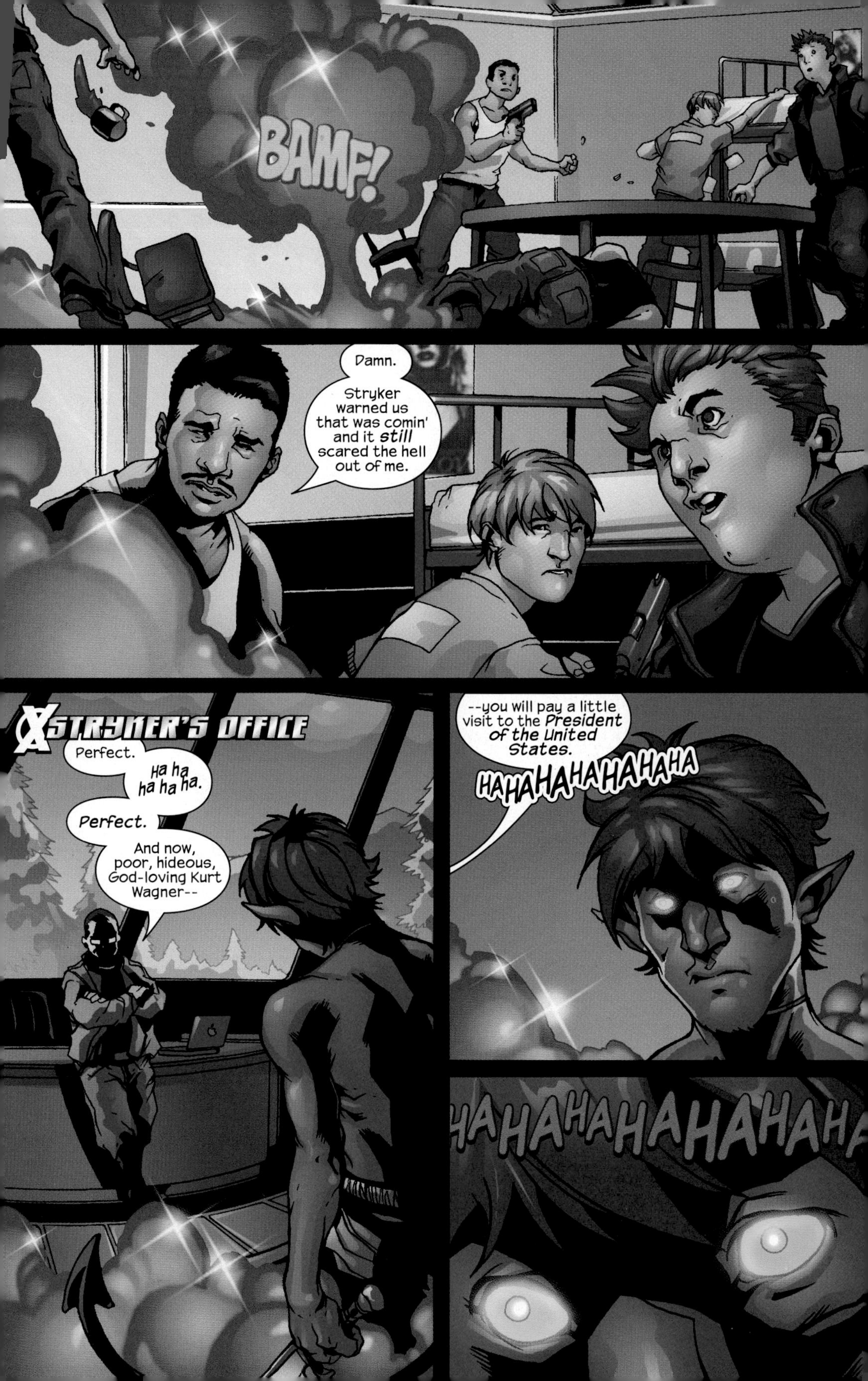
BAMF!
Damn.
Stryker warned us that was comin' and it *still* scared the hell out of me.
STRYKER'S OFFICE
Perfect.
Ha ha ha ha ha.
Perfect.
And now, poor, hideous, God-loving Kurt Wagner--
--you will pay a little visit to the *President of the United States.*
HAHAHAHAHAHAHA
HAHAHAHAHAHAHA

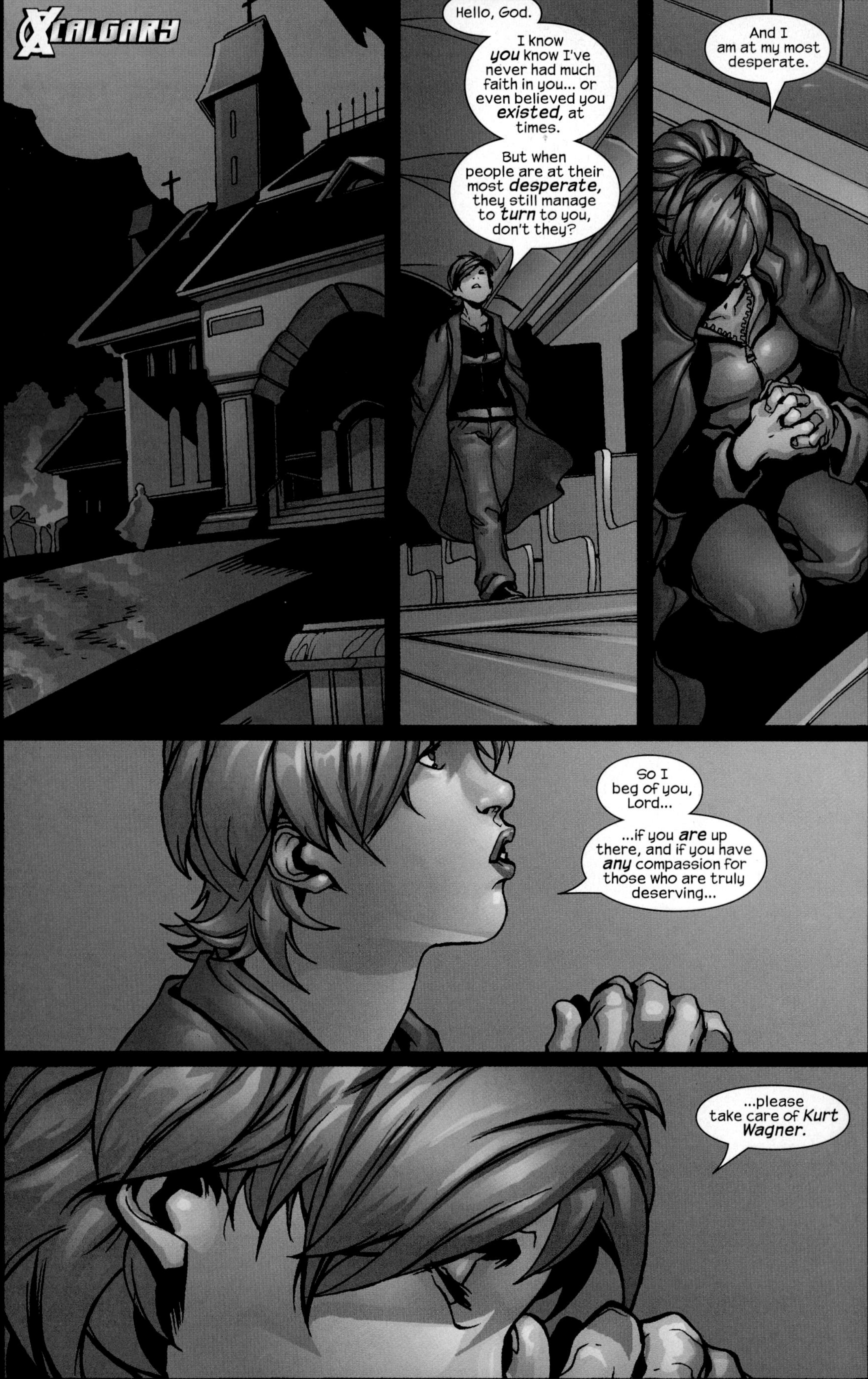
CALGARY
Hello, God.
I know *you* know I've never had much faith in you... or even believed you *existed,* at times.
But when people are at their most *desperate,* they still manage to *turn* to you, don't they?
And I am at my most desperate.
So I beg of you, Lord...
...if you *are* up there, and if you have *any* compassion for those who are truly deserving...
...please take care of *Kurt Wagner.*